STARTING STRATEGIES

STRATEGIES 1

Teacher's Book

Ingrid Freebairn

Longman

Longman Group Limited
London

*Associated companies, branches and
representatives throughout the world*

© Longman Group Limited 1977

All rights reserved. No part of this
publication may be reproduced, stored in
a retrieval system or transmitted in any
form or by any means, electronic,
mechanical, photocopying, recording, or
otherwise, without the prior permission
of the copyright owner.

First published 1977
Third impression 1980

ISBN 0 582 51915 2

Printed in Singapore by
Ban Wah Press

Contents

Introduction
 i) Who the course is for
 ii) What the course tries to do
 iii) The ideas behind the course
General description of the course
General teaching notes
Guide to general teaching procedures

UNIT 1. My name's Sally
Set 1. Ask somebody's name and say your name
Set 2. Ask and say where places and people are

UNIT 2. I'm a journalist
Set 1. Greet people formally and introduce yourself
Set 2. Ask and say what somebody's job is (1)
 Say what your job is

UNIT 3. Hello and Goodbye!
Set 1. Introduce people (1) and greet informally
Set 2. Ask and say what somebody's job is (2)
Set 3. Ask and say somebody's name

UNIT 4. Looking for a flat (1)
Set 1. Ask and talk about marital status
Set 2. Spelling
Set 3. Say your telephone number

UNIT 5. Looking for a flat (2)
Set 1. Ask and say where places are

UNIT 6. Consolidation Unit

UNIT 7. I'm from Melbourne
Set 1. Introduce people (2)
Set 2. Ask and talk about nationality
Set 3. Ask and say where people are from

Unit 8. Where exactly do you live?
Set 1. Ask and say where people live
 Say where you live
Set 2. Ask and say where people live exactly

UNIT 9. One bed, one sit., K & B
Set 1. Show and ask about places
Set 2. Express satisfaction and dissatisfaction
Set 3. Ask and talk about cost (1)

UNIT 10. Coffee time
Set 1. Offer, accept and refuse
Set 2. Ask people for things and give people things
Set 3. Ask and talk about cost (2)

UNIT 11. Do you like tea with lemon?
Set 1. Ask and say the time (1)
Set 2. Ask what people like and say what you like
Set 3. Ask and say what people like

UNIT 12. Consolidation Unit

UNIT 13. Train to Coventry
Set 1. Ask and say the time (2)
Set 2. Ask and talk about fixed times

UNIT 14. Shopping in Coventry
Set 1. Ask people to do things
 Agree to do things
 Say you can't do things
Set 2. Ask what people would like and say what you would like
Set 3. Ask for and give specific information
Set 4. Talk about the weather

UNIT 15. Happy Birthday!
Set 1. Ask and talk about dates
Set 2. Ask for and make suggestions
 Agree and disagree with suggestions
Set 3. Express pleasure

UNIT 16. A nice weekend
Set 1. Ask people what they want to do
 Say what you want to do
Set 2. Ask and talk about the past

UNIT 17. An invitation
Set 1. Answer the telephone, say your name and start a conversation
Set 2. Arrange to meet somebody
Set 3. Invite people to do things
 Accept and refuse invitations to do things

UNIT 18. Going to work
Set 1. Ask and say how people get to work
 Say how you get to work
Set 2. Ask and say how often people do things
 Say how often you do things
Set 3. Ask and say how far away places are
Set 4. Ask and say how long journeys take
Set 5. Ask and say how much things cost

UNIT 19. Focus on people at work
Set 1. Ask and say what people do every day
 Say what you do every day
Set 2. Ask people about their jobs
 Say who people work for and where they work
 Say who you work for and where you work

UNIT 20. Consolidation

Index of functions: How to say it
Grammar review
Active Vocabulary (in topic areas)
Passive Vocabulary (Unit by Unit)
Alphabetical list of both Active and Passive Vocabulary

Introduction

i) Who the course is for

The course is for:
- complete beginners who are learning English for the first time;
- 'false' beginners who have tried to learn some English before, but want to start again from the beginning.

The course is also ideally suited to a class of learners of mixed ability – a common feature even of beginners' classes. It offers basic practice work for average learners and more challenging activities for faster learners.

ii) What the course tries to do

The main aims of the course are to:
- give the students a feeling that they are learning useful language from the very beginning.
- provide the students, in as short a time as possible, with the language they need in order to communicate successfully in a wide range of situations.
- train them to listen to and read real spoken and written language.
- train them to understand a wide range of accents.
- give a picture of a real community in contemporary Britain.
- contribute towards the students' educational, social and personal development.

iii) The ideas behind the course

1. The functional approach and the selection of functions

Most adult language learners have in common a desire to be able to communicate intelligibly in the chosen language. At advanced levels of language learning, it is less easy to predict accurately what exactly the learner wants to communicate, or in what situation he is likely to find himself. At an elementary level, however, one can more confidently draw up a list of the most basic communicative needs of a foreign language learner. He needs, for example, to be able to identify himself and give personal facts about himself. He needs to be able to ask factual questions concerning his environment (times of trains, location of places etc.) and understand the answers to these questions. He needs to be able to exchange ideas, express moods and emotions.

This course takes as its main starting point for language development, what a learner wants to do through language. (As a working label, these communicative acts – identifying oneself, giving personal facts about oneself etc. – are referred to throughout the Teacher's Book as *language functions*.)

2. The grading of the functions

To decide on a grading of functions which suits the needs of every learner is impossible. What seems very important to one learner may seem much less important to another. It depends on several factors: the learner's age, background and personality, the country in which he is learning English, the purpose for which he intends to use it, and so on. A purely functional course can, in any case, run the risk of looking rather like a tourist phrase book; the learner may see the immediate application of the language, but will not be given any insight into the way the language works. The result is that he cannot readily create language to suit his needs in different situations.

Although it is true that a learner can often master a fairly complex piece of language if he considers it important or useful, it is dangerous to ignore completely a systematic presentation of language.
As far as we know, no research has been done on how the learner would be affected if structural grading were abandoned in favour of a purely functionally-graded syllabus. Until any definite results emerge, we still think it is right to grade learning material by taking simple structures before more difficult ones, introducing the present simple before the past tense, simple clauses before complex ones. Beyond this, the learner's needs should nevertheless take priority over supposedly 'correct' structural grading. There is no real reason, either linguistic or pedagogic, why the present simple should not be introduced before the present continuous, the past before the future, or the *going to* future before the present continuous. Within this context, it seems to us to be right to place the functions in order of importance first, and consider the grading of the structures involved as the second stage.

3. Language functions and their realisation

A criticism often levelled at the so-called 'new' functional course books is that they are merely structural courses with functional labels tacked on to the structures. Following this is the criticism that functional courses wrongly represent a function with only one phrase or structure. Of course there are innumerable ways of expressing one function. Intonation alone can very often convey a function, regardless of the words being uttered. For example:

> *My mother is coming to lunch.*
> *Is she?*

Here, *Is she?* is used to indicate surprise. There are, however, numerous other ways of indicating surprise in this context e.g. *What! Oh, that's a surprise!/Really?/ Your mother is coming to lunch!* In the last of these, surprise is again indicated by intonation alone.

A language course moving from an elementary to an advanced level ought to give the learner insights into the different ways of expressing important language functions. At an elementary level, it is impossible to cover thoroughly more than one way of expressing a function, except in the case of short phrases e.g. greeting, leave-taking, thanking etc. Here the need for more than one expression is important even at an elementary level, and the learning load is comparatively light. Otherwise, the choice of language to express a function has been based on general usefulness, frequency and applicability.

4. Authentic material

The emphasis so far has been on the spoken word and the learner's productive needs. However it is not enough to assume that a learner's needs are covered if he can communicate in the spoken language alone. A foreigner on holiday in Britain may well find that his initial language activity will involve reading, understanding and filling in a form, understanding a spoken announcement, reading and understanding notices and so on. It is important, then, to train the learner to understand the spoken and written language in the forms which he is most likely to meet; that is, authentic spoken and written language.

In terms of listening practice, authenticity should relate not only to different varieties of spoken language (conversation, interviews, announcements etc.) but also to different accents and dialects. A foreigner arriving in Britain to attend a language course may find, to his disappointment and confusion, that the only person who talks with a recognisable and intelligible (to him) received pronunciation, is his language teacher – and even that cannot be taken for granted. Exposure to this type of pronunciation alone will not only give a false impression of how the average Briton speaks, but may well cause him to give up all hope of being able to communicate with native speakers of English.

5. Productive and receptive skills

Implicit in this aim to familiarise the learner with authentic spoken and written material is the belief that a learner, even at the beginner's level, need not, and indeed should not, be presented only with language that is within his productive range. A learner's receptive skills are noticeably better than his productive skills at any stage in the language learning process. This notion tends to be suppressed, in the belief that it is confusing for the learner to be in contact with forms that are not fully within his productive range. But since this is an inevitable part of anyone's day-to-day language experience, it is better that the learner be prepared for it.

The special features of Starting Strategies can be summarised as follows:

The selection of language functions is based on the learner's needs.

The grading of language functions is based primarily on the learner's immediate needs, but at the same time follows a basic framework of structural progression.

Authentic spoken and written material is linked either functionally or thematically to the main body of the material.

Language to be learned actively is to be distinguished from language to be recognised passively.

General description of the course

The course consists of:
i) **the Students' Book.**
ii) **the Teacher's Book.**
iii) **the set of tapes.** (dialogues and practice materials).
iv) **songs** (available in LP, tape or cassette form).
v) **a set of wall pictures**

i) The Students' Book
The Students' Book is divided into 20 Units. Each Unit (except Units 6, 12 and 20) consists of:
a) Presentation material (a dialogue or text).
b) Classroom exercises, divided into Sets.
c) Extension material.
d) Open dialogue.
e) Oral exercise examples.
f) Language summary page.

Units 6, 12 and 20 are Consolidation Units which bring together and revise the language presented in the preceding Units. They include extension activities, fill-in exercises, games and songs.

a) Presentation material
In most Units the language functions to be practised are presented in the form of a dialogue. The dialogue is sometimes divided into sections which exemplify the functions or groups of functions to be practised in the Unit.

The setting for the dialogues is a documentary film company in Manchester. The characters introduced are seen both in their varied work situations and in their out-of-work leisure activities. Although the dialogue has continuity of setting and character, there is no serialised story; the dialogues can be presented independently of one another.

b) Classroom exercises
The classroom exercises practise the specific language functions presented in the dialogue. Each section of the dialogue focuses on one or two particular language functions; it is immediately followed by practice materials for these functions. The majority of exercises follow a three-phase pattern:
1. re-presentation and organisation of the language in focus.
2. controlled practice.
3. transfer of language to the students' own experience or to a related problem.

c) Extension material
The extension material is designed to develop reading, listening, writing and communicative skills.

The reading and listening material is as authentic as possible i.e. the type of material is authentic but the language has been edited in places. The material is linked functionally or thematically to the Unit. Some of the language contained in the extension material is for passive recognition only.

The various writing activities try to reflect the actual uses of written language. The students are asked only to write what they might, in real life, be required to write.

d) Open dialogue
The open dialogue relates to one or more of the language functions presented in the Unit. It is designed to give the student an opportunity to use, in a freer conversational setting, the language which he has already practised.

e) Oral exercise examples
The title and two examples of each Oral Exercise are written out in full in the Students' Book. Italics indicate the part which they are meant to take.

f) Language summary page
This final section of each Unit contains a checklist of the functions introduced in the Unit with example sentences, a summary of the grammar printed out in the form of a substitution table and a list of the vocabulary from the Unit that is to be actively learnt.

ii) The Teacher's Book
The Teacher's Book consists of:
a) Introduction.
b) General description of the course.
c) Guide to general teaching procedures.
d) Summary of the teaching contents of each Unit.
e) Detailed teaching notes for each Unit.
f) Tapescript of the practice materials.
g) Indexes of the functions, structures and vocabulary, both active and passive, introduced in the course.

iii) The set of tapes
A set of tapes accompanies the course. The tape material for each Unit is divided into two parts: A and B.
Part A includes:
a) the complete dialogue in two versions: without pauses and with pauses (for repetition).
b) the listening passage(s). Instructions for related activities appear in the Students' Book.
c) speechwork exercises. These exercises practise some important features of stress, intonation and pronunciation related to the Unit. They use only familiar vocabulary. The stress and intonation exercises provide additional structural practice based on the language from the Unit.
d) the open dialogue: recorded with pauses for the students to give their own responses.

Part B consists of a set of oral exercises to practise the main structural features from the Unit. These are recorded in three phases: listen – speak – check performance with model response.

iv Songs (with teaching notes)
A set of songs "Cloudsongs" accompanies the course. The songs are designed to expand and exploit topics, functions and structures covered in the course book. They also help to develop aural comprehension and build up confidence and fluency. Moreover they are important in that they provide a pleasant and relaxing activity after concentrated classroom language work.

v) Wall Pictures/Overhead Transparencies(OHP)
A set of 10 wall pictures accompanies certain Units of the course. Detailed teacher's notes indicate where in these Units they are to be used. In most cases the pictures are simply a magnified version of the illustrations already printed in the Students' Book. They do not introduce any new vocabulary or characters. As such, they are an optional but useful extra teaching aid. It is easier to illustrate, practise and check vocabulary and structures when the students are all looking at the same picture. If these pictures are not available, teachers can use home-made flash cards (pictures cut out from magazines and pasted on to cardboard), blackboard sketches, actions, or can simply rely on the illustrations in the book.

General teaching notes

Catering for the learners' needs
There is a strong movement in language teaching today, shifting the decision about what should be learnt from the teacher to the student. The danger of a course book of this nature is that the needs of the students are prescribed by the writer. Naturally one cannot hope to satisfy the needs of every individual student or every group of students. It is essential for the teacher to assess independently the needs of his particular group of students in the light of their linguistic, educational and socio-cultural background and to relate these factors to the material presented in this course book. Some of the language presented may not be essential to a particular group, at least at this early stage. Some may need to be expanded. The decision should, we feel, be made by the teacher and students together.

The importance of group work
Another trend in language teaching is the shift in emphasis from 'teaching' to 'learning'. Research shows that learning is most effective in small groups, as opposed to large groups (10 or more) or individually. Many of the teacher's notes for particular exercises in Starting Strategies included suggestions for pair work, group work and 'cross-group reporting'.

Cross-group reporting can be illustrated as follows. Take a class of 15 students. The class is divided into three groups of five to work on some group activity. Each student in each of the three groups is given a letter: A, B, C, D, E. When the group activity is completed, the groups re-form: all A's go to one group, all the B's to another and so on, until there are five new groups of three students each. The role of each student in the new cross-groups is to report to the other members of his group the findings of his original group. The following diagram illustrates the arrangement more clearly:

```
First working groups        Cross-groups
  A     A     A         A   B   C   C   E
  E B   E B   E B       AA  BB  CC  DD  EE
  DC    DC    DC
```

This kind of work has several advantages. Firstly, each individual student carries the responsibility of reporting his original group's results and must therefore be an active listener, if not speaker, in the original group. Secondly, everybody is forced to speak in the cross-group. Thirdly, the arrangement enables students to get to know more than one or two people in the class.

Active and passive vocabulary
Throughout the course a distinction is made between active and passive vocabulary. The rationale is elaborated in the section *Productive and receptive skills* (see Introduction page v). A further distinction is made between vocabulary that is introduced passively in one Unit, but actively in a later Unit, and vocabulary that is only introduced passively. This is indicated in the complete vocabulary list at the back of the Teacher's Book. For example, 'coffee *6*, **10**' means that the word *coffee* is introduced passively for the first time in Unit 6, but is only presented actively from Unit 10 onwards; 'landlord *5*' means that the word *landlord* appears for the first time in Unit 5 but is not taken up actively during the rest of the course. A complete Unit by Unit list of passive vocabulary is also printed at the back, with an indication of where, if at all, the words are reintroduced actively.

The students will probably want to know the meaning of most, if not all, passive vocabulary that is printed in their books. The quickest and most economical explanation of the meaning is best. Reference to a dictionary can be useful, especially in multi-lingual groups, and when the students are studying a text silently. Unfamiliar words which occur on the tape can often be ignored if the students themselves do not notice them and demand an explanation. Students should not be required to produce the words actively or memorise them. The learning load for each Unit should be no greater than that specified in the summary page at the end of each Unit in the Students' Book.

Use of the mother tongue in monolingual classes.
For many years teachers have been discouraged from resorting to the use of the mother tongue in language classes. The advantages of as much exposure to the target language as possible are obvious, and exclusive use of the target language has not been a problem while the emphasis has been on structural teaching, for very little (or no) description of what students are going to learn in a lesson is expected to be given to them. However with the shift of emphasis from structural to functional teaching, where students are often told explicitly what they are going to learn, strict adherence to the target language seems no longer relevant.

In fact, functional teaching seems to be especially suitable for monolingual classes where the teacher can use the mother tongue freely to present the learning goals of each lesson, to simplify explanation of the passive vocabulary items in certain texts, and to give the background setting for dialogues, listening and reading passages.

Constant shifts from one language to another can, of course, be unsettling for students in the long run. The teacher should decide in advance at what stage or on what occasions he might use the mother tongue and then keep strictly to this decision. The students will then know when they are allowed to use the mother language and when not.

Symbols used in the teacher's notes
SB   Students' Book.
TB   Teacher's Book.
T–S   The teacher asks a question or makes a statement; the student answers or responds.
S–T   The student asks a question or makes a statement; the teacher answers or responds.
S1–S2, One student asks another student a question. The
S2–S3 second student answers. Then the second student
etc. asks a third student a similar question and so on, in the form of a chain. The chain need not work in a logical order from left to right; students can choose to whom they want to put a question each time.

Teaching terms and techniques
The following terms and techniques are referred to in the teacher's notes:
1. *'Practise the intonation of the model exchange.'*
The model exchange is the piece of language which is highlighted by a picture strip or box before an exercise. It is usually a two-line exchange. The teacher takes each line separately and practises the intonation by the 'back-chaining' method e.g.

TEACHER: *Listen please: What time does the train leave? train leave?... does the train leave?... what time does the train leave?*

2. *'Practise the pronunciation of the words chorally and individually.'*
The teacher proceeds as follows:
TEACHER: *Say after me please: water.*
CLASS: *water.*
TEACHER: *Again.*
CLASS: *water.*
TEACHER: *Mary.*
MARY: *water.*
TEACHER: *Peter.*
PETER: *water.*

If the class is large, select only two or three students to repeat individually.

3. *'Students work in pairs simultaneously.'*
The teacher divides the class into pairs and labels each member of each pair A and B. Students ask and answer questions according to the exercise first A–B, then B–A. All the pairs are active at the same time. The teacher goes round and listens to the performance of as many pairs as possible, correcting when necessary.

If there is an uneven number in the class, the teacher can either make one group of three or take part himself as a member of a pair. If this is a permanent situation, it is important that the same student is not always the 'odd-man-out'.

As most of the classroom work is conducted in pairs, it is essential to rearrange the seating of the students after 3 or 4 lessons so that they will get a chance of working with different partners. This also helps to avoid personal conflicts that can arise between individual students.

Guide to general teaching procedures

Before teaching any Unit or part of a Unit, the teacher should look at the summary of the main teaching points which precedes each Unit.
This will indicate:
1. the new functions which are to be learnt.
2. the main structures on which the functions are based.
3. the vocabulary items which are to be actively learnt.
4. the stress, intonation and pronunciation features practised in the tape material.

This guide assumes that the teacher is aware of the relevant language items in focus. As the format for each Unit tends to vary, this guide can only serve as a general reference section. Where an exercise or text needs special attention, a teacher can refer to the additional teaching notes accompanying each unit of the course. For ease of reference, the classwork (Sets and Extension) pages of the Students' Book are reproduced in a reduced size in the Unit by Unit notes.

a) DIALOGUE
1. Introduce setting and context.
2. Play tape of first section (if the dialogue is divided, sections are shown in the tapescript).

3. Explain new vocabulary and expressions.
4. Play tape again.
5. Ask simple questions about the dialogue. This is probably not possible in the very early Units as students have not enough language yet to understand the questions.

b) SETS AND EXERCISES

If the students have a monolingual background, it may save time to explain the functional titles and the instructions for each exercise in the mother tongue. If the students have a multilingual background, it is essential to make it very clear, using the given examples, what the language function is, and what the students are expected to do in the exercises.

1. Read model exchange printed in SB. A suggested intonation pattern is printed in the individual notes for each Unit.
2. Students listen and repeat chorally and individually.
3. Present the new vocabulary using either the pictures in SB or, preferably, real objects, pictures from magazines, blackboard drawings or overhead pictures. This is not essential, but makes it easier to check vocabulary.
4. Students repeat the new words chorally and individually.
5. Check comprehension of new words.
6. Give another model example of the exercise, using one of the new vocabulary items.
7. Select one or two students and give further examples; students provide either the stimulus or the response.
8. Students work in pairs.
9. Check the students' performance by listening to them as they practise with each other, or by asking one or two pairs to perform in front of the rest of the class. It is sometimes useful to re-form the pairs for this purpose.

c) EXTENSION MATERIAL: Reading texts

There are two types of reading texts. The first consists of authentic-type materials like advertisements, notices, timetables, graphs, charts etc., where the purpose is to read or skim for specific information. Activities accompanying them are either printed in SB or are suggested in the individual teacher's notes.

The second type of text consists of connected prose passages: pieces of information about some aspect of British life, letters, newspaper articles etc. For this type of text the following procedure is recommended:

1. Introduce the topic of the text, preferably by asking questions that will lead to the text.
2. Present the key vocabulary, both active and passive. This may sometimes be combined with the previous stage.
3. Read the text aloud; the students follow it in their books.
4. Write a set of simple comprehension questions on the blackboard or have them prepared already on an overhead projection.

Alternative A

5a. Students read the text again, silently (possibly with the aid of a dictionary) and work out the answers to the questions.
6a. Students ask and answer the comprehension questions orally, working S1–S2, S2–S3 etc. round the class.

Alternative B

5b. Students work in small groups, studying the text and finding the answers to the questions, which they all write down.
6b. Students re-form their groups (see page vi on Cross-group reporting) and report their answers to the cross-groups.

Alternative C

Set questions on the text for homework. Correction of answers would then take place during the next lesson.

EXTENSION MATERIAL: Writing activities

1. Give clear instructions, preferably with a model example on the blackboard.
2. Ask students to work individually, in pairs or in groups, depending on the type of writing to be done.
3. Check progress while they are working. When the work is completed, the students may check each others' work. You may wish to collect in written work occasionally, especially if the work is set as homework.

d) OPEN DIALOGUE

The open dialogue is centred on one or more of the functions practised in the Unit. The students should be encouraged to give 'true' answers, using the correct structure or situational phrase where applicable. A practice model should be given so that students know what is expected of them.

1. Set the situation clearly.
2. Ask one student to read the printed side of the dialogue (or read it yourself in the early Units). Give the response yourself.
3. Change parts with the student. This time, you read the printed part; the student responds. Make sure that the student's responses are true, as he may think that he has to say the same as you.
4. Practise the same exchange with another student giving the responses. This should establish that more than one answer is possible.
5. Divide the students into pairs and ask them to practise the dialogue, changing parts afterwards. Go round and listen. This last activity may be carried out in the language laboratory if one is available (see following section).

e) TAPE MATERIAL: Speechwork

Speechwork can be carried out in the classroom or the language laboratory. If practised in class, ask for choral and individual repetition of each item.

TAPE MATERIAL: Oral Exercises

The oral exercises can be done in the classroom or the language laboratory. If practised in class, play the two model examples printed in the SB, and do one extra example yourself.

Practise the model responses with the students chorally and individually, making sure that the intonation is as close to the original as possible. Work through the whole exercise selecting individuals and/or groups to respond to each stimulus. There is an average of six examples in each exercise.

Where the exercise makes use of visuals from the SB (instructions preceding the oral exercise will indicate if this is so) students use them so that they can also give the stimulus e.g. Unit 15, Oral Exercise 4. Write a few examples on the blackboard and ask the students to practise saying both halves (stimulus and response). Divide the class into pairs and ask them to do the exercise using the visuals in their books, changing parts at the end.

N.B. There are no individual notes on either the Speechwork or the Oral Exercises. This does not mean that they are less important than the other activities. On the contrary, they are an essential accompaniment to the basic classroom work. This practice should, if possible, precede any work on extension material.

TAPE MATERIAL: Open dialogue
See above for instructions about preparation. If a language laboratory is used, the students can practise giving individual responses in the pauses and listen to correct themselves if necessary. The teacher, monitoring the students, cannot hope to listen to everybody's efforts. Select a few students each time and keep a check on which students you have listened to.

TAPE MATERIAL: Listening activity
As in the reading text, much of the language used will be outside the students' productive capacity. The instructions for activities which accompany the listening passage appear in SB and help the students to focus their attention on the important facts to be drawn from the passage.
1. Play the tape to yourself or read the tapescript before the lesson.
2. Check what questions or activities accompany the passage.
3. Present any new 'key' words for general comprehension of the passage.
4. Play the tape through once without stopping.
5. Prepare the students for the activity, making sure they know what to do.
6. Play the tape again stopping in relevant places. Do not stop to explain the meaning of all new words and expressions.
7. Check answers.
   Stage 6 could be done in the language laboratory. The students can stop the tape as often as they like. In real life, of course, one does not have the opportunity to listen again to something one did not understand at a first hearing. The teacher should control the number of times that students listen to a given passage. As the course progresses, students should decrease the number of times they go over the listening passage. Classroom practice is in this context preferable. It also prevents the student from stopping the tape himself when he meets a language item which is not immediately recognisable.

UNIT 1 My name's Sally

	Skills	Functions	Example Sentences	Main Structures
SET 1	1. Speaking 2. Writing	Ask and say your name	*What's your name?* *Sally Baker.*	*What's your name?*
SET 2	1. Speaking 2. Speaking 3. Speaking 4. Speaking 5. Speaking	Ask and say where places and people are	*Where's Kent Road?* *It's over there.* *Where's Mr Freeman?* *He's over there.* *Where's Mrs Richards/* *Miss Young?* *She's over there.*	Where's + name of person? Where's + name of place? He/She/It's over there.
		Attract attention Thank	*Excuse me! Where's ....?* *...Thank you.*	
EXTENSION	1. Writing 2. Writing 3. Listening	Write questions in bubbles for characters asking directions. Write names for different purposes in different ways. Dialogue (not in Students' Book).		

OPEN DIALOGUE

ORAL EXERCISES		
1. Ask where places and people are		Kent Road. *Where's Kent Road?*
2. Say where people and places are (1)		Where's Mr Freeman? *Mr Freeman's over there.*
3. Say where places and people are (2)		Where's Kent Road? *It's over there.*
4. Say where people and places are (3)		Where's Mr Freeman? *Mr Freeman is over there.*

SPEECHWORK

A STRESS
　　Miss Young   . ●
　　Mr Freeman   . . ● .
　　Kent Road   ● ●

B INTONATION   ˈWhere's Miss Young? ↗
C PRONUNCIATION /ɪ/ Mr Simmons

ACTIVE VOCABULARY

name	Mr	yes
road	Mrs	please
park	Miss	thank you
station		excuse me
teacher	your	over there
What		
Where		

Unit 1

DIALOGUE

The pictures indicate that this is a formal situation – a girl is asked her name at a reception desk, so titles (*Miss* Sally Baker, *Mr* Freeman) are used.

SET 1 Ask somebody's name and say your name

Ex 1 What's your name?   Sally Baker.

Give an example using your own name.
Practise intonation of the question with the whole class.
Practise with one student T–S, with another S–T (see Guide to General Teaching Procedures page vii).
Students work simultaneously in pairs, giving own names, then in a chain round the class.
Students make their own name cards to place in front of them if you think this is useful.

Ex 2 Write another example on the blackboard, giving your own name and signature.
Students fill in their own names and signatures.
Go round the class to check students have understood the meaning of *signed*.
(Students with general writing difficulties can look at the alphabet in Unit 4 to check how letters are formed.)

DIALOGUE

Room One is a passive item of vocabulary (see General Guide). Numbers 1–9 are introduced in Unit 4; names of rooms are introduced in Unit 9.

SET 2 Ask and say where places and people are

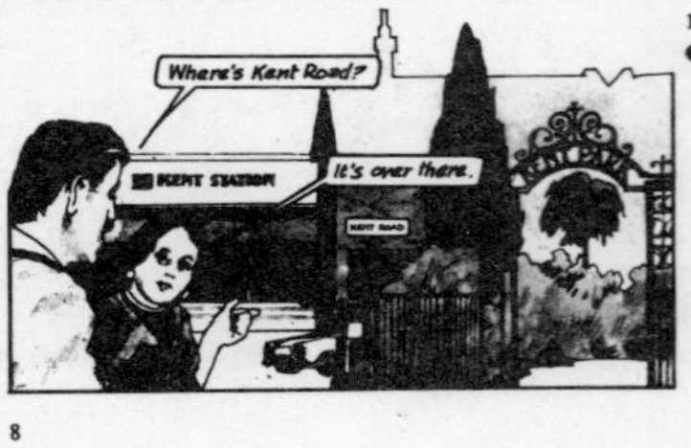

Ex 1 Where's Kent Road?   It's over there.

Illustrate meaning of *road/park/station*.
Practise pronunciation of *Kent Road/Park/Station*.
Read model exchange.
Students repeat chorally.
Practise with one student T–S, with another S–T.
Students work simultaneously in pairs with the three examples, taking different parts in turn.
Check individual students.

Unit 1

Ex 2 Where's Mr Freeman?   He's over there.

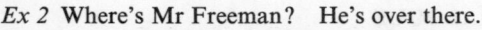

Practise pronunciation of surnames.
Explain and practise pronunciation of *Mr*/mɪstə^r/.
Proceed as in Ex 1 with model exchange and practise.

Ex 3 Where's Mrs Richards?   She's over there.

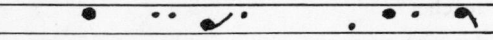

Practise pronunciation of surnames. *Young, Richards* may be difficult.
Explain and practise pronunciation of *Mrs*/mɪsɪz/ and *Miss*.
Proceed as in Ex 2 with model exchange and practice.

Ex 4 Write on the blackboard one or two names of places in your local town. Students can then suggest other places; a list of 6 is enough.
Students choose a place from the list, working simultaneously in pairs.
Check individual pairs.

Ex 5 Given an example using one of the students' names. Give examples of *he/she*.
Students work in pairs simultaneously, or pair by pair so that you can check them.
Or, move tables aside and ask students to walk round and approach each other as if they were at work or in a public building.

EXTENSION

1 *Writing* This aims to consolidate the questions in written form. Students work individually writing the appropriate questions in the empty bubbles. When they have completed the speech bubbles, ask them to compare their answers with those of their partners.

2 *Writing names* The different visual contexts (the memorandum note, the envelope or the doorplate) indicate the different ways of writing a name.
Students should write the suggested names in four different ways. This is also an exercise in accurate copying. Introduce and explain *Ms* (i.e. some women, both married and unmarried, prefer to be addressed as *Ms*/məz/).

3 *Listening* (see tapescript on page 4) This is to consolidate the functions practised in Sets 1 and 2. There is no writing activity connected with it. Look at the tapescript first to set the scene. It might help to write on the blackboard:

   Address: 2 West Road – Where is it?

(Note: if there is time, play the whole dialogue as a continuous listening passage for extra practice. Students should not need to follow the words in their books. This applies to all subsequent Units.)

Open Dialogue See Guide to General Teaching Procedures (page viii) and tapescript (page 4).

Oral Exercises See Guide to General Teaching Procedures (page viii) and tapescript (page 4).

Speechwork See Guide to General Teaching Procedures (page viii) and tapescript (page 4).

2. Ask and answer like this:
   Where's Mr ....?
   He's over there.
   Thank you.

3. Ask and answer like this:
   Where's Mrs/Miss ....?
   She's over there.
   Thank you.

4. Choose a place in your town. Ask and answer like this:
   Excuse me!
   Yes?
   Where's ....?
   It's over there.
   Thank you.

5. Choose a person in your classroom. Ask and answer like this:
   Excuse me!
   Yes?
   Where's ....?
   He's/She's over there.
   Thank you.

UNIT 1
EXTENSION

1. Write the questions in the pictures

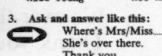
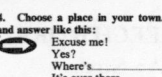
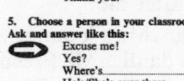

Kent Park   Kent Station   Miss Baker   Mr Freeman   Mr Johnson

2. Write names

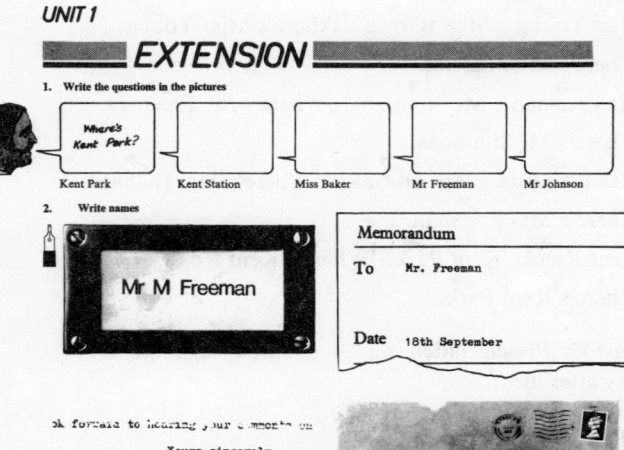

Write these names in the same way:
Sally Baker (Miss)   Tessa Richards (Mrs)
George Blake (Mr)   Your name

OPEN DIALOGUE
Talk to Murray Freeman

MURRAY: Excuse me!
STUDENT: ....
MURRAY: What's your name?
STUDENT: ....
MURRAY: Oh. My name's Murray Freeman. Where's your teacher?
STUDENT: ....
MURRAY: Oh. Thank you.

Unit 1

Tapescript
Part A

1 DIALOGUE
SALLY: Mr Freeman, please.
DOORMAN: Yes. What's your name?
SALLY: Sally Baker. Miss Sally Baker. I'm from the Manchester News.
DOORMAN: One moment, please, Miss Baker.
(phones)
Mr Freeman? Oh, Mr Freeman, Miss Baker's here, from the Manchester News.
He's in Room One, Miss Baker.
SALLY: Thank you.

SALLY: Excuse me!
MAN: Yes?
SALLY: Where's Room One?
MAN: It's over there.
SALLY: Thank you.

2 SPEECHWORK
Part A: Stress
Say after me:
di da…Miss Young…Miss Barnes…
di di da di…Mr Freeman…Mr Simmons…
di di da di…Mrs Richards…Mrs Freeman…
da da…Kent Road…Kent Park…

Part B: Intonation
Say after me:
Miss Young…Miss Barnes…'Where's Miss Young…
'Where's Miss Barnes…
Mr Freeman…Mr Simmons…'Where's Mr Freeman…
'Where's Mr Simmons…
Mrs Richards…Mrs Freeman…'Where's Mrs Richards…
'Where's Mrs Freeman…
'Kent Road…'Kent Park…'Where's 'Kent Road…
'Where's 'Kent Park…

Part C: Pronunciation
Say after me:
/ɪ/…/ɪ/…it…it…it's over there…
Miss…Mister…Mrs…
Mr Simmons…it's Mr Simmons…
Mrs Richards…it's Mrs Richards…

3 LISTENING
MURRAY: Now, what's the address?
TESSA: Number 2, West Road.
MURRAY: West Road. Where's West Road, I wonder.
TESSA: Excuse me!
MAN: Yes?
TESSA: Where's West Road?
MAN: West Road? Um…Yes, it's over there.
TESSA: Thank you very much.

4 OPEN DIALOGUE
Talk to Murray Freeman.
MURRAY: Excuse me!
STUDENT: ....
MURRAY: What's your name?
STUDENT: ....
MURRAY: Oh, my name's Murray Freeman. Where's your teacher?
STUDENT: ....
MURRAY: Oh, thank you.

Part B ORAL EXERCISES

Exercise 1 Ask where places and people are.
Kent Road
Where's Kent Road?
Mr Freeman
Where's Mr Freeman? Now go on.
Kent Park
Where's Kent Park?
Miss Baker
Where's Miss Baker?
Kent Station
Where's Kent Station?
Mrs Richards
Where's Mrs Richards?

Exercise 2 Say where people and places are (1).
Listen carefully.
Where's Mr Freeman?
Mr Freeman's over there.
Where's Kent Road?
Kent Road's over there. Now go on.
Where's Mr Blake?
Mr Blake's over there.
Where's Kent Park?
Kent Park's over there.
Where's Kent Station?
Kent Station's over there.

Exercise 3 Say where places and people are (2).
Where's Kent Road?
It's over there.
Where's Mr Freeman?
He's over there.
Where's Miss Baker?
She's over there. Now go on.
Where's Kent Station?
It's over there.
Where's Mrs Richards?
She's over there.
Where's Mr Simmons?
He's over there.

Unit 1

Where's Kent Park?
It's over there.
Where's Miss Young?
She's over there.

Exercise 4 Say where people and places are (3).
Listen carefully.
Where's Mr Freeman?
Mr. Freeman is over there.
Where's Kent Road?
Kent Road is over there. Now go on.
Where's Mr Blake?
Mr Blake is over there.
Where's Kent Park?
Kent Park is over there.
Where's Mrs Richards?
Mrs Richards is over there.
Where's Kent Station?
Kent Station is over there.

UNIT 2 I'm a journalist

	Skills	Functions	Example Sentences	Main Structures
SET 1	1. Speaking	Greet people formally Introduce yourself	*How do you do!* *My name's Sally Baker.*	*My name's* + name *I'm* + name
SET 2	1. Speaking 2. Speaking	Ask and say what someone's job is	*What does Murray do?* *He's a film director.*	*What does he do?* *He's a/an...*
	3. Speaking	Ask and say what your job is	*What do you do?* *I'm a journalist.*	*What do you do?* *I'm a...*
EXTENSION	1. Reading 2. Writing 3. Listening	Publicity brochure: read the instructions and greetings Crossword puzzle based on names of professions Consolidation dialogue		
OPEN DIALOGUE				
ORAL EXERCISES	1. Greet people formally		How do you do! My name's Murray Freeman. *How do you do, Mr Freeman.*	
	2. Ask people their names and greet them		*What's your name?* Young. Miss Jackie Young. *How do you do, Miss Young.*	
	3. Ask about people's jobs		That's Murray over there. *What does Murray do?*	
	4. Say what people do		What does Murray do? *He's a film director.*	

SPEECHWORK

		ACTIVE VOCABULARY	
A STRESS	typist • . she's a typist • . • .	journalist film director cameraman	secretary technician van driver typist
B INTONATION	Jackie, ↗ Jackie Young ↗	How do you do! One moment my too	do
C PRONUNCIATION	/iː/ he, Sheila		

Unit 2

DIALOGUE

Emphasise that we say *How do you do* to people we have not met before if they are a) recognisably older or b) if they are superior in a professional situation e.g. employer/employee. Notice that there are two alternative ways of introducing oneself: *My name's...* and *I'm...* This unit concentrates on the first way but the second way is equally acceptable. *How do you do* and *What do you do?* are structurally similar and may cause confusion but the exercises will provide practice, especially in the differing intonation patterns: a fall for *How do you do* and a rise for *What do you do?*

SET 1 Greet people formally and introduce yourself

Ex 1 How do you do, Mr Freeman. My name's Sally Baker.

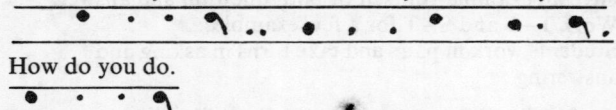

How do you do.

Using your own name, give this example: *How do you do. My name's...*
Students repeat chorally *How do you do.*
Go round the class practising *My name's...* and concentrate on a falling intonation.
Individual students introduce themselves to you. Perhaps students should get out of their seats and go up to you to introduce themselves. Shaking hands is optional.

I'm a journalist

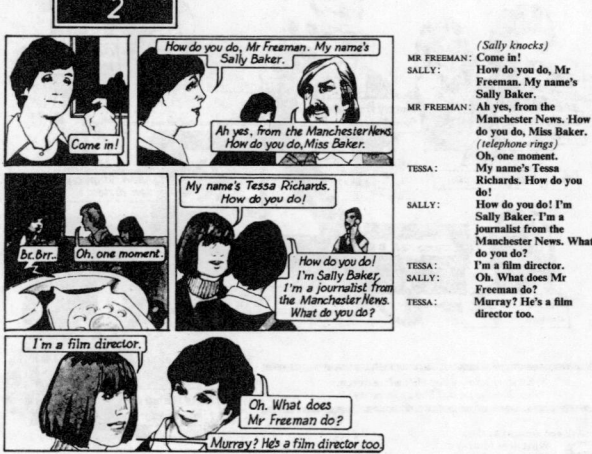

MR FREEMAN: (Sally knocks) Come in!
SALLY: How do you do, Mr Freeman. My name's Sally Baker.
MR FREEMAN: Ah yes, from the Manchester News. How do you do, Miss Baker.
(telephone rings)
TESSA: Oh, one moment. My name's Tessa Richards. How do you do!
SALLY: How do you do! I'm Sally Baker. I'm a journalist from the Manchester News. What do you do?
TESSA: I'm a film director.
SALLY: Oh. What does Mr Freeman do?
TESSA: Murray? He's a film director too.

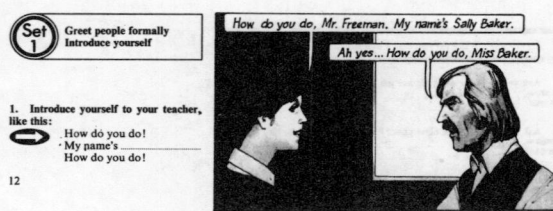

Unit 2

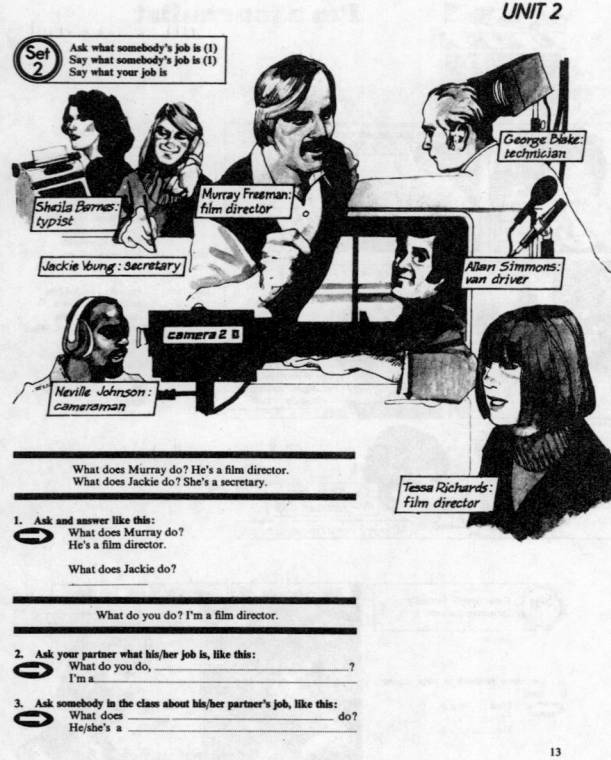

What does Murray do? He's a film director.
What does Jackie do? She's a secretary.

1. Ask and answer like this:
   What does Murray do?
   He's a film director.

   What does Jackie do?
   _____

   What do you do? I'm a film director.

2. Ask your partner what his/her job is, like this:
   What do you do, _____?
   I'm a _____.

3. Ask somebody in the class about his/her partner's job, like this:
   What does _____ do?
   He/she's a _____.

13

UNIT 2
EXTENSION

A publicity brochure for Focus Films:

WHO'S WHO in FOCUS FILMS

Meet Murray Freeman, a film director at Focus Films: 'Hello, there, my name's Murray Freeman and I'm a film director at Focus'.
Meet Allan Simmons, a van driver: 'Hi, I'm Allan, I'm a van driver'.
Meet Tessa Richards, a film director: 'Hello, yes, I'm a film director at Focus, too'.
Meet Neville Johnson: 'I'm a cameraman'.
And George Blake: 'I'm a technician'.
And Jackie Young: 'I'm a secretary'.
WE MAKE FILMS AT FOCUS. CALL US ON THIS NUMBER **(061) 334·1564**

Word Puzzle: Guess the jobs! Don't look at page 13!

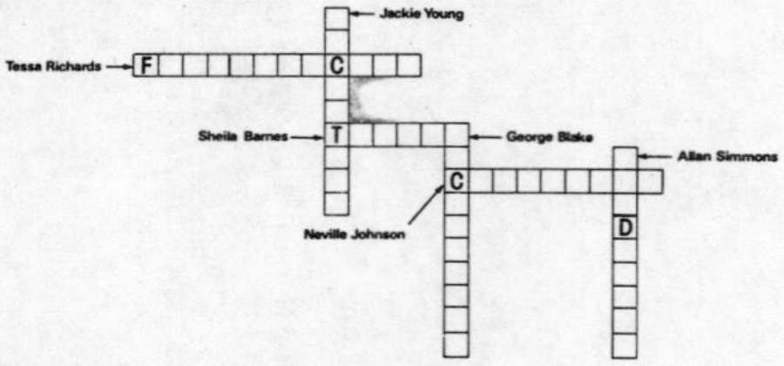

OPEN DIALOGUE

Talk to Murray Freeman

MURRAY: Excuse me!
STUDENT: _____
MURRAY: What's your name?
STUDENT: _____
MURRAY: Oh, my name's Murray Freeman. How do you do!
STUDENT: _____
MURRAY: What do you do?
STUDENT: _____
MURRAY: Oh yes. Where's your teacher?
STUDENT: _____
MURRAY: Oh, thank you.

14

SET 2 Ask and say what somebody's job is
Ask and say what your job is

Spend some time before attempting the exercises on the pronunciation of both first names and surnames, and on the stress, pronunciation and meaning of the various jobs. The names of the characters will recur throughout the book so do not expect students to remember them at this stage. Concentrate on the jobs in this unit. Use the wall picture/OHP (1) to show characters at work to illustrate the meaning of the jobs, or refer to pictures in the students' books.

Ex 1 What does Murray do? He's a film director.

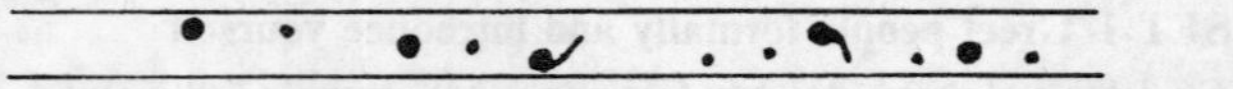

Give an example yourself of both question and answer.
Work T–S and S–T for a few examples.
Students work in pairs and take turns in asking and answering.

Ex 2 What do you do, _____? I'm a film director.

Give an example, using your own name and giving your profession (*teacher*).
If all students are full-time students, proceed immediately with pair-work. If they are not and if they have different jobs, help them first to find the word for their own job if it has not already been mentioned. Some jobs will not be included in the students' book; you will need to help students whose jobs are not included. If necessary, encourage them to use a dictionary.
Help them individually to pronounce their own jobs correctly. The use of *an* before jobs beginning with a vowel is introduced formally in Unit 3, but if a student needs it in this section, explain it to him/her individually. It is not necessary that the whole class understands or learns all the different jobs. They should know their own and that of their partner. Proceed with pair work as in Ex 1.

Ex 3 Ask one or two students about their partners' jobs. Each student asks another student what his partner does; this can be done in a chain round the class.

EXTENSION

Reading: Publicity brochure for Focus Films See Guide to General Teaching Procedures (page viii).

Word puzzle This is to revise the names of jobs and their spellings. Play as a game. Divide the class into pairs and ask them to fill in the crossword without looking at the list of names and jobs in their books. The pair that finishes first wins. The puzzle could also be set as homework to be completed individually.

Key: 1 *film director* 2 *secretary* 3 *typist* 4 *technician*
5 *cameraman* 6 *van driver*

Listening (See tapescript page 9)
This revises and consolidates the main functions of Units 1 and 2. There is no writing activity attached.

Open Dialogue See General Guide and tapescript (page 9).

Oral Exercises See General Guide and tapescript (page 9).

Speechwork See General Guide and tapescript (page 9).

Unit 2

Tapescript
Part A
1 DIALOGUE

	(Sally knocks)
MR FREEMAN:	Come in!
SALLY:	How do you do, Mr Freeman. My name's Sally Baker.
MR FREEMAN:	Ah yes, from the Manchester News. How do you do, Miss Baker.
	(telephone rings)
	Oh, one moment.
TESSA:	My name's Tessa Richards. How do you do!
SALLY:	How do you do! I'm Sally Baker. I'm a journalist from the Manchester News. What do you do?
TESSA:	I'm a film director.
SALLY:	Oh. What does Mr Freeman do?
TESSA:	Murray? He's a film director too.

2 SPEECHWORK
Part A: Stress
Say after me:
da di…typist…student…teacher…driver…
di di da di…she's a typist…I'm a student…
she's a teacher…he's a driver…

Part B: Intonation
Say after me:
Jackie…Jackie Young…Murray…Murray Freeman…
Tessa…Tessa Richards…George…George Blake…
Allan…Allan Simmons…Sheila…Sheila Barnes…

Part C: Pronunciation
Say after me:
/iː/…/iː/…he…she…me…please…Sheila…
Mr Freeman…Mr Freeman please…teacher…
he's a teacher…she's a teacher…

3 LISTENING

TESSA:	Oh, Sheila, I'm looking for Miss Young. Where is she?
SHEILA:	Miss Young? One moment. Oh yes, she's over there.
TESSA:	Thank you. Er…Excuse me. Miss Young?
JACKIE:	Yes?
TESSA:	How do you do! My name's Tessa, Tessa Richards.
JACKIE:	How do you do!
TESSA:	Come and meet George Blake. He's over there.

4 OPEN DIALOGUE
Talk to Murray Freeman.

MURRAY:	Excuse me!
STUDENT:	……………………
MURRAY:	What's your name?
STUDENT:	……………………
MURRAY:	Oh, my name's Murray Freeman. How do you do.
STUDENT:	……………………
MURRAY:	What do you do?
STUDENT:	……………………
MURRAY:	Oh yes. Where's your teacher?
STUDENT:	……………………
MURRAY:	Oh, thank you.

Part B ORAL EXERCISES

Exercise 1 Greet the people at Focus Films formally.

How do you do! My name's Murray Freeman.
How do you do, Mr Freeman.

How do you do! My name's George Blake.
How do you do, Mr Blake. Now go on.

How do you do! My name's Mrs Richards. Tessa Richards.
How do you do, Mrs Richards.

How do you do! My name's Neville Johnson.
How do you do, Mr Johnson.

How do you do! My name's Allan Simmons.
How do you do, Mr Simmons.

How do you do! My name's Miss Young. Jackie Young.
How do you do, Miss Young.

Exercise 2 Ask the people at Focus Films their names, and greet them.

What's your name?
Young. Miss Jackie Young.
How do you do, Miss Young.

What's your name?
Freeman. Mr Murray Freeman.
How do you do, Mr Freeman. Now go on.

What's your name?
Richards. Mrs Tessa Richards.
How do you do, Mrs Richards.

What's your name?
Blake. Mr George Blake.
How do you do, Mr Blake.

What's your name?
Baker. Miss Sally Baker.
How do you do, Miss Baker.

Exercise 3 Ask about people's jobs.

That's Murray over there.
What does Murray do?

That's Tessa over there.
What does Tessa do? Now go on.

That's Sheila over there.
What does Sheila do?

That's Allan over there.
What does Allan do?

That's George over there.
What does George do?

That's Neville over there.
What does Neville do?

Unit 2

Exercise 4 Say what the people at Focus Films do. Look at page 13.

What does Murray do?
He's a film director.

What does Tessa do?
She's a film director. Now go on.

What does Allan do?
He's a van driver.

What does Sheila do?
She's a typist.

What does George do?
He's a technician.

What does Neville do?
He's a cameraman.

What does Jackie do?
She's a typist.

UNIT 3 Hello and Goodbye!

	Skills	Functions	Example Sentences	Main Structures
SET 1	1. Speaking 2. Speaking 3. Speaking	Introduce people Greet informally	*Neville, this is Sally.* *Sally's a journalist.* *Hello!*	*This is* + name Name + *'s a...*
SET 2	1. Speaking 2. Speaking 3. Speaking 4. Writing 5. Writing	Ask what somebody's job is Say what somebody's job is	*Is Sally a journalist?* *Yes, she is.* *Is Sally a secretary?* *No, she isn't.* *What does she do?* *She's a journalist.* *Sally isn't a secretary. She's a journalist.*	*Is* + Name + *a/an...?* *Yes, he/she is* *No, he/she isn't* Name + *is a*............
SET 3	1. Speaking 2. Speaking	Ask and say somebody's name	*What's his name?* *His name's Neville.*	*His/Her name's* + Name
EXTENSION	1. Writing 2. Listening Writing 3. Speaking 4. Reading	Game: pair names with jobs. Radio programme: host introduces guests. Fill in jobs. Introduce your group (based on listening in Extension 2). Credits and titles for a TV programme.		

OPEN DIALOGUE

ORAL EXERCISES			
	1. Ask people what their jobs are	This is Murray. *What do you do, Murray?*	
	2. Answer questions about jobs	Is Murray a film director? *Yes, he is.*	
	3. Introduce people	Introduce Neville to Murray. *Murray, this is Neville.*	
	4. Say other people's names and jobs	Who's that? *Her name's Sally. She's a journalist.*	

SPEECHWORK		ACTIVE VOCABULARY		
A STRESS	This is Jackie • • ●	engineer	his	hello
		housewife	her	goodbye
		student		
B INTONATION	Jackie, this is Murray (↗ ↘)	doctor	this	and
C PRONUNCIATION	/æ/ Jackie, thank you.	friend	here	no
		job		

Unit 3

Hallo and Goodbye!

NEVILLE: Hello, Tessa!
TESSA: Hello, Neville! Neville, this is Miss Baker.
SALLY: Oh, please call me Sally.
TESSA: All right! Neville, this is Sally. Sally's a journalist.
NEVILLE: Hello!
SALLY: Hello!
MURRAY: Neville!
NEVILLE: Yes, I'm coming, Murray. Goodbye, Sally!
SALLY: Goodbye!
    Is Neville a film director?
TESSA: No, he isn't.
SALLY: What does he do?
TESSA: He's a cameraman.
SALLY: What's his name? I mean his surname?
TESSA: His name? Johnson, Neville Johnson.

Set 1 Introduce people (1) / Greet informally

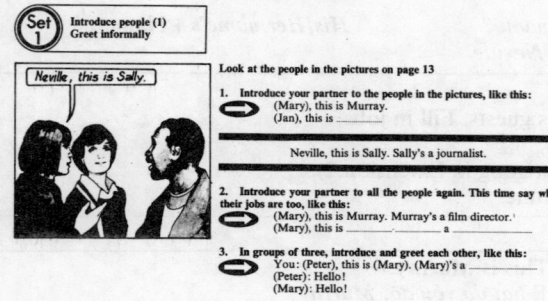

Neville, this is Sally.

Look at the people in the pictures on page 13

1. Introduce your partner to the people in the pictures, like this:
    (Mary), this is Murray.
    (Jan), this is _____

    Neville, this is Sally. Sally's a journalist.

2. Introduce your partner to all the people again. This time say what their jobs are too, like this:
    (Mary), this is Murray. Murray's a film director.
    (Mary), this is _____ a _____

3. In groups of three, introduce and greet each other, like this:
    You: (Peter), this is (Mary). (Mary)'s a _____
    (Peter): Hello!
    (Mary): Hello!

16

Set 2 Ask what somebody's job is (2) / Say what somebody's job is (2)

UNIT 3

1. Sally Baker – She's a journalist.
2. Walter Moaney – He's an engineer.
3. Pat Moaney – She's a teacher.
4. David Richards – He's a teacher too.
5. Doris Blake – She's a housewife.
6. Paul Blake – He's a student.
   Maria Magnani – She's a student too.
   Martha Hunt – She's a doctor.

Is Sally a journalist? Yes, she is.
Is Walter an engineer? Yes, he is.

1. Look at the people in the pictures. Ask and answer like this:
   Is Sally a journalist?
   Yes, she is.

   Is Walter an engineer?
   Yes, he is.

   Is _____ a(n) _____?
   Yes, _____ is.

Is Sally a secretary? No, she isn't.
Is Walter a technician? No, he isn't.

2. Look at the people again. Ask and answer like this:
   Is Sally a secretary?
   No, she isn't.

   Is Walter a technician?
   No, he isn't.

   Is _____ a(n) _____?
   No, _____ isn't.

   Pat – doctor   Paul – engineer
   David – journalist   Maria – teacher
   Doris – teacher   Martha – housewife

17

DIALOGUE

This dialogue shows how to make introductions in a more informal context, using first names and *Hello*.

Explain that we can say *Hello* even when we meet somebody for the first time, if the person is approximately the same age or if they are equal professionally. Of course the introductions could also be followed by *How do you do*, but students probably find *Hello* more natural.

Please call me Sally is not practised in the following exercises but could be practised if students want to be called by shortened names.

SET 1 Introduce people and greet informally

Ex 1 Neville, this is Sally.

Introduce the first few characters to a few students to illustrate this exercise.
Students work in pairs simultaneously.

Ex 2 Neville, this is Sally. Sally's a journalist.

Practise as in Ex 1.

Ex 3 Choose two students in the class and introduce them to each other. Ask them to say *Hello* to each other.
Ask one of them to introduce you to the other (and vice versa).
Students form groups of 3. Each student takes it in turn to introduce the other two in the group.

SET 2 Ask and say what somebody's job is

Ex 1 Is Sally a journalist?   Yes, she is.

Introduce and practise the pronunciation of the new jobs using the wall picture/OHP (1). Check with:
Question: *What does Sally do?* Answer: *She's a journalist*, etc. Explain the use of *a/an*.
Practise the first few examples chorally, ensuring that the intonation of the question and answer is correct.
Ask individual students questions to elicit response *Yes, he is, Yes, she is*.
Students work in pairs taking turns to ask and answer.

Ex 2 Is Sally a secretary?   No, she isn't.

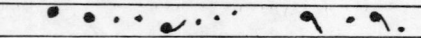

Practise the first few examples chorally. Work as in Ex 1.

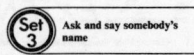

Ex 3 This combines Ex 2 with *What does he/she do?*
Work from the questions in Ex 2, giving an example first yourself. Then ask one student to respond and give another example.
Students work in pairs simultaneously, taking turns to ask and answer.

Ex 4 For class or homework.
Students work individually, writing full sentences.
Stress accurate spelling, the correct position of apostrophes and use of the article.

Ex 5 Students ask each other their names (if not already familiar) and their jobs, and note them down.
Students individually write out the sentences in full.

SET 3 Ask and say somebody's name
Ex 1 What's his name?   His name's Neville.

Show that *his* is used with male persons, *her* with females. Demonstrate the question form by pointing to different men and women in the class and asking *What's his/her name?* Make sure that it is one of the other students – not the one to whom you are referring – who gives the answer. Practise the intonation of the question and answer.
Using the names of the characters on page 13, give an example for the exercise, one for each sex.
After some T–S practice, students work in pairs, taking turns to ask and answer.

Ex 2 Students in turn point to somebody in the class and ask the other students what his/her name is. Accept both full and short answers.

UNIT 3

Is Neville a film director?
No, he isn't.
What does he do?
He's a cameraman.

3. Look at the people again. Ask and answer like this:
   Is Sally a secretary?
   No, she isn't.
   What does she do?
   She's ....

   Is Walter a technician?
   No, he isn't.
   What does he do?
   He's ....

   Ask the questions from Exercise 2.

4. Look at the questions in Exercise 2 again. Write the answers like this:
   Sally isn't a secretary. She's a journalist.
   Walter isn't a technician. He's an engineer.
   Pat .... She's a ....

   David ....
   Doris ....
   Paul ....
   Maria ....
   Martha ....

5. Write notes on 3 people in the class, like this:
   Peter Black – student
   Jan White – secretary
   Now write full sentences:
   Peter Black is a student
   Jan White is a secretary

Set 3 Ask and say somebody's name

What's his name? What's her name?
His name's Neville. Her name's Tessa.

1. Look at the pictures on page 13. Ask and answer like this:
   What's his/her name?
   His/her name's ....

2. Ask your partner about someone else in the class:
   What's . . .

Unit 3

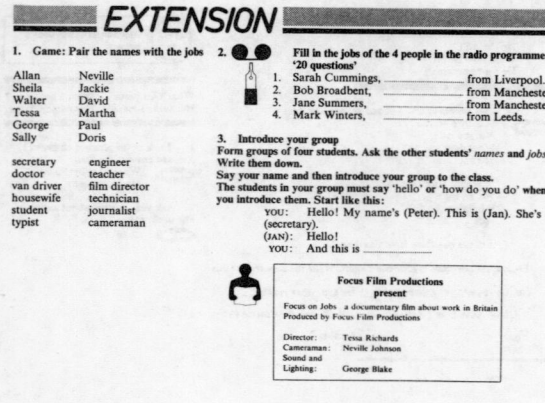

EXTENSION

1 *Game: Pair the names with the jobs* Give an example by writing out the first job with the correct name beside it.
Students work individually in the same way.
Give a time limit and check the answers.

2 *Listening and writing* Radio programme – host introduces a panel of guests.
Play the tape once.
Refer the students to the activity – filling in the people's jobs.
Play the tape again, possibly pausing after each person's job is mentioned so that students have time to write down the answers.
Check answers.

3 *Introduce your group* This activity is based on the listening passage.
Students form groups of 4.
One student is the host, the other 3 are the panel of guests. The host finds out from each of the 3 students their names, jobs and where they are from, and notes them down.
The host introduces himself and the panel to the rest of the class. The members of the panel can say *Hello* or *How do you do* as they are introduced.

4 *Reading* Credits and titles for a TV programme.
Students read silently.
Draw their attention to those things which they have already learnt, not passive items, by asking simple direct questions e.g. *What's the name of the film? Who's the director?/the cameraman?/the technician?* Explain *'documentary film'* – a nonfiction film taken exclusively from reality, usually on subjects of social or political interest.

Open Dialogue See General Guide and tapescript (page 15).

Oral Exercises See General Guide and tapescript (page 15).

Speechwork See General Guide and tapescript (page 15).

Tapescript
Part A

1 DIALOGUE
NEVILLE: Hello, Tessa!
TESSA: Hello, Neville! Neville, this is Miss Baker.
SALLY: Oh, please call me Sally.
TESSA: All right! Neville, this is Sally. Sally's a journalist.
NEVILLE: Hello!
SALLY: Hello!
MURRAY: Neville!
NEVILLE: Yes, I'm coming, Murray. Goodbye, Sally!
SALLY: Goodbye!

　　　　Is Neville a film director?
TESSA: No, he isn't.
SALLY: What does he do?
TESSA: He's a cameraman.
SALLY: What's his name? I mean his surname?
TESSA: His name? Johnson, Neville Johnson.

2 SPEECHWORK
Part A: Stress
Say after me:
da di…di di da di…Jackie…this is Jackie…Neville…this is Neville…Murray…this is Murray…Tessa…this is Tessa…

Part B: Intonation
Say after me:

Jackie…Murray…Jackie, this is Murray…
Tessa…Jackie…Tessa, this is Jackie…
George…Neville…George, this is Neville…
Sheila…Allan…Sheila, this is Allan…
Murray…Walter…Murray, this is Walter…

Part C: Pronunciation
Say after me:
/æ/…/æ/…thank you…Jackie…thank you Jackie…Allan…thank you Allan…van driver…Allan's a van driver…

3 LISTENING
This is Radio 1.
And now 'Twenty Questions'. And here to introduce the programme is your host Brian Trafford.
Good evening, everybody. This is Brian Trafford here in Manchester to introduce the first programme in the series Twenty Questions. Here on the panel this evening we have four guests…
Sarah Cummings, a secretary from Liverpool.
SARAH: How do you do!
And on her left, Bob Broadbent, an engineer from Manchester.
BOB: Hello!
And then we have Jane Summers, a housewife, also from Manchester.
JANE: Hello!
And last but not least, Mark Winters, a technician from Leeds.
MARK: How do you do!
(Applause)
And now for the first object. Object No 1 is mineral…

4 OPEN DIALOGUE
You visit Focus Films with a friend. Talk to Tessa.
TESSA: Hello!
STUDENT: ....
TESSA: What's your name?
STUDENT: ....
TESSA: Well, I'm Tessa. And this is Jackie. Jackie's a secretary.
JACKIE: Hello!
STUDENT: ....
TESSA: Where's your friend?
STUDENT: ....
TESSA: What's your friend's name?
STUDENT: ....
TESSA: Oh, please introduce me.
STUDENT: ....
TESSA: How do you do. Oh, here's Murray.
MURRAY: Hello!
STUDENT: ....
MURRAY: Well, Tessa, it's time to start.
TESSA: Oh, all right. Well, goodbye!
STUDENT: ....

Part B ORAL EXERCISES

Exercise 1 Ask these people what their jobs are.
This is Murray.
What do you do, Murray?
This is Tessa.
What do you do, Tessa? Now go on.
This is Neville.
What do you do, Neville?
This is Sheila.
What do you do, Sheila?
This is George.
What do you do, George?
This is Allan.
What do you do, Allan?

Exercise 2 Answer Sally's questions about people's jobs at Focus Films.
Is Murray a film director?
Yes, he is.
Is Allan a technician?
No, he isn't. Now go on.
Is Sheila a typist?
Yes, she is.
Is Neville a cameraman?
Yes, he is.

Unit 3

Is Tessa a secretary?
No, she isn't.

Is Jackie a technician?
No, she isn't.

Exercise 3 Introduce people.

Introduce Neville to Murray.
Murray, this is Neville.

Introduce Sally to Murray.
Murray, this is Sally. Now go on.

Introduce Tessa to Murray.
Murray, this is Tessa.

Introduce Sheila to Murray.
Murray, this is Sheila.

Introduce Allan to Murray.
Murray, this is Allan.

Introduce George to Murray.
Murray, this is George.

Exercise 4 Say other people's names and jobs. Look at the people on page 17.

Who's that?
Her name's Sally. She's a journalist.

Who's that?
His name's Walter. He's an engineer. Now go on.

Who's that?
Her name's Pat. She's a teacher.

Who's that?
His name's David. He's a teacher.

Who's that?
Her name's Doris. She's a housewife.

Who's that?
His name's Paul. He's a student.

UNIT 4   Looking for a flat (1)

	Skills	Functions	Example Sentences	Main Structures
SET 1	1. Speaking 2. Speaking 3. Speaking 4. Speaking 5. Speaking	Ask and talk about marital status	*Are you married?* *No, I'm not.* *Yes, I am.* *Is he/she married?* *Yes, he/she is.* *No, he/she isn't.*	*Are you married?* *Is he/she married?* *Yes, I am. No, I'm not.* *Yes, he/she is. No, he/she isn't.*
SET 2	1. Speaking 2. Speaking 3. Speaking	Spelling	(Letters of alphabet)	
SET 3	1. Speaking 2. Speaking 3. Writing 4. Speaking and Writing	Say your telephone number Numbers 0–9	(telephone numbers) *What's your telephone number? It's 507–8912.*	*What's your . . . ?* *It's . . .*
		Greet somebody in the morning	*Good morning!*	
EXTENSION	1. Reading and Writing	Write part of letter of application for a job based on model letter.		
	2. Listening and Writing	Fill in facts on form while listening to dialogue at flat agency.		
	3. Listening and Writing	Fill in telegram form while listening to telephone conversation between sender and telephone operator.		
	4. Writing	Fill in telegram form.		
	5. Speaking	Telephone telegram using form completed in Activity 4.		
	6. Reading	Reading Text: Sally Baker is a journalist.		

OPEN DIALOGUE

ORAL EXERCISES			
	1. Spell people's names		My name's Freeman. Can you spell that please? *F R double E M A N.*
	2. Respond to greetings		Good morning! *Good morning!*
	3. Repeat numbers		The code number for Manchester is 061. *061.*
	4. Answer correctly		Are you a teacher? *No, I'm not.*

SPEECHWORK

		ACTIVE VOCABULARY	
A STRESS	Yes, I am ●•●	flat	Good morning
		bedroom	Congratulations
B INTONATION	031 9028	surname	send
		address	married
C PRONUNCIATION	/ʌ/ number, one	telephone number	double
		telegram	small

one	four	seven	only
two	five	eight	
three	six	nine	

Looking for a flat (1)

TOWN AND COUNTRY FLAT AGENCY Application Form

Name Jackie Young Mr/Mrs/Miss Occupation Secretary
Address 4. Drummond Street, Trafford Park, Manchester 17. Size of flat wanted 1 bedroom
Tel. No. Trafford Park (061) 872 4679 Offer 3 Gordon Road, Manchester 8

MAN: Good morning! Can I help you?
JACKIE: Good morning! Yes. I'm looking for a small flat. One bedroom only.
MAN: Yes . . . just a minute. . . . What's your name, please?
JACKIE: Jackie Young.
MAN: Are you married?
JACKIE: No, I'm not.
MAN: And your address? What's your address?
JACKIE: 4, Drummond Street, Trafford Park, Manchester 17.
MAN: Is that D R U double M O N D?
JACKIE: Yes, that's right.
MAN: What's your telephone number?
JACKIE: Trafford Park four-six-seven-nine.
MAN: What's the code number?
JACKIE: Oh-six-one eight-seven-two.
MAN: And what do you do, Miss Young? What's your occupation?
JACKIE: I'm a secretary.

21

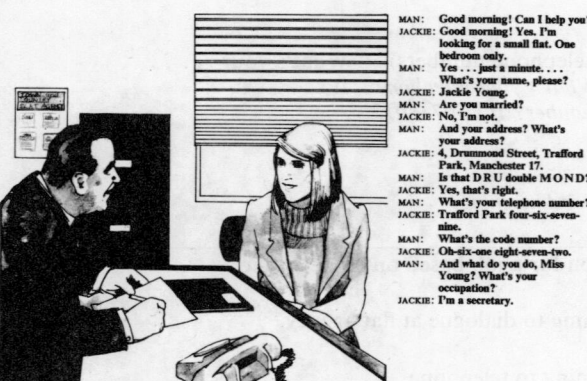

DIALOGUE

Note: This unit is relatively long and contains a lot of new material. Be prepared to spend an extra lesson to ensure that all of it is covered as thoroughly as possible. The spelling and numbers alone will probably take up a complete lesson.

Set the scene at the flat agency. Let the students look at the application form for a few minutes silently. Explain *bedroom* with a sketch on a blackboard. Explain *code number* by giving an example of a local code number. Play the dialogue and ask the students to look at the application form while they listen. The passive items should be self-explanatory if they understand the dialogue.

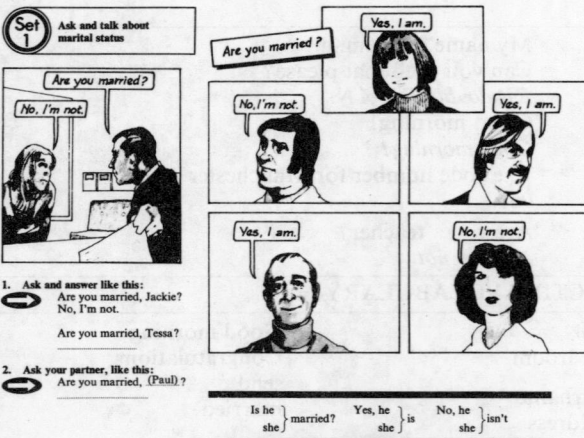

UNIT 4

Set 1 Ask and talk about marital status

1. Ask and answer like this:
Are you married, Jackie?
No, I'm not.

Are you married, Tessa?
....

2. Ask your partner, like this:
Are you married, (Paul)?
....

Is he / she married? Yes, he / she is. No, he / she isn't

3. Look at the people in Exercise 1. Ask and answer like this:
Is Jackie married?
No, she isn't.

Is Tessa married?
....

4. Quiz. Ask your partner/the class and answer:
Is Muhammed Ali married?
Yes .... *or* No ....

Ask about:

Elizabeth Taylor *Jimmy Carter* *Prince Charles*

5. Think of a person and ask in the same way:
Is .... married?
Yes .... *or* No ....

22

SET 1 Ask and talk about marital status

Ex 1 Are you married? No, I'm not.

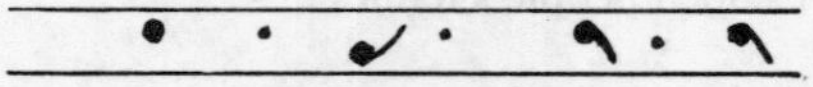

Give an example of the question and both positive and negative replies. Use a wedding ring to illustrate this if necessary.
Students repeat questions and answers chorally.
Give two examples of the exercise.
Students work in pairs, asking and answering.

Ex 2 (Omit the exercise if you feel it might be embarrassing.) Give an example by asking one of the students.
Students work in pairs.

Ex 3 Is he married? Yes, he is.

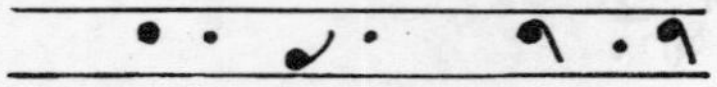

Proceed as in Ex 1.

Ex 4 This can be done either as a classroom quiz with you reading out the names in question form, or the students can find out the answers and write them down as part of their homework. Add other names that are suitable or topical.

Ex 5 Students work in pairs, asking each other about their friends or about other famous people.
Students take turns to ask and answer.

SET 2 Spelling: the Alphabet
Presentation and practice of the letters in groups of sounds on the blackboard should precede practice in the conventional order. The letters which need extra practice are all the vowels *A E I O U* plus *H J K G Y Q R*.

Set 2 aims to present and practise the letters of the alphabet in a restricted context of names and addresses. Spelling is often difficult for foreign learners and it is advisable to spend a few minutes at the beginning or end of the following 4 or 5 lessons practising and revising the letters. Special games to practise spelling can be used. See *Language Teaching Games and Contexts*, W. R. Lee, Oxford University Press.

Ex 1 Write the first group of letters on the blackboard and say them.
Students repeat chorally and individually.
Proceed with the second group in the same way.
Mix letters from the first and second groups for choral and individual repetition.
Proceed with all the groups in the same way, first practising the letters from the same group thoroughly and then mixing letters from different groups.
For individual checking, point to a letter in one of the groups and ask a student to pronounce it. Continue with other students and other letters.
Read the alphabet through in the right order, in groups of five letters, the students repeating chorally.
Students read the alphabet in chain form, i.e. S1 says *A*, S2 says *B*, S3 says *C*, and so on.

Ex 2 Common abbreviations.
This exercise is best used as a checking exercise. Individual students read out the abbreviations; the other students correct them if necessary. If students want to say the country to which the abbreviations belong, do not insist on the English version/pronunciation at this stage.

Ex 3 Students work in pairs. S1 says:
My surname is *(BARNES) B A R N E S*.
S2 writes it down as he hears it. S1 says:
My address is *3 Chiswick Road, C H I S W I C K*.
S2 writes it down as he hears it.
Students check with each other that the names are spelt correctly.
They change parts.

Unit 4

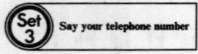

1. Say these numbers

    507-8912 = five-oh-seven eight-nine-one-two
    63324 = six-double-three-two-four
    015-9984 =
    44013 =
    01-286-5260 =

2. Ask and answer with your partner, like this:
    What's your telephone number?
    It's   four-six-seven-nine
    (4679)

3. Fill in this form for yourself

    SURNAME (BLOCK CAPITALS)_____ MR/MRS/MISS/MS
    MAIDEN NAME _____
    FIRST NAMES _____
    ADDRESS _____
    TELEPHONE NUMBER _____
    OCCUPATION _____

4. Fill in the form for your partner. Remember to ask the right questions

    SURNAME (BLOCK CAPITALS)_____ MR/MRS/MISS/MS
    MAIDEN NAME _____
    FIRST NAMES _____
    ADDRESS _____
    TELEPHONE NUMBER _____
    OCCUPATION _____

24

SET 3 Say your telephone number
Numbers 0–9

Write the numbers (or use flash-cards) on the board and say them. Do not write the numbers in words; they are printed in the students' books and to point the spelling out at this stage may interfere with pronunciation.
Students repeat chorally and individually.
Check by pointing at numbers in scrambled order. Students say the numbers individually.

Ex 1 Write your telephone number on the blackboard and say *My telephone number is...*
Write another number with a double figure in it e.g. 63324 to show that we say double 3. Write a number with the figure 0 in it e.g. 507–8912 to show that we say *oh*, not *zero* or *nought*.
Ask students to look at each of the numbers in their books and then say them. Let them think first how to say the numbers, then ask them to speak. Make up more numbers of your own if more practice is needed.

Ex 2 What's your telephone number?   It's 507–8912

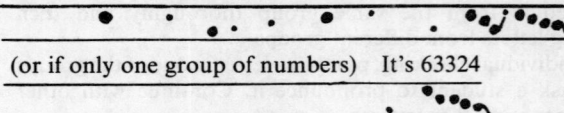

(or if only one group of numbers)   It's 63324

Give an example of the model exchange using your own number.
Students repeat questions only chorally.
Students work in pairs, taking turns to ask and answer. Ask them to write down each other's number.
Check by asking *What's (Mary's) number?*   Answer: *It's...*

Ex 3 Fill in a form for yourself as an example.
Explain maiden name and its applicability.
Students work individually.

Ex 4 Students work in pairs, asking their partner to spell while they write in the form.

Unit 4

EXTENSION

1 *Reading and writing* Show the city of Manchester on the map on page 42.
Read through the passage once, then again, pausing the second time for choral repetition.
Students write their own paragraph about themselves.

2 *Listening – application form* The passage is similar to the original dialogue and should not cause difficulty. Refer students to the original application form at the beginning of the Unit so that they can see how they are to fill it in.
Play the tape once. Play again, stopping at relevant places so students can fill in each item.
Write a model on the blackboard for the students to check their completed form.

3 *Listening – telegram* Explain the meaning of telegram. Students listen to the tape and fill in the name and address of the person to whom the telegram is sent, the ending *Love* and the name of the sender *Ann*. The message *Congratulations* is already printed, but will need explaining.

4 Students working individually write the name and address of somebody they know in the space provided.
They can copy the word *Congratulations* from the previous telegram.

5 Students work in pairs. One student reads the part of the telephone operator.
The other phones in the telegram, using the form he/she has already filled in (Ex 3). This time he/she will have to spell *Congratulations* aloud.
Students change parts.

Open Dialogue See General Guide and tapescript (page 22).

Oral Exercises See General Guide and tapescript (page 23).

Speechwork See General Guide and tapescript (page 22).

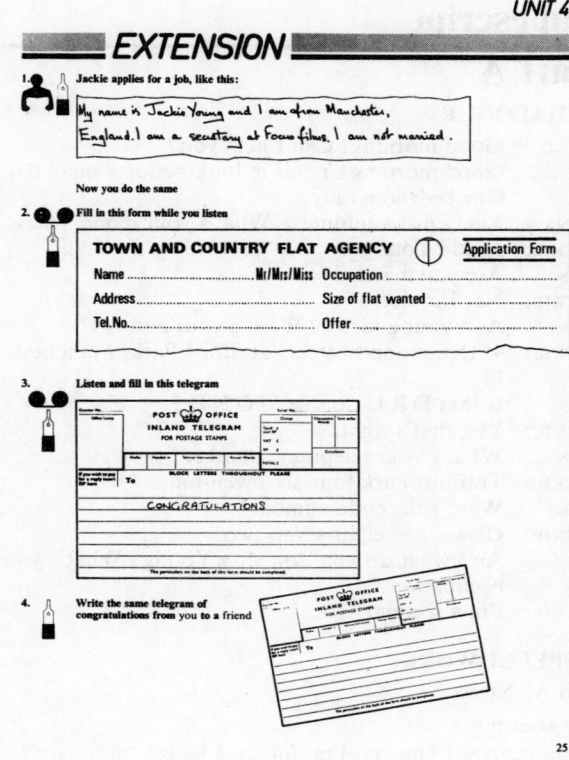

Unit 4

Tapescript
Part A

1 DIALOGUE
MAN: Good morning! Can I help you?
JACKIE: Good morning! Yes. I'm looking for a small flat. One bedroom only.
MAN: Yes… just a minute… What's your name, please?
JACKIE: Jackie Young.
MAN: Are you married?
JACKIE: No, I'm not.
MAN: And your address? What's your address?
JACKIE: 4, Drummond Street, Trafford Park, Manchester 17.
MAN: Is that D R U double M O N D?
JACKIE: Yes, that's right.
MAN: What's your telephone number?
JACKIE: Trafford Park four-six-seven-nine.
MAN: What's the code number?
JACKIE: Oh-six-one eight-seven-two.
MAN: And what do you do, Miss Young? What's your occupation?
JACKIE: I'm a secretary.

2 SPEECHWORK
Part A: Stress
Say after me:
da di da…yes I am…no I'm not…yes he is… no he isn't… yes she is…no she isn't…

Part B: Intonation
Say after me:
one two three four …five six seven eight …one three five seven …two four six eight …one three five …two four six eight …two four six …one three five seven … oh three one …nine oh two eight …seven five six … one four oh nine …

Part C: Pronunciation
Say after me:
/ʌ/…/ʌ/…number…telephone number…
one…double…double one two one…Miss Young…
hello…Murray…hello Murray…one moment…
come in…hello Murray, come in…

3 LISTENING (1)
Listen and fill in the form on page 25.
MAN: Good morning! Can I help you?
WALTER: Yes, I'm looking for a flat.
MAN: Mmm. What size?
WALTER: Two bedrooms, I think.
MAN: Two bedrooms…mmm…just a minute please… where's the application form…ah…here…now, your name, please.
WALTER: Moaney. Walter Moaney.
MAN: Can you spell that?
WALTER: MOANEY.
MAN: N E Y…Married?
WALTER: Yes, I am.
MAN: Address?
WALTER: 5 Station Road.
MAN: And your telephone number?
WALTER: 5 4 2 3 1 6 8.
MAN: Once again, please.
WALTER: 5 4 2 3 1 6 8.
MAN: Thank you. And what do you do, Mr Moaney? What's your occupation?
WALTER: I'm an engineer.
MAN: Right…well…let's see…two bedrooms…what about this…8 West Road…
WALTER: Sorry…where…what address?
MAN: 8 West Road. That's near the station and the shops.
WALTER: Mmm…Yes, I'll go and see it.

LISTENING (2)
Listen to this telephone conversation and write down the telegram which Ann sends to her mother.
TELEPHONE OPERATOR: Yes, can I help you?
ANN: Yes, I'd like to send a telegram, please.
TEL. OP: What is your number, please?
ANN: 061 823 4978.
TEL. OP: 061 823 4978. Yes. Who is the telegram to, please?
ANN: To Mrs Carfax. C A R F A X.
TEL. OP: Carfax…yes…and the address?
ANN: 8 Dalton Road, Leeds.
TEL. OP: Can you spell Dalton, please?
ANN: Yes. D A L T O N.
TEL. OP: 8 Dalton Road, Leeds. And what is the message?
ANN: Congratulations. Love, Ann. That's A double N.
TEL. OP: I'll read that to you. Mrs Carfax, 8 Dalton Road, Leeds. Congratulations. Love, Ann.
ANN: That's fine. Thank you Goodbye.
TEL. OP: Goodbye.

4 OPEN DIALOGUE
Talk to the man at the flat agency.
MAN: So you want a small flat with one bedroom. I'd like some information, please. What's your name?
STUDENT: ....
MAN: Can you spell that, please?
STUDENT: ....
MAN: Are you married?
STUDENT: ....
MAN: And what's your address?
STUDENT: ....
MAN: And telephone number?
STUDENT: ....
MAN: Yes. And what do you do?
STUDENT: ....
MAN: Well, here's a flat…one bedroom, small, near the park *and* the station. Here's the address.
STUDENT: ....
MAN: Well, goodbye for now.
STUDENT: ....

Unit 4

Part B ORAL EXERCISES

Exercise 1 Spell people's names.
Look at the people and their names on page 13.
My name's Freeman.
Can you spell that please?
F R double E M A N.

My name's Simmons.
Can you spell that please?
S I double M O N S. Now go on and spell the names for the different people at Focus Films.

My name's Young.
Can you spell that please?
Y O U N G.

My name's Johnson.
Can you spell that please?
J O H N S O N.

My name's Barnes.
Can you spell that please?
B A R N E S.

My name's Richards.
Can you spell that please?
R I C H A R D S.

Exercise 2 Listen to how these people greet you.
Then you greet them.

Good morning!
Good morning!

My name's Freeman. How do you do!
How do you do! Now go on.

My name's Murray. Hello!
Hello!

My name's Tessa Richards. How do you do!
How do you do!

Good morning!
Good morning!

Oh, hello!
Hello!

How do you do!
How do you do!

Goodbye!
Goodbye!

Exercise 3 Listen to these numbers and repeat them.

The code number for Manchester is 061.
061. Now you repeat the numbers.

The number you want is 674 5563.
674 5563.

The code number for Bristol is 0753.
0753.

The number for Focus Films is 983 2756.
983 2756.

Exercise 4 Give personal information.
Are you a teacher?
No, I'm not.
Are you a student?
Yes, I am.
Is Sally married?
No, she isn't.
Is Tessa married?
Yes, she is. Now go on and answer correctly.
Are you a teacher?
....
Are you married?
....
Are you a student?
....
Is Tessa a teacher?
....
Is Allan married?
....
Is Jackie married?
....

UNIT 5 Looking for a flat (2)

	Skills	Functions	Example Sentences	Main Structures
SET 1	1. Speaking 2. Speaking 3. Writing and Speaking 4. Memory game 5. Writing 6. Speaking – roleplay	Ask and say where places are Say goodbye formally Thank somebody politely	*The post office is opposite the school.* *Where's the post office?* *It's opposite the school.* *Goodbye!* *Thank you very much!*	Where's the . . . ? It's + opposite + the near in front of next to behind
EXTENSION	1. Reading and Writing 2. Listening 3. Reading	Write a message based on a model, arranging a place to meet, and saying where it is. Identify places through listening to sounds and voices. Reading Text: Jackie Young goes to a flat agency.		

OPEN DIALOGUE

ORAL EXERCISES	1. Ask where places are	Ask the policeman where the bank is. *Excuse me, where's the bank?*
	2. Confirm where places are (using map)	Is the bank next to the hotel? *Yes, that's right. Next to the hotel.*
	3. Say where places are (using map)	Excuse me, where's the bank? *It's next to the hotel.*
	4. Answer questions about places (using map)	Is the school opposite the bank or the hotel? *It's opposite the bank.*
	5. Correct statements about places (using map)	The bank's opposite the park. *No, it isn't, it's opposite the school.*

SPEECHWORK

A STRESS	next to the bank ● ● ● ●	ACTIVE VOCABULARY		
B INTONATION	Excuse me, where's the bank?	next to behind in front of opposite near	bank cinema hotel school office	post office restaurant police station supermarket cafe
C PRONUNCIATION	/e/ yes, next	woman man map thank you very much I don't know	young nice	or want

24

Unit 5

DIALOGUE

The three-line exchange between Jackie and the policeman is not recorded. Read it yourself and refer students to the map of the town. Use the wall picture/OHP (2) if available. *Policeman* is part of this unit's active vocabulary.
Point to the places e.g. *Post Office, bank*; say the words. Students repeat chorally and individually.
If you have access to bigger pictures of these individual buildings use them to illustrate the meaning of the words.

SET 1 Ask and say where places are

It may be more effective to demonstrate the different space relations with real objects or people, or by drawing diagrams on the blackboard. The diagrams in the book will help to reinforce the concepts. With a movable object you can quickly practise the correct use of the preposition.

Ex 1 The students should be able to see the map and the exercise at the same time. The wall picture/OHP would help. Give the answers to the first two examples.
Students in pairs work out the answers first and write them in.
Check answers by asking individual students to read them aloud.

Ex 2 Where's the post office?   It's opposite the school.

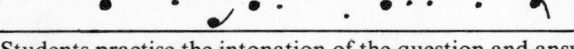

Students practise the intonation of the question and answer chorally and individually.
Students in pairs take turns to ask and answer.
Check afterwards by asking individual students.

Ex 3 Students should sketch only one part of their town if it is large. In reality this exercise may elicit few of the prepositions mentioned, but will provide practice in accurate copying and labelling.
Students then work in pairs as in Ex 2.

Ex 4 This can be done in pairs, with one student checking the other student's memory.

Ex 5 Individual work to practise the spelling of names of places.

DIALOGUE

This dialogue continues the conversation in Unit 4, in the Town and Country Flat agency. The words and phrases underlined are to be substituted in Ex 6, where students use other places, other telephone numbers etc.

Ex 6 Students use the addresses and telephone numbers from the agent's list to make their own conversation.
They should be able to state the position of the flat from the map.
Students work in pairs, using the printed dialogue to guide them, substituting the underlined words and phrases.
Students change parts and use the second address – and so on.

Looking for a flat (2)

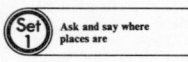 Ask and say where places are

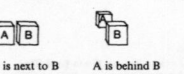

A is next to B   A is behind B   A is in front of B   A is opposite B   A is near B

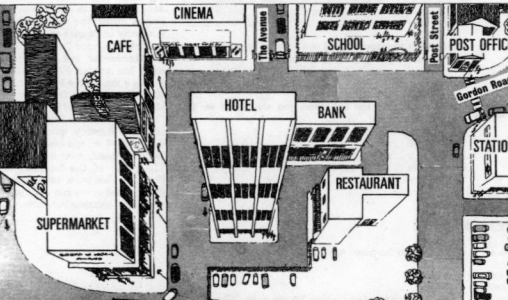

28

1. Say where places are
   → The post office is opposite the school

   Talk about the other places in the same way

   The bank/the hotel
   The restaurant/the hotel
   The bank/the restaurant
   The school/the bank
   The station/the restaurant
   The park/the police station
   The police station/the supermarket
   The supermarket/the cafe
   The hotel/the cafe

2. Ask and say where places are
   → Where's the post office?
   It's opposite the school.
   or
   It's near the station.
   Look at the map and ask and answer about:

   the post office, the bank, the park, the station, the police station, the cinema.

3. Draw a map of part of your town. Write in the names of the streets, mark the bank etc.
   With a partner, ask and answer as in Exercise 2.

4. Memory Game
   Look at the map for one minute. Then shut your book and say where places are. How many can you remember? Your partner can help you.

5. Word Game
   What are these places? Write them down.
   1. MICANE   4. TASTNIO
   2. NAKB   5. HOLOSC
   3. LTOEH   6. ETASUNRRTA

UNIT 5

MAN: What do you do Miss <u>Young</u>?
JACKIE: I'm a <u>secretary</u>.
MAN: Oh, a <u>secretary</u>.
JACKIE: That's right.
MAN: Where?
JACKIE: At <u>Focus Films</u>.
MAN: I see.
JACKIE: I'm looking for a small <u>one</u>-bedroom flat near my office.
MAN: Now let's see. Ah yes, here's one. It's in <u>Gordon Road</u>. Yes, and it's a <u>one</u>-bedroom flat.
JACKIE: <u>Gordon Road</u>? Where is <u>Gordon Road</u> exactly?
MAN: Here, look at the map. <u>Gordon Road</u> is here, <u>next to the station</u>.
JACKIE: That's good.
MAN: Yes. Well here's the address and the telephone number: <u>3, Gordon Road, Manchester 8, 334 8956</u>.
JACKIE: Thank you very much. Goodbye.
MAN: Goodbye.
         Hello, hello! <u>334 8956</u>? Oh, good, <u>Mrs Parker</u>?
(phones) A <u>young woman</u> is coming to see the flat. <u>Jackie Young</u>.
         Yes, that's right. <u>She's a secretary at Focus Films</u>.
         Oh, <u>no, she isn't married</u>. Yes. Good, good, <u>she's</u> very nice. Thank you <u>Mrs Parker</u>. Goodbye.

Read the dialogue again with a partner. Say what you do and offer a flat from the list below.

Town and Country Flat Agency

① 7 LEE ROAD
1 bedroom (woman preferred)
Tel:(061) 334 4579
Mrs Galloway

③ 9 THE AVENUE
2 bedrooms
Tel:(061) 334 3981
Mrs Jones

② 6 FREEDOM WAY
1 bedroom (man preferred)
Tel:(061) 334 2091
Miss Robson

④ GORDON ROAD
1 bedroom (man or woman)
Tel:(061) 334 8956
Mrs Parker

Unit 5

UNIT 5
EXTENSION

1. Jackie's mother, Mrs Young, is in Manchester. She wants to see Jackie for lunch. Jackie writes her a message

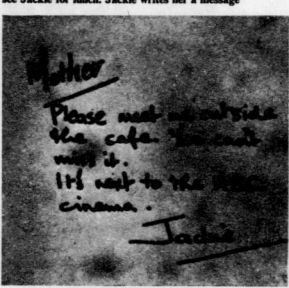

Now write a message like this to a friend. Choose a place to meet on the map on page 28. Say where it is

Jackie Young Goes to a Flat Agency
Jackie Young is a new secretary at Focus Films, the documentary film company in Manchester.
Jackie is from Trafford, a suburb of Manchester, but she wants a flat near her job at Focus Films. She wants a small one-bedroom flat and she wants a nice landlady or landlord. She goes to a flat agency.
The man at the 'Town and Country Flat Agency' gives Jackie the address of a one-bedroom flat in Gordon Road, next to the station. The name of the landlady is Mrs Parker. The man telephones Mrs Parker and gives her Jackie's name and some information about her.

2. Listen to the tape and say where you are. There are five different places
1. I'm in a ....
2. I'm at a ....
3. I'm in a ....
4. I'm in a ....
5. I'm in a ....

OPEN DIALOGUE
You are at the station on the map. A stranger talks to you

STRANGER: Excuse me!
STUDENT: ....
STRANGER: Can you help me. I'm looking for the bank. Where is it?
STUDENT: ....
STRANGER: Oh, is it? Thank you. And then can you tell me – is the cinema near the bank?
STUDENT: ....
STRANGER: Oh, good. Well, thank you very much. Goodbye.
STUDENT: ....

30

EXTENSION

1 *Reading and Writing* Explain the words *mother*, *lunch*, *message* and *you can't miss it*.
Write your own message on the blackboard as an example, choosing a different place on the map.
Students write their messages individually.

2 *Listening* Play the tape once only, pausing after each scene to give the students time to write in their answers.
As most of the comprehension revolves around identifying sounds, this is a fairly easy activity, to be treated as a game.
Key: 1 park   2 station   3 cinema   4 restaurant   5 bank

Open Dialogue See General Guide and tapescript (page 27).

Oral Exercises See General Guide and tapescript (page 27).

Speechwork See General Guide and tapescript (page 27).

Unit 5

Tapescript
Part A

1 DIALOGUE
MAN: What do you do, Miss Young?
JACKIE: I'm a secretary.
MAN: Oh, a secretary.
JACKIE: That's right.
MAN: Where?
JACKIE: At Focus Films.
MAN: I see.
JACKIE:: I'm looking for a small one-bedroom flat near my office.
MAN: Now let's see. Ah yes, here's one. It's in Gordon Road. Yes, and it's a one-bedroom flat.
JACKIE: Gordon Road? Where is Gordon Road exactly?
MAN: Here, look at the map. Gordon Road is here, next to the station.
JACKIE: That's good.
MAN: Yes. Well here's the address and the telephone number: 3, Gordon Road, Manchester 8. 334 8956.
JACKIE: Thank you very much. Goodbye.
MAN: Goodbye.

MAN: Hello, hello! 334 8956? Oh, good, Mrs Parker? A young woman is coming to see the flat. Jackie Young. Yes, that's right. She's a secretary at Focus Films. Oh, no, she isn't married. Yes. Good, good, she's very nice. Thank you Mrs Parker. Goodbye.

2 SPEECHWORK
Part A: Stress
Say after me:
da...bank...park...da di...station...da di di...cinema...
da di di da...next to the bank...next to the park...
da di di da di...next to the station...
da di di da di di...next to the cinema...

Part B: Intonation
Say after me:
bank ...｜where's the bank ...park ...where's the park ...
hotel...｜where's the hotel...station...where's the station...
excuse me ...excuse me, where's the bank...excuse me,
｜where's the park...excuse me, ｜where's the hotel...excuse me,
｜where's the station...

Part C: Pronunciation
Say after me:
/e/.../e/...yes...next...next to...Kent...Kent Road...Yes it's next to Kent Road...seven...number seven...number seven Kent Road...

3 LISTENING
Sounds of five different places: 1 park 2 station 3 cinema 4 restaurant 5 bank.

4 OPEN DIALOGUE
You are at the station on the map on page 28. A stranger talks to you.
STRANGER: Excuse me!
STUDENT: ....
STRANGER: Can you help me? I'm looking for the bank. Where is it?
STUDENT: ....
STRANGER: Oh, is it? Thank you. And can you tell me – is the cinema near the bank?
STUDENT: ....
STRANGER: Oh good. Well, thank you very much. Goodbye.
STUDENT: ....

Part B ORAL EXERCISES

Exercise 1 Ask where places are.

Ask the policeman where the bank is.
Excuse me, where's the bank?
Ask the policeman where the post office is.
Excuse me, where's the post office? Now go on.
Ask the policeman where the police station is.
Excuse me, where's the police station?
Ask the policeman where the cinema is.
Excuse me, where's the cinema?
Ask the policeman where the supermarket is.
Excuse me, where's the supermarket?
Ask the policeman where the hotel is.
Excuse me, where's the hotel?
Ask the policeman where the station is.
Excuse me, where's the station?

Exercise 2 Say where places are.
Look at the map on page 28.

Excuse me, can you help me?
Is the bank next to the hotel?
Yes, that's right. Next to the hotel.
Is the post office opposite the school?
Yes, that's right. Opposite the school. Now go on.
Is the restaurant behind the hotel?
Yes, that's right. Behind the hotel.
Is the hotel opposite the cafe?
Yes, that's right. Opposite the cafe.
Is the station near the park?
Yes, that's right. Near the park.
Is the bank in front of the restaurant?
Yes, that's right. In front of the restaurant.
Is the police station next to the park?
Yes, that's right. Next to the park.
Is the supermarket near the cinema?
Yes, that's right. Near the cinema.
Is the school opposite the bank?
Yes, that's right. Opposite the bank.

Unit 5

Exercise 3 Say where places are again.
Look at the map on page 28. Help the tourist.
Excuse me, where's the bank?
It's next to the hotel.
Excuse me, where's the post office?
It's opposite the school. Now go on.
Excuse me, where's the park?
It's next to the police station.
Excuse me, where's the restaurant?
It's behind the bank.
Excuse me, where's the station?
It's near the park.
Excuse me, where's the school?
It's opposite the post office.

Exercise 4 Answer the questions. Look at the map again.
Is the school opposite the bank or the hotel?
It's opposite the bank.
Is the cinema near the school or the restaurant?
It's near the school. Now go on.
Is the hotel in front of the bank or the restaurant?
It's in front of the restaurant.
Is the park next to the post office or the police station?
It's next to the police station.
Is the restaurant behind the hotel or the school?
It's behind the hotel.

Exercise 5 Say the correct places.
Look at the map again.
Is the bank opposite the park?
No, it isn't, it's opposite the school.
Is the school opposite the hotel?
No, it isn't, it's opposite the bank. Now go on.
Is the supermarket opposite the station?
No, it isn't, it's opposite the hotel.
Is the police station opposite the bank?
No, it isn't, it's opposite the supermarket.
Is the school opposite the cafe?
No, it isn't, it's opposite the bank.
Is the cinema opposite the police station?
No, it isn't, it's opposite the school.

UNIT 6 Consolidation Unit

	Skills	Activity	Functions revised
DIALOGUE	Listening	Tourist asks information bureau to find him a hotel room.	Attract attention Ask and say where places are
1.	Speaking	Students read the dialogue in pairs, substituting own names.	Say name, address and telephone number Spelling
2.	Speaking–roleplay	Repeat the dialogue in new situations, using the original dialogue as framework, and new information from the Tourist Information Guide.	Thanking
3.	Listening	Extended version of original dialogue.	
4.	Writing	Fill in a registration form for tourist accommodation.	
5.	Writing and Speaking	Fill in questions in a dialogue. Then practise dialogue with new information.	
6.	Spelling	Fill in missing words in a context, where first letter is provided.	
7.	Vocabulary Classification	Grouping of words into different vocabulary areas from a jumbled list.	
8.	Spelling	Spelling game similar to 'Hangman'.	
9.	Reading	Reading Text: Elizabeth Hotel Service Guide.	

SPEECHWORK		ACTIVE VOCABULARY		
A Stress	in the centre • • ● •	airport	taxi	reserve
		air terminal	bus	work
B Intonation	I'm looking for a hotel	centre	room	remember
		shopping centre	table	
C Pronunciation	/əʊ/ road, hotel	car park	price	
		hostel		
		bar	cheap	outside
		country		
		tourist	expensive	
		river	fairly	

Unit 6

Consolidation Unit

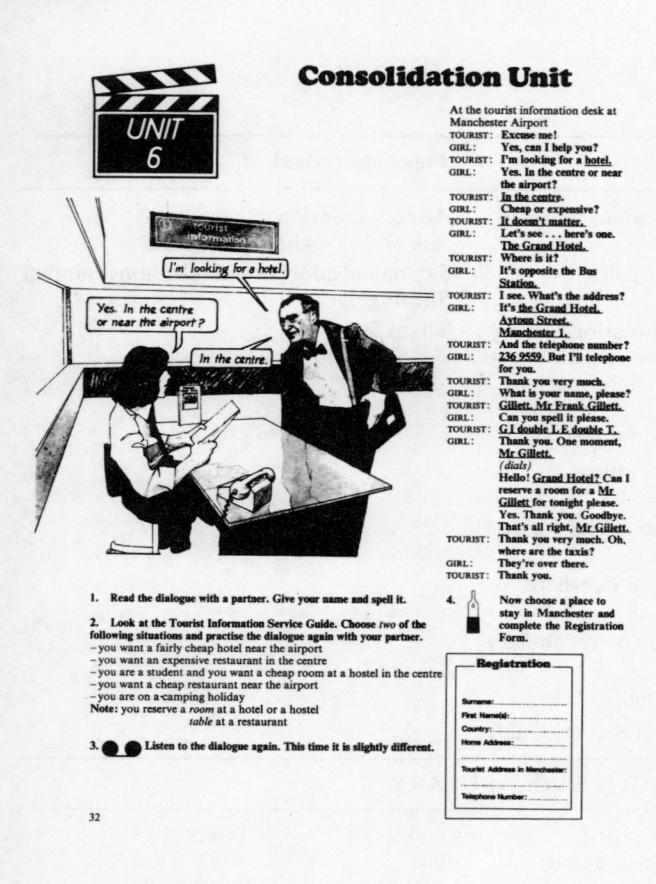

At the tourist information desk at Manchester Airport

TOURIST: Excuse me!
GIRL: Yes, can I help you?
TOURIST: I'm looking for a hotel.
GIRL: Yes. In the centre or near the airport?
TOURIST: In the centre.
GIRL: Cheap or expensive?
TOURIST: It doesn't matter.
GIRL: Let's see . . . here's one. The Grand Hotel.
TOURIST: Where is it?
GIRL: It's opposite the Bus Station.
TOURIST: I see. What's the address?
GIRL: It's the Grand Hotel, Aytoun Street, Manchester 1.
TOURIST: And the telephone number?
GIRL: 236 9559. But I'll telephone for you.
TOURIST: Thank you very much.
GIRL: What is your name, please?
TOURIST: Gillett. Mr Frank Gillett.
GIRL: Can you spell it please.
TOURIST: G1 double I,E double T.
GIRL: Thank you. One moment, Mr Gillett.
(dials)
Hello! Grand Hotel? Can I reserve a room for Mr Gillett for tonight please. Yes. Thank you. Goodbye. That's all right, Mr Gillett.
TOURIST: Thank you very much. Oh, where are the taxis?
GIRL: They're over there.
TOURIST: Thank you.

1. Read the dialogue with a partner. Give your name and spell it.

2. Look at the Tourist Information Service Guide. Choose *two* of the following situations and practise the dialogue again with your partner.
   – you want a fairly cheap hotel near the airport
   – you want an expensive restaurant in the centre
   – you are a student and you want a cheap room at a hostel in the centre
   – you want a cheap restaurant near the airport
   – you are on a camping holiday

   Note: you reserve a *room* at a hotel or a hostel
         a *table* at a restaurant

3. 🎧 Listen to the dialogue again. This time it is slightly different.

4. Now choose a place to stay in Manchester and complete the Registration Form.

Registration

Surname:
First Name(s):
Country:
Home Address:
Tourist Address in Manchester:
Telephone Number:

UNIT 6

MANCHESTER AIRPORT TOURIST INFORMATION SERVICE

HOTELS

NAME	Grand Hotel	Hotel Piccadilly	Excelsior Hotel	Tatton Arms Hotel
ADDRESS	Aytoun Street Manchester 1	Piccadilly Plaza Manchester 1	Wythenshawe Manchester 22	Mill Lane Northenden Manchester 22
TELEPHONE	(061) 236 9559	(061) 236 8414	(061) 437 5811	(061) 998 4750
POSITION	In the centre opposite to the bus station	In the centre near the bus station	Near the airport opposite the car park	Near the airport and near M6 motorway
PRICE for single room	£12.20	£16.25	£11.50	from £3.00

RESTAURANTS

NAME	WHEELS	THE KNIFE AND FORK	MULLIGANS	THE PICCADILLY
ADDRESS	5, Whitworth Street Manchester 1	9, London Road Manchester 1	Wythenshawe Manchester 22	67, Princess Street Manchester 1
TELEPHONE	675 8859	678 0576	673 8876	674 9054
POSITION	In the centre next to the Palace Theatre	In the centre opposite Piccadilly Station	Near the airport	In the centre near the air terminal
CATEGORY	****	****	*	**

HOSTEL AND STUDENT ACCOMMODATION

NAME	NATIONAL UNION OF STUDENTS (N.U.S.) HOSTEL	YOUNG MEN'S AND WOMEN'S CHRISTIAN ASSOCIATION (Y.M.C.A.) (Y.W.C.A.) HOSTEL
ADDRESS	2, Lever Street Manchester 1	6, Blackfriars Street Manchester 1
TELEPHONE	675 4329	657 0045
POSITION	In the centre opposite Piccadilly Gardens	In the centre next to the ABC Cinema

CAMPING SITES

NAME	Blue Skies	Cosmos
ADDRESS	Blackhills Manchester 9	River Road Manchester 7
TELEPHONE	986 3345	895 4396
POSITION	Next to the river outside the city	Near the airport behind the Sports Stadium

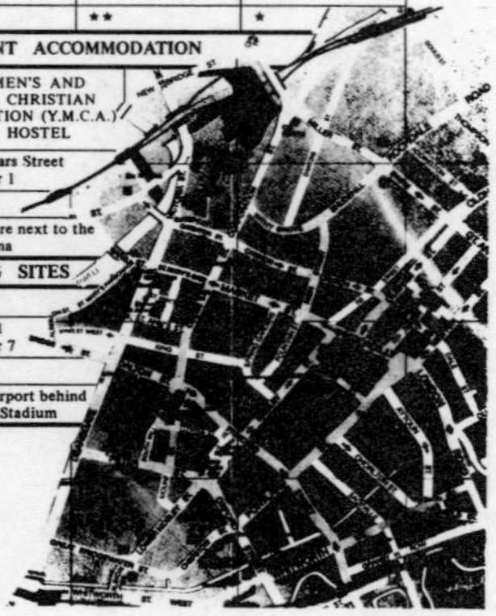

DIALOGUE

The dialogue is central to the first five exercises. Apart from a few new vocabulary items, this dialogue brings together many of the important functions already practised in Units 1–5.

Play the taped version of the dialogue and ask a few comprehension questions.

1 Students read the dialogue in pairs, but substitute their own names for that of *Mr Gillett*.

2 *Role-play Dialogue*
Look at the Tourist Information Service Guide with the whole class. Look at each section in turn and ask questions like:
The Excelsior Hotel – what's the address? What's the telephone number? etc. Correct the pronunciation of the answers both individually and chorally.

Choose one of the situations and ask one of the better students in the class to be the girl behind the information desk.

The student who is the girl behind the desk will need to look at the Guide as well as the original dialogue.

Ask the students to follow the original dialogue while you act your own situation with the chosen student.

This will give students an indication of where and how to substitute. Or make an overhead stencil with gaps for substitution.

Students work in pairs. One student chooses one of the remaining 4 situations and acts it out with his partner. They change parts afterwards and choose one of the 3 remaining situations. Proceed as before.

3 *Listening* Play the extended version of the original dialogue.
This is slightly more complicated but contains the same basic information. Question and answer work should not be necessary.

4 *Writing* Students look at the list of hotels or student hostels in the Guide and fill in the form.
Explain *country* by giving an example. However this will be practised extensively in the next unit.

Reading Divide students into groups of 3–5. Ask them to read the passage together and work out, with the aid of dictionaries, if necessary, the information given in this tourist brochure.
Go round and help each group if necessary. It is unnecessary to ask them to read it aloud.

5 *Fill-in Dialogue* The question *Where do you work?* is a passive item and should be explained at the beginning. Students work individually, checking each other's answers. After checking, students work in pairs on the substitution exercise, choosing two of the three people in the chart.
Key: *What's your name?/What's your surname?/Are you a tourist?/What do you do?/Here in Manchester?/ Where do you work?/Where's the coffee bar?/Coffee?*

6 *Fill-in vocabulary* Students work individually.
Check their answers afterwards.
The number of dashes indicates the number of letters and aims to encourage accurate spelling.
Key: *Name/address/telephone number/code/married/van driver/flat/bedroom flat/station.*

7 *Vocabulary classification* This can be done individually or in groups. The aim of the exercise is to establish the five categories: professions; places/buildings; numbers; prepositions; greetings.
Students can either number the words according to group, (e.g. all prepositions have No 1, all professions have No 2) or they can rewrite them in the right groups. The latter method gives extra copying practice but takes more time.
Key

behind	two	technician	hello
near	nine	secretary	good morning
opposite	five	doctor	goodbye
next to	eight	engineer	how do you do
school			
park			
bank			
station			

Unit 6

Spelling Game Another version of 'Hangman'. The game can be played as a class game using the blackboard, or in groups using paper (if played in groups, give each group leader a different word to prevent groups overhearing each other). One person in the class thinks of a word and writes the number of letters in the word on the blackboard.

e.g. – – – – – –   (*typist*)

Everyone else in the class must guess the word by calling out letters one by one e.g. *F?* If there is an F in the word (in this case there isn't) the person at the blackboard puts the letter in the correct place in the word. If there isn't, he writes the letter at the side of the blackboard and crosses it out. At the same time he draws the first line of the sign STOP. (It can be completed in 13 lines and letters.) Every time a wrong letter is suggested, a line is added to the drawing. When the STOP sign is complete, the group has to stop playing. The aim of the game is to guess the word before the drawing is complete.

Unit 6

Tapescript
Part A

1 DIALOGUE
At the tourist information desk at Manchester Airport

TOURIST: Excuse me!
GIRL: Yes, can I help you?
TOURIST: I'm looking for a hotel.
GIRL: Yes. In the centre or near the airport?
TOURIST: In the centre.
GIRL: Cheap or expensive?
TOURIST: It doesn't matter.
GIRL: Let's see... here's one. The Grand Hotel.
TOURIST: Where is it?
GIRL: It's opposite the bus station.
TOURIST: I see. What's the address?
GIRL: It's the Grand Hotel, Aytoun Street, Manchester 1.
TOURIST: And the telephone number?
GIRL: 236 9559. But I'll telephone for you.
TOURIST: Thank you very much.
GIRL: What is your name, please?
TOURIST: Gillett. Mr Frank Gillett.
GIRL: Can you spell it please?
TOURIST: G I double L E double T.
GIRL: Thank you. One moment, Mr Gillett.
(dials)
Hello! Grand Hotel? Can I reserve a room for a Mr Gillett for tonight please? Yes. Thank you. Goodbye.
That's all right, Mr Gillett.
TOURIST: Thank you very much. Oh, where are the taxis?
GIRL: They're over there.
TOURIST: Thank you.

2 SPEECHWORK
Part A: Stress
Say after me:
di di da di...in the centre...near the centre...
near the station...near the airport...
di di da di di...near the terminal...near the cinema...
near the motorway...

Part B: Intonation
Say after me:
hotel...I'm looking for a hotel...restaurant...I'm looking for a restaurant...hostel...I'm looking for a hostel...camping site...I'm looking for a camping site...

Part C: Pronunciation
Say after me:
/əʊ/.../əʊ/...no...road...hotel...phone...telephone
...Where's the hotel...it's in West Road...Where's West Road...it's over there...Where's the telephone...it's over there...What's the phone number...it's five oh six oh nine...
hello...it's Jo...Jo...J.O....

3 LISTENING
At the Tourist Information Desk at Manchester Airport

TOURIST: Excuse me.
GIRL: Yes, can I help you?
TOURIST: I'm looking for a room, a hotel room.
GIRL: Yes. In the city centre or here near the airport?
TOURIST: In the city centre.
GIRL: Ah, yes, now let's see, here's one, The Elizabeth. It's a very good hotel.
TOURIST: Where is it exactly?
GIRL: Well, look, here it is on the map. It's here next to the Central Station.
TOURIST: I see. What's the address?
GIRL: The address? It's The Elizabeth Hotel, St. Anne's Square, Manchester 1.
TOURIST: And the telephone number?
GIRL: 675 9500 but I'll telephone for you. It's a 4 star hotel.
TOURIST: Thank you very much.
GIRL: Can I have your name please.
TOURIST: Gillett. Frank Gillett.
GIRL: Is that double L?
TOURIST: Yes. It's G I double L E double T.
GIRL: Mr F. Gillett.
TOURIST: That's right.
GIRL: What do you do, Mr Gillett?
TOURIST: I'm a journalist, but I'm here as a tourist.
GIRL: I see. One moment please, Mr Gillett.
(dials)
Hello! Hotel Elizabeth? Reception? Can I make a reservation for a Mr Frank Gillett for today please. Gillett. Double L and double T. O.K! Fine! Thank you. Goodbye!
That's fine, Mr Gillett.
TOURIST: Thank you very much. Now where are the taxis?
GIRL: Over there next to the buses. Can you see?
TOURIST: Oh, yes, over there. Well, thank you and goodbye!
GIRL: Goodbye Mr Gillett.

UNIT 7 I'm from Melbourne

	Skills	Functions	Example Sentences	Main Structures
SET 1	1. Speaking 2. Speaking	Introduce people	*Jackie, meet Allan. He's a van driver.*	Meet + name
SET 2	1. Writing 2. Speaking 3. Speaking and Writing 4. Speaking 5. Word Game	Ask and talk about nationality	*Are you English?* *Yes, I am./No, I'm not. I'm Australian.* *Are they English?* *No, they aren't. They're American. Look at their car.*	Are you/they English? Is he/she English? Yes, I am. No, I'm not. Yes, he/she is. No, he/she isn't. Yes, we/they are. No, we/they aren't.
SET 3	1. Speaking 2. Speaking 3. Speaking	Ask and say where people are from	*Where are you from?* *I'm from London.*	Where are you from? I'm from . . . Are you/they from . . . ? Yes, we/they are. No, we/they aren't. We're/they're from . . .
EXTENSION	1. Listening 2. Reading	Identify nationality of singers. Reading Text: The People of Britain.		

OPEN DIALOGUE

ORAL EXERCISES		
	1. Ask and say where you're from	Where are you from? We're from Manchester. Where are you from?
	2. Give correct information about where people are from	Are Liz and David from London? No, they aren't. They're from Manchester.
	3. Confirm people's nationality	Is he English? Of course he's English. Look at his car.
	4. Spell names of countries	Spell Canada. C A N A D A
	5. Say what nationality people are	What about the people from Manchester? They're English.
	6. Say where places are	Where's Sydney? It's in Australia.

SPEECHWORK			ACTIVE VOCABULARY		
A STRESS	I'm from London • • ● •		England	English	Manchester
B INTONATION	ˈAre you Énglish?		America	American	London
	ˈAre you from Éngland?		Canada	Canadian	Liverpool
C PRONUNCIATION	/ə/ from London from Manchester		Ireland	Irish	Melbourne
			Australia	Australian	Sydney
					New York City
			car	new	meet
			girl	easy	guess
			boy	many	look at
			sister	our	
			brother	their	I must go!
			mother	from	That's right
			father	not	of course

Unit 7

DIALOGUE
Point out that *Morning* is an informal way of saying *Good Morning*. The first part of the dialogue, up to *Jackie: Guess!* relates to Set 1; the second part, up to the end relates to Set 2.

SET 1 Introduce people (2)
Jackie meet Allan. He's a van driver.

Ex 1 Give an example of this alternative way of introducing people (cf Unit 3 Set 1). Students introduce each character to Jackie in turn, speaking individually.

Ex 2 Divide class into groups of 3. Each of the students takes turns to introduce the second to the third.

SET 2 Ask and talk about nationality
Use a map to illustrate these countries and nationalities. The nationalities selected here are all English-speaking.
Students will be asked to give their own nationalities but should only be required to learn those nationalities printed in the book, their own nationality and possibly one or two others relevant to their situation.

Ex 1 Go round and help individual students (if a class of mixed nationality). Help them to pronounce their nationality correctly.

Ex 2 Students work in groups of 4, or walk round and ask 3 other people in the class.

Ex 3 This is the first time students have met *we* and *they*. Show that *we're = we are*; *they're = they are*.
Before doing the exercise, practise *we* and *they* by grouping students into common nationalities and asking them to say what they and the others are, e.g. *We're French, They're Italian, He's German,* etc. The exercise can be done orally in pairs first, then individually in written form.

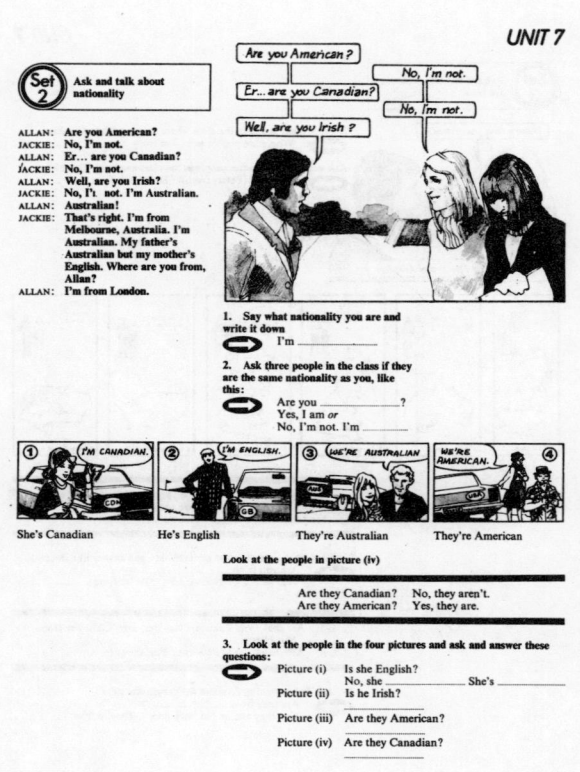

I'm from Melbourne

UNIT 7

ALLAN: Morning, girls!
TESSA: Oh, good morning Allan. Jackie, meet Allan. He's a van driver. Allan, this is Jackie, our new secretary.
ALLAN: Hello, Jackie!
JACKIE: Hello, Allan!
ALLAN: Are you English, Jackie?
JACKIE: No, I'm not.
ALLAN: Where are you from?
JACKIE: Guess!

Set 1 Introduce people (2)

Jackie, meet Allan. He's a van driver.

1. Look at the people on page 13. Introduce all the people to Jackie, like this:
   Jackie, meet Murray. He's a film director.
   Jackie, meet _____ She's a _____

2. Introduce your partner to somebody in the class, like this:
   You: (Peter), meet (Mary) She's (He's) a _____
   (Mary): Hello (Peter)
   (Peter): Hello (Mary)

UNIT 7

Set 2 Ask and talk about nationality

ALLAN: Are you American?
JACKIE: No, I'm not.
ALLAN: Er... are you Canadian?
JACKIE: No, I'm not.
ALLAN: Well, are you Irish?
JACKIE: No, I'm not. I'm Australian.
ALLAN: Australian!
JACKIE: That's right. I'm from Melbourne, Australia. I'm Australian. My father's Australian but my mother's English. Where are you from, Allan?
ALLAN: I'm from London.

1. Say what nationality you are and write it down
   I'm _____

2. Ask three people in the class if they are the same nationality as you, like this:
   Are you _____?
   Yes, I am *or*
   No, I'm not. I'm _____

She's Canadian   He's English   They're Australian   They're American

Look at the people in picture (iv)

Are they Canadian?   No, they aren't.
Are they American?   Yes, they are.

3. Look at the people in the four pictures and ask and answer these questions:
   Picture (i)   Is she English?
                  No, she _____ She's _____
   Picture (ii)   Is he Irish?
                  _____
   Picture (iii) Are they American?
                  _____
   Picture (iv)   Are they Canadian?
                  _____

Unit 7

UNIT 7 (page 38)

4. Look at the pictures. Ask and answer like this:

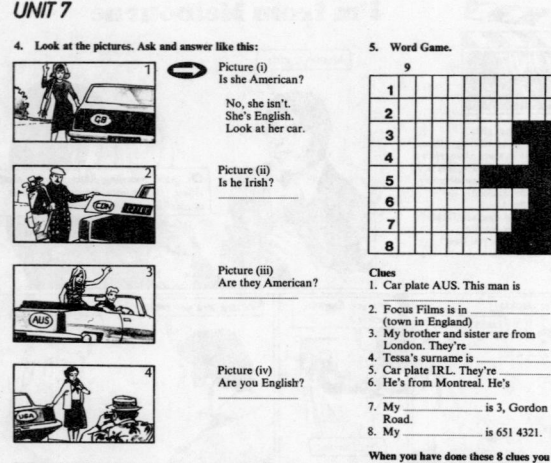

Picture (i)
Is she American?
➔ No, she isn't. She's English. Look at her car.

Picture (ii)
Is he Irish?

Picture (iii)
Are they American?

Picture (iv)
Are you English?

Picture (v)
Are you Canadian?

5. Word Game.

Clues
1. Car plate AUS. This man is _____
2. Focus Films is in _____ (town in England)
3. My brother and sister are from London. They're _____
4. Tessa's surname is _____
5. Car plate IRL. They're _____
6. He's from Montreal. He's _____
7. My _____ is 3, Gordon Road.
8. My _____ is 651 4321.

When you have done these 8 clues you can see the last word, number 9 down. Write down what this word is here: _____

UNIT 7 (page 39)

Set 3 Ask and say where people are from

Where are you from?   I'm from London.

1. Ask three people in the class where they are from, like this:
   ➔ Where are you from? I'm from _____
   Ask and say where other people in the class are from, like this:
   ➔ Where is (Peter) from? He's/She's from _____

1. Liz & David 2. Sue & John 3. Carol & Steve 4. Judy & Michael 5. Angela & Gary 6. Janet & Don

   i) Are you from London? No, we aren't. We're from Manchester.
   ii) Are you from Sydney? No, we aren't. We're from Melbourne.
   iii) Are you from Liverpool? Yes, we are.

2. Look at the people in the pictures. Ask and answer like this:
   ➔ Are you from _____?
   Yes, we are. *or* No, we aren't. We're from _____

   i) Are they from London? No, they aren't. They're from Manchester.
   ii) Are they from Melbourne? Yes, they are.

3. Ask and answer again about the people like this:
   ➔ Are they from _____?
   Yes, they are, *or* No, they aren't. They're from _____

Ex 4 Introduce the new possessive adjectives *our*, *their*, and revise the others. Explain *look at* and *car*.
Give a few examples, then practise as in Ex 3.

Ex 5 Word Game
Students work in pairs. The first pair to complete the crossword with all words spelt correctly has won.
Key: *A*USTRALIAN
      *M*ANCHESTER
      *E*NGLISH
      *R*ICHARDS
      *I*RISH
      *C*ANADIAN
      *A*DDRESS
      *N*UMBER

SET 3 Ask and say where people are from

Ex 1 Where are you from? I'm from London.

Students practise chorally and individually.
Move round the class asking 3 students where they are from, making notes as they ask.
This exercise can be made into a game: the class splits into two teams. You ask both teams e.g. *Where's Peter from?* The team which answers first gets a point.
The person whose name it is, is not allowed to cooperate.

Ex 2 Are you from London?

No, we aren't. We're from Manchester.

The exercise provides extended practice. Use the wall picture/OHP to show towns.
Do choral and individual pronunciation work on the names of the places; do not insist on absolute accuracy – it is more important for students to be fluent in the forms of the verb *to be* at this stage.
Do all the examples with a few students.
Students in pairs repeat the exercise, taking turns to ask and answer.

Ex 3 Students in pairs proceed as in Ex 2. Go round and check.

EXTENSION

Listening Pause after playing each song, while students write in their answers.
Choose one of the songs (if you can print out the words) for singing together as a form of relaxation at the end of the lesson.

Open Dialogue See General Guide and tapescript (page 37).

Oral Exercises See General Guide and tapescript (page 37).

Speechwork See General Guide and tapescript (page 37).

Tapescript
Part A
1 DIALOGUE
ALLAN: Morning, girls!
TESSA: Oh, good morning Allan. Jackie, meet Allan. He's a van driver. Allan, this is Jackie, our new secretary.
ALLAN: Hello, Jackie!
JACKIE: Hello, Allan!
ALLAN: Are you English, Jackie?
JACKIE: No, I'm not.
ALLAN: Where are you from?
JACKIE: Guess!

ALLAN: Are you American?
JACKIE: No, I'm not.
ALLAN: Er... are you Canadian?
JACKIE: No, I'm not.
ALLAN: Well, are you Irish?
JACKIE: No, I'm not. I'm Australian.
ALLAN: Australian!
JACKIE: That's right. I'm from Melbourne, Australia. I'm Australian. My father's Australian but my mother's English. Where are you from, Allan?
ALLAN: I'm from London.

2 SPEECHWORK
Part A: Stress
Say after me:
di di da di...I'm from London...I'm from England...I'm from Melbourne...she's from London...she's from Sydney...we're from Ireland...they're from England...he's from Brighton...

Part B: Intonation
Say after me:
English...are you English...from England...are you from England...
American...are you American...from America...are you from America...
Canadian...are you Canadian...from Canada... are you from Canada...

Part C: Pronunciation
Say after me:
/ə/ ... /ə/ ... London ... Manchester ... Canada ... America ... from London...from Manchester...from Canada...from America...to London...to Manchester...to Canada... to America...from London to Manchester...from London to Canada...

3 LISTENING
Listen to these four people singing. What nationality are they?
Are they English, American, Irish or Australian?

Song No. 1 American
    2 Irish
    3 English
    4 Australian

4 OPEN DIALOGUE
Bill, an American boy, comes to see you at school. Talk to him.
BILL: Hi! My name's Bill.
STUDENT: ....
BILL: Oh, are you English?
STUDENT: ....
BILL: Oh, where are you from? Which town?
STUDENT: ....
BILL: Oh, well, I'm from New York City, in the United States. Say, is your teacher English?
STUDENT: ....
BILL: Well, I must go. Goodbye.
STUDENT: ....

Part B ORAL EXERCISES

Exercise 1 Say where you are from. You are the people in the pictures on page 39.

Liz and David: where are you from?
We're from Manchester. Where are you from? Now go on.

Sue and John: where are you from?
We're from Melbourne. Where are you from?

Carol and Steve: where are you from?
We're from Liverpool. Where are you from?

Judy and Michael: where are you from?
We're from England. Where are you from?

Angela and Gary: where are you from?
We're from America. Where are you from?

Janet and Don: where are you from?
We're from Canada. Where are you from?

Exercise 2 Give correct information about where people are from. Look at the pictures again.

Are Liz and David from London?
No, they aren't. They're from Manchester.

Are Sue and John from Liverpool?
No, they aren't. They're from Melbourne. Now go on.

Are Carol and Steve from Manchester?
No, they aren't. They're from Liverpool.

Are Judy and Michael from Australia?
No, they aren't. They're from England.

Are Angela and Gary from Ireland?
No, they aren't. They're from America.

Are Janet and Don from England?
No, they aren't. They're from Canada.

Unit 7

Exercise 3 Confirm people's nationality.

Is he English?
Of course he's English. Look at his car.
Is she American?
Of course she's American. Look at her car. Now go on.
Are they Australian?
Of course they're Australian. Look at their car.
Are they Irish?
Of course they're Irish. Look at their car.

Exercise 4 Spell the names of countries.

Spell Canada.
C A N A D A Now go on.
Spell America.
A M E R I C A
Spell Australia.
A U S T R A L I A
Spell England.
E N G L A N D
Spell Ireland.
I R E L A N D

Exercise 5 Say what nationality people are. Look at the pictures on page 39. Listen.

Sue and Larry are from Washington. They're American.
What about the people from Manchester?
They're English.
What about the people from Melbourne?
They're Australian. Now go on.
What about the people from Liverpool?
They're English.
What about the people from England?
They're English.
What about the people from the U.S.A?
They're American.
What about the people from Canada?
They're Canadian.

Exercise 6 Say where places are.

Where's Sydney?
It's in Australia.
Where's Liverpool?
It's in England. Now go on.
Where's New York?
It's in America.
Where's Manchester?
It's in England.
Where's Montreal?
It's in Canada.
Where's Dublin?
It's in Ireland.
Where's Los Angeles?
It's in America.

UNIT 8 Where exactly do you live?

	Skills	Functions	Example Sentences	Main Structures
SET 1	1. Speaking 2. Speaking 3. Speaking 4. Speaking	Ask and say where people live Say where you live	*Where do you live?* *I live in Trafford.*	*Where do you live?* *I/We/They live in* + place name
SET 2	1. Speaking 2. Speaking 3. Speaking 4. Speaking 5. Speaking	Ask and say exactly where people live	*Where do you live?* *I live in the north of England.* *Where exactly do you live?* *I live in a suburb north of London.*	*I* *the north/south of ...* *We* + *live in* + *a suburb of* *They* *in a suburb, north/ south of ...*
EXTENSION	Game	Students direct each other using compass directions across a classroom of obstacles (instructions in Teacher's Book only).		
	1. Reading and 2. Writing	Item in the Focus magazine about new staff – Jackie introduces herself. Students write their own piece using this model.		
	3. Listening	Consolidation dialogue based on Units 7 and 8.		
	4. Listening	TV Quiz show. Interviewing a contestant. Students fill in Sally Maxwell's personal details on form.		
	5. Reading	Reading Text: Towns and cities in Britain.		

OPEN DIALOGUE

ORAL EXERCISES		
	1. Say where you live	Mr and Mrs Ace, do you live in London? *Well, we live in a suburb of London.*
	2. Say exactly where people live (1)	Mr and Mrs Ace live in a suburb of London. *Yes, in a suburb north of London.*
	3. Ask exactly where people live	We're from the north of England. *Oh, I'm from the north too. Where exactly do you live?*
	4. Say where places are	Where's Newcastle exactly? *It's in the north of England.*
	5. Say exactly where people live (2)	Where exactly do Mr and Mrs Ace live? *They live north of London, in a suburb.*

SPEECHWORK			ACTIVE VOCABULARY		
A STRESS	north of England ●.●. I live in the north of England .●..●.●.		Brighton Newcastle Edinburgh Bristol Leeds Southampton Cambridge	north south east west suburb parents	now but exactly in live what about?
B INTONATION	Yes, I am No, he isn't				
C PRONUNCIATION	/θ/ three, thank you				

Unit 8

Where exactly do you live?

Allan Simmons is still talking to Jackie.

JACKIE: Where do you live? I mean, where do you live now?
ALLAN: I'm from London, but I live in Manchester now.
JACKIE: I live in Trafford.
ALLAN: Trafford?
JACKIE: It's a suburb west of Manchester.
ALLAN: Oh yes, that's right.

Set 1 — Ask where people live / Say where you live

Where do you live?
I live in Trafford.

1. Look at the single people on the map. Ask and answer like this:
   Where do you live, (Jane)?
   I live in (Manchester).

2. Now ask your partner:
   Where do you live, _____?
   I live in _____.

   Where do you live?
   We live in London.

3. Look at the couples on the map. Ask and answer like this:
   Where do you live, Mr and Mrs Ace?
   We live in London.

   Where do they live?
   They live in London.

4. Look at the couples again. Ask and answer like this:
   Where do Mr and Mrs Ace live?
   They live in London.

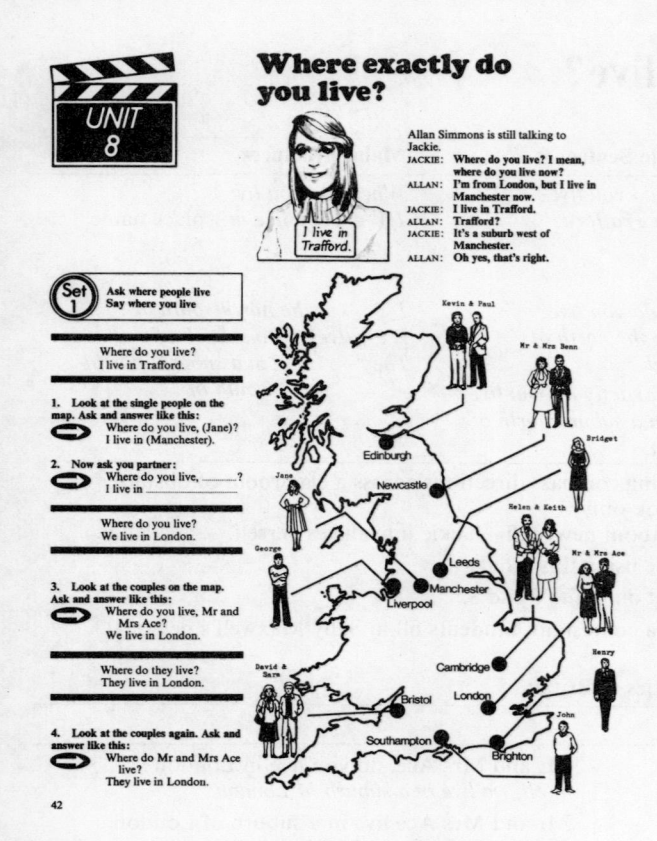

42

Set 2 — Ask and say where people live exactly

Where do you live? I live in the north of England.

1. Look at the map on page 42 again. Ask the people from Brighton, Newcastle, Bristol and Cambridge where they live, like this:
   Where do you live, Henry?
   I live in the _____ of England.

2. Ask your partner where he/she lives, like this:
   Where do you live, _____?
   I live in the _____ of _____.

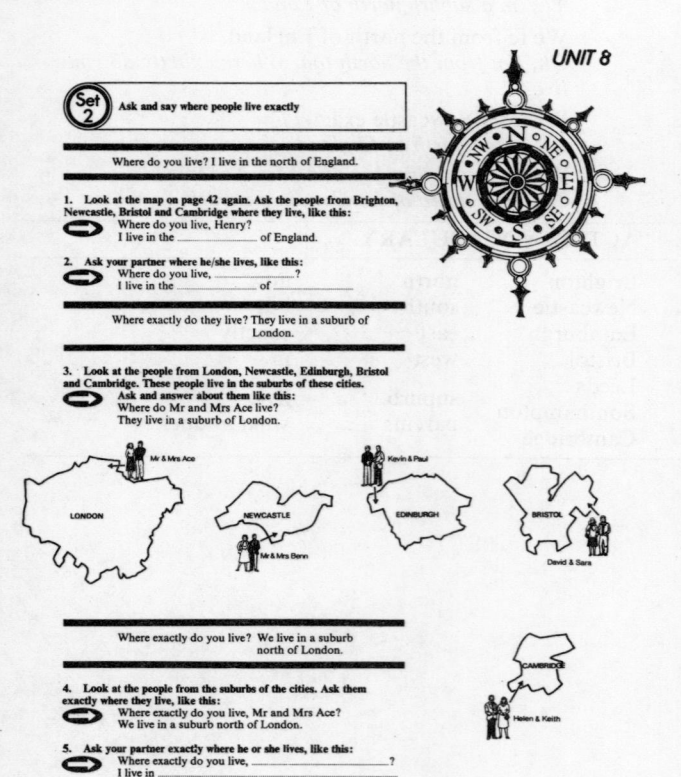

   Where exactly do they live? They live in a suburb of London.

3. Look at the people from London, Newcastle, Edinburgh, Bristol and Cambridge. These people live in the suburbs of these cities. Ask and answer about them like this:
   Where do Mr and Mrs Ace live?
   They live in a suburb of London.

   Where exactly do you live? We live in a suburb north of London.

4. Look at the people from the suburbs of the cities. Ask them exactly where they live, like this:
   Where do you live, Mr and Mrs Ace?
   We live in a suburb north of London.

5. Ask your partner exactly where he or she lives, like this:
   Where exactly do you live, _____?
   I live in _____.

43

DIALOGUE

This dialogue continues the conversation between Jackie and Allan from Unit 7.
Illustrate the meaning of *suburb* by giving a local example. Show the direction *West* on the blackboard, but do not teach the compass points until Set 2.
It is possible to present the first three lines of the dialogue, then the Set 1 exercises, then the remaining three lines of the dialogue and the exercises in Set 2.

SET 1 Ask where people live and say where you live

Use the map of Britain on page 42, or the wall picture/OHP (3), to present and practise the pronunciation of names of different cities and the people in them.

Ex 1 Where do you live?   I live in Trafford.

Practise the intonation of the question form.
Do the first example of the exercise.
Work T–S; check answer and pronunciation.
Students work in pairs.

Ex 2 Students work in pairs and ask each other.
If students are not studying in their homelands, ask them to say their home town now. This also applies to other exercises.

Ex 3 & 4 Proceed as Ex 1.

SET 2 Ask and say where people live exactly

Ex 1 Where do you live?   I live in the north of England.

Practise the pronunciation of N S E W.
Check comprehension by drawing compass points without labelling them. Ask individual students to name the direction as you point to a point on the compass.
This can be practised with a map of the students' country pointing to various parts.
Practise *I live in the north of England*, making sure that stress and rhythm are acceptable.
Do the first example of the exercise.
Work T–S; then students work in pairs.

Ex 2 Students ask each other. This can be done as a chain round the class, so that every student may hear where everybody else lives.

Ex 3 Where exactly do they live?

They live in a suburb of London.

Practise rhythm and stress.
Work as in Ex 1.

Ex 4 Work as in Ex 1.

Ex 5 Work as in Ex 2.

Unit 8

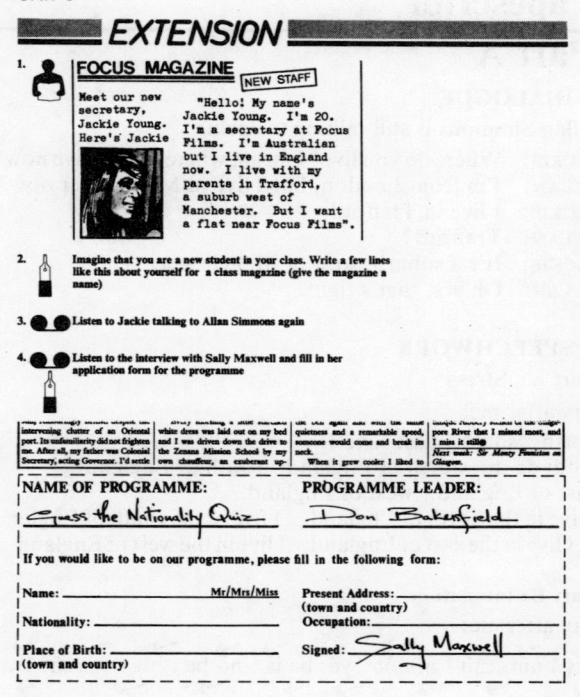

EXTENSION

Game Make sure there are enough chairs to make the game sufficiently complicated.

Clear the classroom of tables and chairs; put 8–9 chairs in different places in the room. Blindfold one student. Direct him/her from one end of the room to the other so that he/she doesn't bump into any of the chairs.

Direct him like this:

Take 4 steps north. Now take 2 steps north-west . . . etc.

Each person can take turns to call out a direction.
If the blindfolded person touches a chair, then another student takes his place and starts from the beginning.
Make sure every student gets a chance to speak.

1 & 2 *Reading and Writing* Read passage twice, pausing the second time for choral repetition.

Ask students to write a similar paragraph about themselves. As numbers over 9 have not yet been taught, students should write only the figure of their age (which can be fictitious). Students work individually. Check writing in class or collect it to correct outside the class.

3 *Listening (1)* This combines the dialogues of Units 7 and 8 in a slightly expanded form. The last few lines are completely new, but contain no new material and present no problems. Treat as consolidation listening.

4 *Listening (2)* Explain the setting: a quiz programme from television.

Play the tape once without stopping.
Go through the form which is to be filled in; give examples of place of birth (town and country).
Play tape again, stopping at convenient places to give the students time to fill in the details.
Check answers at the end; play tape again if necessary.

Open Dialogue See General Guide and tapescript (page 43).

Oral Exercises See General Guide and tapescript (page 43).

Speechwork See General Guide and tapescript (page 42).

Unit 8

Tapescript
Part A

1 DIALOGUE
Allan Simmons is still talking to Jackie.

JACKIE: Where do you live? I mean, where do you live now?
ALLAN: I'm from London, but I live in Manchester now.
JACKIE: I live in Trafford.
ALLAN: Trafford?
JACKIE: It's a suburb, west of Manchester.
ALLAN: Oh yes, that's right.

2 SPEECHWORK
Part A: Stress
Say after me:

north…south…east…west…
da di da di…north of England…south of England…
east of England…west of England…
I live in the north of England… I live in the south of England
…I live in the east of England…I live in the west of England…

Part B: Intonation
Say after me:

yes I am…no I'm not…yes he is…no he isn't…yes she is…
no she isn't…yes we are…no we aren't…yes they are…
no they aren't…

Part C: Pronunciation
Say after me:

/θ/…/θ/…three…your room number is three oh three…
thank you…thanks…north…I live in the north…
south…I live in the south…do you live in the north or the south?…

3 LISTENING (1)
ALLAN: Morning all, morning girls!
TESSA: Oh, good morning, Allan. Jackie, meet Allan. He's a van driver. Allan, this is Jackie. She's a secretary, a new secretary.
ALLAN: Ah, so you're our new secretary – hello.
JACKIE: Hello.
ALLAN: Mmm, that's lovely – say it again.
JACKIE: Say what again?
ALLAN: Say hello again.
JACKIE: Hello.
ALLAN: You aren't English, are you? Or are you?… *Are* you English, Jackie?
JACKIE: No, I'm not.
ALLAN: Where are you from then?
JACKIE: Guess!
ALLAN: Guess? Oh … oh, all right. Um, are you … American?
JACKIE: No!
ALLAN: Irish, then?
JACKIE: No, I'm not Irish. I'll tell you. I'm Australian.
ALLAN: Australian. You're an Aussie! You're from down under!
JACKIE: That's right. I'm from Melbourne.
ALLAN: Melbourne!
JACKIE: Well, where are you from, Allan? You aren't from Manchester.
ALLAN: No, I'm from London – but I live here now – in Manchester. But where do you live? I mean, where do you live now?
JACKIE: In Trafford.
ALLAN: Trafford … wait a moment … that's a suburb of Manchester, isn't it?
JACKIE: Mmm. It's a suburb west of Manchester to be exact.
TESSA: Allan! Allan!
ALLAN: Coming!
TESSA: Are you ready? Are you ready to go?
ALLAN: Yes, I am.
TESSA: Here's the address.
ALLAN: Is that B A R T or B A N T?
TESSA: It's an R. B A R T O N. Barton Road. It's in the south of Manchester.
ALLAN: Right! Where's my map of Manchester … ah, here it is. Bye, everyone. Goodbye, Jackie.
JACKIE: Oh … oh … Goodbye, Allan. (Allan goes out) Er…Tessa…is Allan married?
TESSA: Allan? Married? Oh no … Allan isn't married!

LISTENING (2)
Listen to the tape and fill in the form in your books.
(Radio/TV quiz show from USA)

HOST: And now, ladies and gentlemen, the next contestant for the Guess The Nationality Quiz is Sally Maxwell … (applause) …
SALLY: How do you do.
HOST: How do you do and pleased to meet you. Now tell us about yourself … first question … are you married? … (faint laughter) …
SALLY: No, no I'm not.
HOST: You're not married … Well, Miss Maxwell …
SALLY: Please call me Sally …
HOST: Of course … Sally, you aren't American, are you?
SALLY: No, I'm not. I'm English.
HOST: From London?
SALLY: No, I'm from the north of England, from Newcastle. (with put-on northern accent)
HOST: (imitating) Newcastle … that's wonderful … ha ha … but you live here in San Francisco?
SALLY: Yes, well, I live in a suburb of San Francisco.
HOST: And what do you do, Sally? Tell us …
SALLY: I'm a teacher.
HOST: Wonderful! Hear that, ladies and gentlemen? Sally's a teacher. That's really wonderful … So, here she is, ladies and gentlemen, Sally Maxwell from Newcastle in England … she's a teacher and she lives here with us in San Francisco. And Sally is now going to answer the sixty four thousand dollar question … are you ready, Sally?
SALLY: Yes.
HOST: Here it is! (Fade out) … What nationality is Richard Burton?

4 OPEN DIALOGUE
Talk to Allan Simmons.

ALLAN: Hello, I'm Allan, Allan Simmons. What's your name?
STUDENT: ....
ALLAN: Are you a student?
STUDENT: ....
ALLAN: Are you English?
STUDENT: ....
ALLAN: Oh, well, *I'm* English. I'm from the south of England, London, actually. What about you? Where are you from?
STUDENT: ....
ALLAN: Really? I live in Manchester now. Where do you live?
STUDENT: ....
ALLAN: And your parents? Where do they live?
STUDENT: ....
ALLAN: Where is that exactly?
STUDENT: ....
ALLAN: Oh, yes. Well, I must go now. Goodbye for now!
STUDENT: ....

Part B ORAL EXERCISES

Exercise 1 Say where you live. You are the people in the pictures on page 43.

Mr and Mrs Ace, do you live in London?
Well, we live in a suburb of London.
Mr and Mrs Benn, do you live in Newcastle?
Well, we live in a suburb of Newcastle. Now go on.
Kevin and Paul, do you live in Edinburgh?
Well, we live in a suburb of Edinburgh.
David and Sara, do you live in Bristol?
Well, we live in a suburb of Bristol.
Helen and Keith, do you live in Cambridge?
Well, we live in a suburb of Cambridge.

Exercise 2 Say exactly where people live
Look at page 43.

Mr and Mrs Ace live in a suburb of London.
Yes, in a suburb north of London.
Mr and Mrs Benn live in a suburb of Newcastle.
Yes, in a suburb south of Newcastle. Now go on.
Kevin and Paul live in a suburb of Edinburgh.
Yes, in a suburb north-west of Edinburgh.
David and Sara live in a suburb of Bristol.
Yes, in a suburb east of Bristol.
Helen and Keith live in a suburb of Cambridge.
Yes, in a suburb south-west of Cambridge.

Exercise 3 Express interest and ask exactly where people live.

We're from the north of England.
Oh, I'm from the north too. Where exactly do you live?
We're from the south of Canada.
Oh, I'm from the south too. Where exactly do you live? Now go on.
We're from the north-west of Ireland.
Oh, I'm from the north-west too. Where exactly do you live?
We're from the centre of Bristol.
Oh, I'm from the centre too. Where exactly do you live?
We're from the south-west of Australia.
Oh, I'm from the south-west too. Where exactly do you live?

Exercise 4 Say where places are.

Where's Newcastle exactly?
It's in the north of England.
Where's Southampton exactly?
It's in the south of England. Now go on.
Where's Bristol exactly?
It's in the west of England.
Where's Brighton exactly?
It's in the south of England.
Where's Cambridge exactly?
It's in the east of England.

Exercise 5 Say exactly where people live.
Look at the pictures on page 43.

Where exactly do Mr and Mrs Ace live?
They live north of London, in a suburb.
Where exactly do Mr and Mrs Benn live?
They live south of Newcastle, in a suburb. Now go on.
Where exactly do David and Sara live?
They live east of Bristol, in a suburb.
Where exactly do Helen and Keith live?
They live south-west of Cambridge, in a suburb.
Where exactly do Kevin and Paul live?
They live north-west of Edinburgh, in a suburb.

UNIT 9 One bed., one sit., K and B

	Skills	Functions	Example Sentences	Main Structures
SET 1	1. Speaking 2. Speaking 3. Speaking 4. Listening 5. Drawing and Speaking	Show and ask about places	*This is the bedroom and that's the sitting room.* *Is this the bathroom?* *Yes, it is.* *Is this the kitchen?* *No, it isn't, that's the kitchen over there.*	This/that is the . . . Is this/that the . . . ? Yes, it is/No, it isn't This is the + adjective + noun
SET 2	1. Reading and Writing 2. Speaking 3. Speaking 4. Speaking 5. Speaking 6. Speaking 7. Speaking	Express satisfaction and dissatisfaction	*Mmm! It's nice and big!* *Oh! It isn't very big!*	
SET 3	1. Reading and Writing 2. Speaking	Ask about and say cost Count to twenty	*How much is it?* *It's fourteen pounds.*	
EXTENSION	1. Reading and Writing	Advertisement for the sale of a house, including list of rooms, Students make a list of rooms in their own house.		
	2. Reading and 3. Writing	Letter from a couple who buy the house in previous activity. Students write letter using this model.		
	4. Listening	Dialogue between two couples in a new house. Students list the names of rooms.		
	5. Reading	Reading Text: An English House.		

OPEN DIALOGUE

ORAL EXERCISES

1. Show where rooms are (1)	Can you show me the sitting room? Yes, this is the sitting room.	
2. Show where rooms are (2)	Is this the sitting room? No, it isn't. That's the sitting room over there.	
3. Ask about rooms	You want to find the bedroom. Is this the bedroom?	
4. Ask about prices	How much is it? £13? Yes, that's right. £13.	
5. Express satisfaction	Is your hotel room big? Yes, it's nice and big.	
6. Express dissatisfaction	Is your hotel room big? No, it isn't very big.	

SPEECHWORK

A STRESS   That's the bedroom ● • ●•
           This is the bedroom • • • ●•

B INTONATION   ˈThis is the ˈbedroom ↗
               and ˈthat's the ˈbathroom ↘

C PRONUNCIATION /ð/ that, flat

ACTIVE VOCABULARY

house	kitchen	garden	upstairs
bathroom	toilet	terrace	downstairs
sitting room	hall	beach	show
dining room	garage	sea	
classroom			Dear
pound	big	clean	Love
week	hot	tasty	
food	cold	comfortable	
temperature	warm	very	
weather			
how much?			
Numbers (Ten to twenty)			

Unit 9

DIALOGUE

Explain *upstairs* (passive vocabulary).
Demonstrate the difference between *this* and *that* with gestures. Practise also with names e.g. *This is John and that's Mary.*
Use the wall picture/OHP (4) of the rooms in a house as you work through the dialogue.

SET 1 Show and ask about places

Ex 1 This is the bedroom and that's the sitting room.

Practise the pronunciation of names of rooms first.
Then practise the pronunciation of the sentence above.
Give an example using the wall picture/OHP.
Students work in pairs, taking turns to show different places.

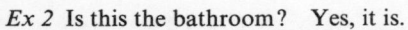

Ex 2 Is this the bathroom?   Yes, it is.

Practise the intonation of the question and answer.
Proceed as in Ex 1.

Ex 3 Is this the kitchen?

No, it isn't. That's the kitchen over there.

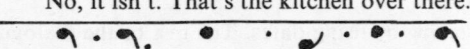

Practise as in Ex 1 and 2.

Ex 4 Listening (1)
Students guess the names of the places where people are from the sound effects on the tape. Students write down the answers.
Answers: 1 bathroom 2 garage 3 garden 4 kitchen 5 toilet 6 sitting room 7 bedroom.

Ex 5 If students live in a house on two floors, show how to draw 2 separate plans for *Upstairs* and *Downstairs*.

SET 2 Express satisfaction and dissatisfaction

Ex 1 Mmm! It's nice and big.

Practise the pronunciation of the new adjectives.
Students work in pairs, filling in the words of Mr and Mrs Ferm.
Practise the intonation of *Mmm! It's nice and big.*
Check the answers by asking individual students to read out what Mr and Mrs Ferm say in each picture.

One bed, one sit, K&B

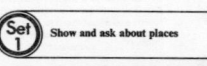

UNIT 9

Jackie goes to see the flat in Gordon Road. Mrs Parker opens the door.

JACKIE: How do you do! I'm Jackie Young. I'm from the Town and Country Flat Agency.
MRS PARKER: Oh yes, the Flat Agency. Come in. The flat's upstairs.
JACKIE: Thank you.
MRS PARKER: This is the bedroom.
JACKIE: Yes.
MRS PARKER: And that's the sitting room.
JACKIE: Mmm! It's nice and big. Is this the bathroom?
MRS PARKER: Yes, it is.
JACKIE: Oh! It isn't very big. Is this the kitchen?
MRS PARKER: No, it isn't. That's the kitchen over there. This is the toilet.
JACKIE: Oh, I see. Well, thank you very much.
MRS PARKER: That's all right.

Set 1 Show and ask about places

This is the bedroom and that's the sitting room.

Look at the plan of the flat

1. Show your partner the different places like this:
   This is the bedroom and that's the sitting room
   This is the bathroom and that's the bedroom

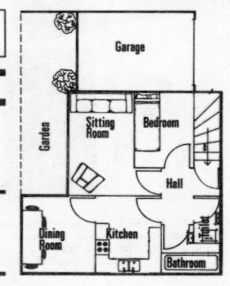

   hall/sitting room
   kitchen/dining room
   bedroom/kitchen
   bathroom/toilet
   garage/garden

UNIT 9

Is this the bathroom?
Yes, it is.

2. Look at the flat again and ask and answer about the places like this:
   Is this the _____?
   Yes, it is.

   Is this the kitchen?
   No, it isn't. That's the kitchen over there.

3. Look at the flat and ask and answer about the places like this:
   Is this the _____?
   No, it isn't. That's the _____ over there.

4. Listen and say which room or place the people are in
   1. In the _____
   2. In the _____
   3. In the _____
   4. In the _____
   5. In the _____
   6. In the _____
   7. In the _____

5. Draw a plan of your house or flat. Tell your partner about the rooms.

Set 2 Express satisfaction and dissatisfaction

Mmm! It's nice and big!

1. Look at this advertisement for a holiday in Spain

   SUNSHINE TOURS ONE WEEK ON THE COSTA BRAVA SPAIN
   SPECIAL REDUCTIONS ONLY £65
   HOTEL Casa Blanca
   ENJOY
   a comfortable hotel
   a big terrace
   tasty food
   a clean beach
   warm sea temperature —26°C

   For further details write to:
   Sunshine Tours Ltd. (Special Reduction: Spain)
   5 Market Street
   Manchester   Tel: 061/543 7698

Mr and Mrs Ferm go and stay at the Hotel Casa Blanca. They are very satisfied with the holiday. Look at the photographs from their holiday and write what they say

Mmm, it's nice and warm

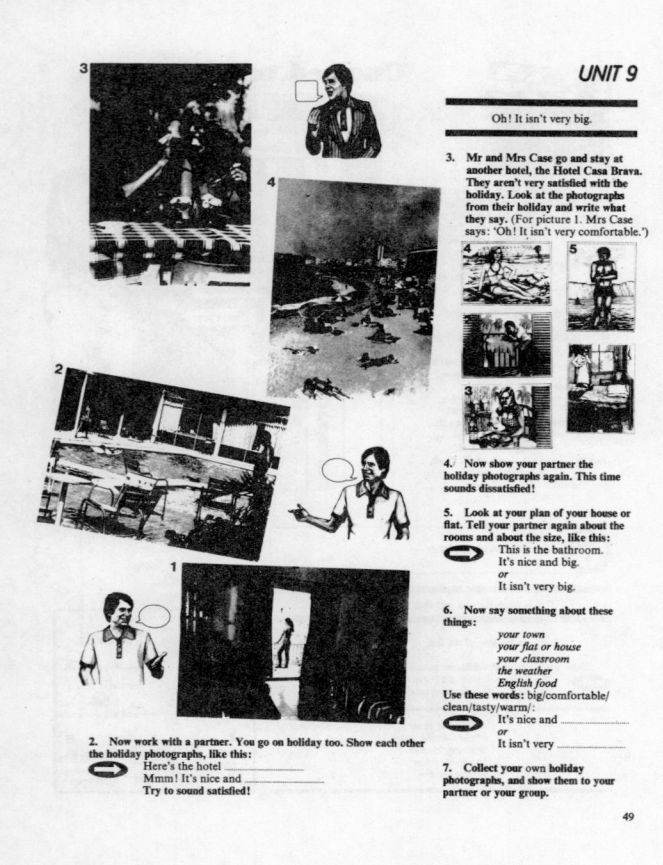

Unit 9

Ex 2 Students work in pairs.
Go round to check; make sure the students sound satisfied.

Ex 3 Oh! It isn't very big.

Work as in Ex 1, but this time sound dissatisfied.

Ex 4 Work as in Ex 2.

Ex 5 If necessary, draw a plan of your own home and talk about the places, to give an example.
Students work in pairs.

Ex 6 Explain *weather*.
Allow a few minutes for preparation – students can consult each other if they like.
Ask individual students what they think of the items. Get several comments on each item.

Ex 7 Students use adjectives learnt in previous exercises. Do not introduce new vocabulary.

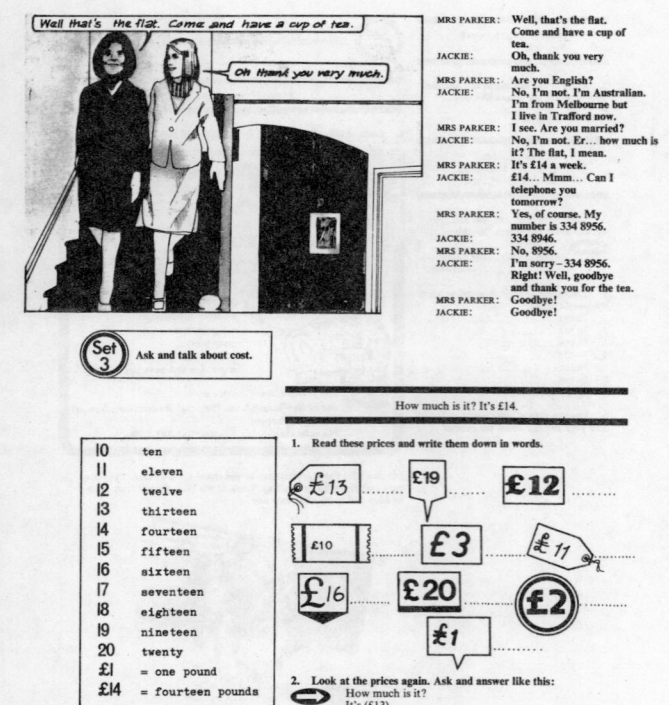

DIALOGUE

Explain *tomorrow* by using dates. The rest of the dialogue should be explained through the pictures.

SET 3 Ask and talk about cost

Practise the numbers as in Unit 4. Check the students pronounce the *-een* of *thirteen* etc. clearly, to save later confusion over *thirty*, *forty* etc.
Revise numbers 1–9 at the same time, possibly with a chain exercise; recite even numbers only, then odd numbers.
Or try simple adding exercises.

Ex 1 Practise the pronunciation of *pound*.
Students read the prices first, then write the prices in full, possibly for homework.

Ex 2 How much is it? It's fourteen pounds.

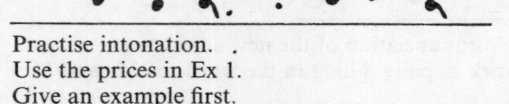

Practise intonation.
Use the prices in Ex 1.
Give an example first.
Students work in pairs, taking turns to ask and answer.

EXTENSION

1 Students look at the list of rooms and extras while they read the advertisement.
They list the rooms in their own homes.

2 Students read letter and address on envelope silently. Ask questions about Cathy and Martin's new house to test comprehension.

3 This is the first exercise in writing a simple letter and addressing an envelope.
Draw attention to the layout of both letter and envelope i.e. where to put the address, date, salutation etc. Explain that *love* is used quite widely as an ending to a close friend or relative, but *Yours* is more neutral.
Students can use the list of rooms in their own homes when they write their own letters.

4 *Listening (2)* Play tape through once, then again stopping after each of the rooms as shown.
Answers: 1 *hall* 2 *sitting room* 3 *kitchen* 4 *big bedroom* 5 *small bedroom* 6 *bathroom* 7 *toilet* 8 *garden*.

Open Dialogue Before starting the dialogue, write on the blackboard the order in which students are to show the rooms, so that the dialogue runs smoothly.
Unlike before, students take the initiative in this dialogue.

Oral Exercises See General Guide and tapescript (page 49).

Speechwork See General Guide and tapescript (page 48).

Unit 9

47

Unit 9

Tapescript
Part A

1 DIALOGUE
Jackie goes to see the flat in Gordon Road. Mrs Parker opens the door.

JACKIE:	How do you do! I'm Jackie Young. I'm from the Town and Country Flat Agency.
MRS PARKER:	Oh yes, the Flat Agency. Come in. The flat's upstairs.
JACKIE:	Thank you.
MRS PARKER:	This is the bedroom.
JACKIE:	Yes...
MRS PARKER:	And that's the sitting room.
JACKIE:	Mmm! It's nice and big. Is this the bathroom?
MRS PARKER:	Yes, it is.
JACKIE:	Oh! It isn't very big. Is this the kitchen?
MRS PARKER:	No, it isn't. That's the kitchen over there. This is the toilet.
JACKIE:	Oh, I see. Well, thank you very much.
MRS PARKER:	That's all right.
MRS PARKER:	Well, that's the flat. Come and have a cup of tea.
JACKIE:	Oh, thank you very much.
MRS PARKER:	Are you English?
JACKIE:	No, I'm not. I'm Australian. I'm from Melbourne but I live in Trafford now.
MRS PARKER:	I see. Are you married?
JACKIE:	No, I'm not. Er...how much is it? The flat, I mean.
MRS PARKER:	It's £14 a week.
JACKIE:	£14... Mmm... Can I telephone you tomorrow?
MRS PARKER:	Yes, of course. My number is 334 8956.
JACKIE:	334 8946.
MRS PARKER:	No, 8956.
JACKIE:	I'm sorry – 334 8956. Right! Well, goodbye and thank you for the tea.
MRS PARKER:	Goodbye!
JACKIE:	Goodbye!

2 SPEECHWORK
Part A: Stress
Say after me:
da di...bedroom...bathroom...kitchen...garden...
da di da di...that's the bedroom...that's the bathroom...
that's the kitchen...that's the garden...
di di di da di...this is the bedroom...this is the bathroom...
this is the kitchen...this is the garden...

Part B: Intonation
Say after me:
bedroom...bathroom...ǃthis is the bedroom and ǃthat's the bathroom
kitchen...toilet...ǃthis is the kitchen and ǃthat's the toilet...
sitting room...dining room...ǃthis is the sitting room and ǃthat's the dining room...
garage...garden...ǃthis is the garage and ǃthat's the garden...

Part C: Pronunciation
Say after me:
/ð/.../ð/...this...that...the bedroom...the kitchen...
the toilet...is this the bedroom...is this the kitchen...
is this the toilet...is that the bedroom...is that the kitchen...
is that the toilet...that's right...yes, that's right...

3 LISTENING (1)
Listen and say where these people are.
1 bathroom
2 garage
3 garden
4 kitchen
5 toilet
6 sitting room
7 bedroom

LISTENING (2)
Listen to the tape and write down the list of rooms and places in your books. Tessa and David Richards go to see Murray and Anna Freeman in their new house.

MURRAY:	Tessa! David! Hello!
TESSA:	Hello! Hello, Anna!
ANNA:	Hello, you two. Come in.
DAVID:	Thanks. So this is your new house!
ANNA:	Yes, do you like it?
DAVID:	(laughing) I don't know yet. Can you show us round?
MURRAY:	Of course! Well, let's start here... This is the hall... and here's the sitting room...
TESSA:	Mmm! It's beautiful!
MURRAY:	And that's the kitchen...
TESSA:	Oh, let's have a look... Oh yes, it's nice and big, isn't it?
ANNA:	Yes, I like big kitchens. The bedrooms and the bathroom are upstairs... here... that's our bedroom, the big bedroom...
DAVID:	Oh yes...
ANNA:	And that's the small bedroom for the children.
TESSA:	What's this room?
MURRAY:	Oh, that's the bathroom. And that's the toilet next to it.
TESSA:	Aha! A bathroom *and* a toilet!
ANNA:	(laughing) Come and see the garden. It isn't very big but it's nice for the kids.
MURRAY:	Well, that's it... do you like it?
TESSA:	Oh yes, it's really nice.

4 OPEN DIALOGUE

Talk to Tessa. Show her your flat or house. Show her the sitting room, the bedroom, the kitchen and the bathroom.

TESSA: Hello!
STUDENT: ....
TESSA: Is this your new flat?
STUDENT: ....
TESSA: Do show me round . . . What's this room?
STUDENT: ....
TESSA: Oh yes, it's nice and big.
STUDENT: ....
TESSA: Mmm! It looks very comfortable. Is this the kitchen?
STUDENT: ....
TESSA: It's very nice. And what's this room?
STUDENT: ....
TESSA: Oh yes. Well, it's lovely. Thank you. Goodbye!
STUDENT: ....

Part B ORAL EXERCISES

Exercise 1 Show where rooms are (1)

Can you show me the sitting room?
Yes, this is the sitting room.

Can you show me the kitchen?
Yes, this is the kitchen. Now go on.

Can you show me the bathroom?
Yes, this is the bathroom.

Can you show me the dining room?
Yes, this is the dining room.

Can you show me the garage?
Yes, this is the garage.

Can you show me the garden?
Yes, this is the garden.

Exercise 2 Show where rooms are. (2)

Is this the sitting room?
No, it isn't. That's the sitting room over there.

Is this the kitchen?
No, it isn't. That's the kitchen over there. Now go on.

Is this the toilet?
No, it isn't. That's the toilet over there.

Is this the bathroom?
No,, it isn't. That's the bathroom over there.

Is this the dining room?
No, it isn't. That's the dining room over there.

Is this the bedroom?
No, it isn't. That's the bedroom over there.

Exercise 3 Ask about rooms.

You want to find the bedroom.
Is this the bedroom?

You want to find the bathroom.
Is this the bathroom? Now go on.

You want to find the kitchen.
Is this the kitchen?

You want to find the toilet.
Is this the toilet?

You want to find the dining room.
Is this the dining room?

You want to find the sitting room.
Is this the sitting room?

Exercise 4 Ask about prices (see page 50).

How much is it? £13?
Yes, that's right. It's £13.

How much is it? £19?
Yes, that's right. It's £19. Now go on.

How much is it? £12?
Yes, that's right. It's £12.

How much is it? £10?
Yes, that's right. It's £10.

How much is it? £3?
Yes, that's right. It's £3.

Exercise 5 You are on holiday. Express satisfaction about things.

Is your hotel room big?
Yes, it's nice and big.

And is it clean?
Yes, it's nice and clean. Now go on.

What about the food? Is it tasty?
Yes, it's nice and tasty.

And the swimming pool. It's clean I hope.
Yes, it's nice and clean.

What about the weather. Is it hot?
Yes, it's nice and hot.

And I hope your bed is comfortable?
Yes, it's nice and comfortable.

Exercise 6 You are still on holiday. This time express dissatisfaction.

Is your hotel room big?
No, it isn't very big.

And clean, I suppose?
No, it isn't very clean. Now go on.

What about the food? Is it tasty?
No, it isn't very tasty.

And the swimming pool. Is it clean?
No, it isn't very clean.

What about the weather? Is it hot?
No, it isn't very hot.

And I hope your bed is comfortable?
No, it isn't very comfortable.

UNIT 10 Coffee Time

	Skills	Functions	Example Sentences	Main Structures
SET 1	1. Speaking 2. Speaking 3. Speaking 4. Speaking	Offer, accept and refuse	*Would you like a cup of coffee?* *Yes, please.* *And a biscuit?* *No, thank you.*	*Would you like . . . ?* *a cup of/a glass of* etc.
SET 2	1. Speaking 2. Speaking 3. Speaking	Ask people for things and give people things	*Can I have a cup of coffee, please?* *Yes, here you are.*	*Can I have . . . please?* *one cup two cups* *one glass two glasses* *one sandwich two sandwiches*
SET 3	1. Reading 2. Speaking 3. Speaking	Ask and talk about cost Numbers 20–100	*How much is a cup of coffee?* *It's 12p.* *A sandwich and a cup of tea, please.*	
EXTENSION	1. Listening	Extended version of the original dialogue.		
	2. Listening	Conversation in a pub between Murray, Tessa and Peter. Students fill in sentences.		
	3. Reading	Reading Text: Memorandum.		

OPEN DIALOGUE

ORAL EXERCISES		
	1. Offer people something to eat or drink	Ah, here's Murray! Offer him a cup of coffee. *Would you like a cup of coffee, Murray?*
	2. Ask for something to eat or drink	A cup of tea or a cup of coffee? *Can I have a cup of coffee, please?*
	3. Ask for something – for yourself and for a friend	I think I'd like a cup of tea. *Right! Can I have two cups of tea, please?*
	4. Ask the price of things	I think I'll have a cup of coffee. *How much is it?*
	5. Say how much things cost	How much is a coffee? *It's 12 pence.*
	6. Rhyme (to practise rhythm and stress of *coffee, tea, biscuits*)	

SPEECHWORK		ACTIVE VOCABULARY		
A STRESS	a cup of tea •●• a cup of coffee •●•●	cup	coffee	red
		glass	tea	white
B INTONATION	ˈCan Iˈhave aˈcup of teˌa, please?	packet	water	strong
C PRONUNCIATION	/w/ water, wine	cafeteria	milk	modern
		biscuit	wine	yes, please
		cake	beer	no, thanks
		sandwich	orange juice	can I have . . .
			chocolate	just
		pay	pence	here you are
		speak	money	right
				Bye!
				Don't worry!
		twenty-one	thirty	
		twenty-two	forty	
		twenty-three etc.	fifty etc.	
			a hundred	

Unit 10

DIALOGUE

Would you like . . . ? should be taught as a phrase without grammatical analysis. The pictures make it clear that the phrase is used when offering; it has nothing to do with likes and dislikes (expressed by *Do you like . . . ?*).

SET 1 Offer, accept and refuse

Present and practise the new vocabulary.
Pay particular attention to stress and intonation.

Ex 1 Would you like a cup of coffee?

Practise the question form chorally and individually.
Give a few examples of how to change the item being offered.
Students practise chorally first; you give the call-word e.g. *cup of tea* and the whole class says *Would you like a cup of tea?* and so on through the list.
Ask individual students to offer something from the pictures.
The wall picture/OHP (5) may be used here.

Ex 2 Yes, please.

Practise the intonation of this response.
Work in a chain round the class S1–S2, S2–S3, where the students offer and accept the offer.
Students work in pairs, offering and accepting in turns.

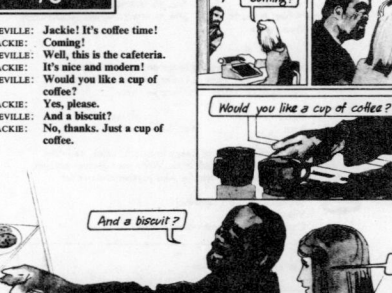

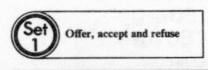

Ex 3 No, thanks.

Practise the intonation of this reponse.
Work as in Ex 2.

Ex 4 Read the model dialogue.
Practise the last response together: *No, thanks. Just a . . .* with a few examples from the list of food and drink.
Select a student and ask him to respond; you read the offering part, he reads the response, using the first examples from the exercise.
Change parts.
Students work in pairs, taking turns to offer and accept.

DIALOGUE

Explain pence. Say that it is written and often pronounced p/pi:/. Numbers 20–100 will be practised in this Set.

SET 2 Ask people for things and give people things

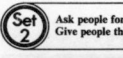

Ex 1 Can I have a cup of coffee, please?   Yes, here you are.

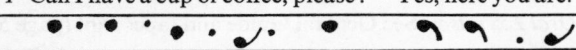

Practise the request and response chorally and individually.
The rising intonation indicates politeness and should be emphasised.
Work as in Set 1, Ex 1 and 2.

Unit 10

UNIT 10

Can I have two cups of coffee, please? Yes, here you are.

one cup – two cups one glass – two glasses
one biscuit – two biscuits one sandwich – two sandwiches
one cake – two cakes

2. Now ask for TWO of everything in the pictures, like this:
   Can I have two cups of coffee, please?
   Two cups of coffee. Yes, here you are.

   Can I have two _____, please?
   Two _____. Yes, here you are.

3. Look again at the pictures of things to eat and drink, and offer your partner something to eat and drink. When your partner accepts, ask for two of the same thing: one for your partner and one for yourself. Here is an example:
   Would you like a sandwich?
   Yes, please.
   Can I have two sandwiches, please?

Set 3 Ask and talk about cost

Numbers 20–100
20 twenty   21 twenty one
22 twenty two   23 twenty three
30 thirty   40 forty   50 fifty
60 sixty   70 seventy   80 eighty
90 ninety   100 a hundred

35p = thirty-five pence (or p.)
£1.35 = one pound thirty-five (pence)
£2.35 = two pounds thirty-five (pence)
£2.00 = two pounds

(i) 59p (ii) 86p (iii) £3.45
(iv) £1.99 (v) £27.00
(vi) £100.00 (vii) £2.75

1. Read these prices

56

UNIT 10

Focus Cafeteria
PRICE LIST

DRINKS
Coffee   12p
Tea   10p
Milk   10p
Orange Juice 12p
Chocolate   15p
Coca Cola   12p

SNACKS
Cakes   10p each
Biscuits   8p
(per packet)
Sandwiches   22p each

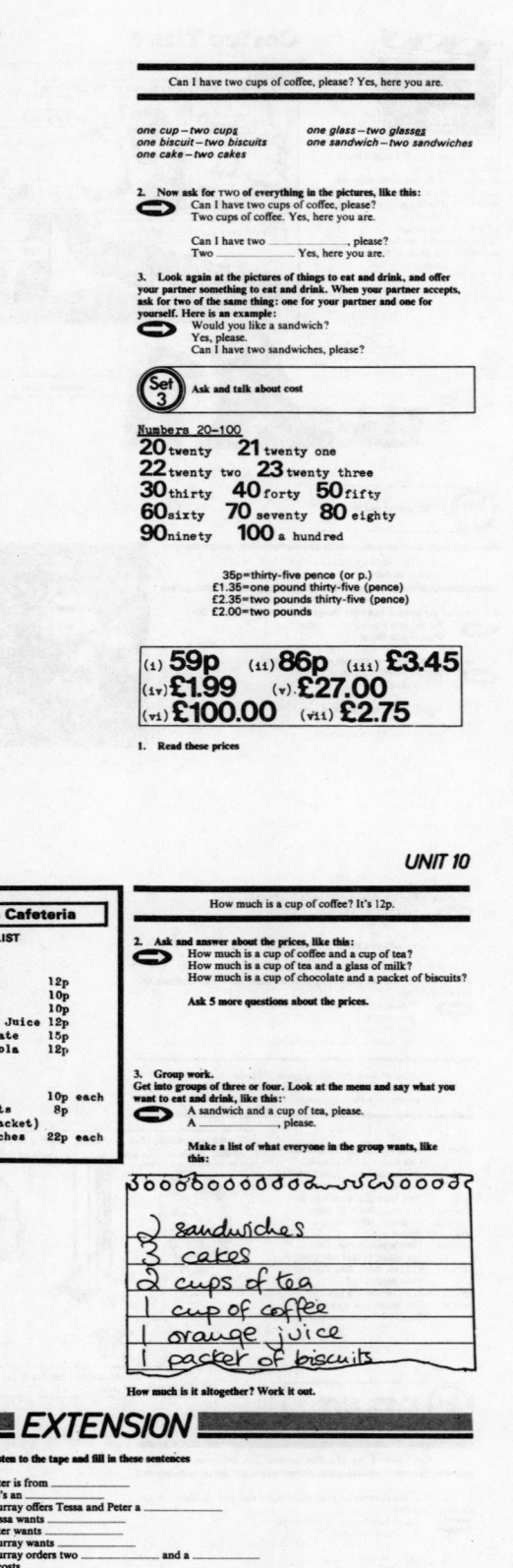

How much is a cup of coffee? It's 12p.

2. Ask and answer about the prices, like this:
   How much is a cup of coffee and a cup of tea?
   How much is a cup of tea and a glass of milk?
   How much is a cup of chocolate and a packet of biscuits?

   Ask 5 more questions about the prices.

3. Group work.
   Get into groups of three or four. Look at the menu and say what you want to eat and drink, like this:
   A sandwich and a cup of tea, please.
   A _____, please.

   Make a list of what everyone in the group wants, like this:

   2 sandwiches
   3 cakes
   2 cups of tea
   1 cup of coffee
   1 orange juice
   1 packet of biscuits

   How much is it altogether? Work it out.

EXTENSION

Listen to the tape and fill in these sentences
Peter is from _____
He's an _____
Murray offers Tessa and Peter a _____
Tessa wants _____
Peter wants _____
Murray wants _____
Murray orders two _____ and a _____
It costs _____

57

Ex 2 Can I have two cups of coffee, please?

Yes, here you are.

Give other examples of plural formation here using words familiar to the students. Do not introduce irregular plurals yet.
Students work in pairs, taking turns to ask and answer.

Ex 3 Give an example so that students realise that the last line of the dialogue is addressed to a third person.
Students work in groups of 3, changing parts several times.

SET 3 Ask and talk about cost
Numbers 20–100

Revise numbers 1–20.
Concentrate on the stress pattern of 30, 40, 50 etc. so that they are not confused with 13, 14, 15 etc. Practise the numbers in multiples of 5 and 10, and odd numbers, from 20 to 50 at least.

Ex 1 Demonstrate how to read prices.
Students practise saying the prices silently and then aloud.

Ex 2 Present and practise the 3 new words on the list – *orange juice*, *coca-cola* and *chocolate*. Ask about the prices of the individual items so that the students get simple practice in reading prices.
Point out the difference between the patterns *It's 12p* and *They're 12p each*.
Students work in pairs asking the more complicated questions printed in the exercise.
They should be able to invent 5 new similar questions for each other to answer. Students will correct each other if they add up wrongly.

Ex 3 Students work in groups of 3 or 4. They must first decide what they want from the list, and appoint one person in the group to take the order for the whole group. They help to add up the sum and see what the whole order will cost.

EXTENSION

1 *Listening* Play the extended version of the dialogue as listening consolidation.

2 *Listening* A conversation in a pub between Murray, Tessa and Peter, a friend of Murray's from New York. Murray takes their orders for drinks.
Play the tape once without stopping, then again pausing at relevant places.
Check afterwards.

Open Dialogue See General Guide and tapescript (page 54).

Oral Exercises See General Guide and tapescript (page 54).

Ex 6 Rhyme
Read the rhyme through, emphasising the stressed syllables and the rhythm. Beat time as you read.
Students then repeat line after line, possibly beating time too.
Then read the whole rhyme through twice, together with the students. The second time read a little faster than the first.

Speechwork See General Guide and tapescript (page 53).

Unit 10

Tapescript
Part A

1 DIALOGUE

NEVILLE: Jackie! It's coffee time!
JACKIE: Coming!
NEVILLE: Well, this is the cafeteria.
JACKIE: It's nice and modern!
NEVILLE: Would you like a cup of coffee?
JACKIE: Yes, please.
NEVILLE: And a biscuit?
JACKIE: No, thanks. Just a cup of coffee.
NEVILLE: Good morning, Mrs Jenkins. Can I have a cup of coffee please – no, can I have two cups of coffee, please?
MRS JENKINS: Two cups of coffee. Yes, here you are. That's 24 pence.
NEVILLE: 24 pence. Here you are.
MRS JENKINS: Thank you.
NEVILLE: Here's your coffee, Jackie. It's white. Is that all right?
JACKIE: Oh yes, that's fine, thanks. How much is it?
NEVILLE: It's 12p. But I'll pay.
JACKIE: Oh, thank you very much. Mmm! It's nice and strong.

2 SPEECHWORK

Part A: Stress

Say after me:

di da di da...a cup of tea...a glass of beer...a glass of milk...a glass of wine...
di da di da di...a cup of coffee...a glass of water...a cup of tea and a cup of coffee...a glass of beer and a glass of water...a glass of wine and a glass of water...a glass of milk and a cup of coffee...

Part B: Intonation

Say after me:

tea please...beer please...milk please...wine please...
a 'cup of tea please...a 'glass of beer please...
a 'glass of milk please...a 'glass of wine please...
'can I 'have a 'cup of tea please?...can I 'have a 'glass of beer 'please?...'can I 'have a 'glass of wine 'please?...'can I 'have a 'glass of milk 'please?...

Part C: Pronunciation

Say after me:

/w/.../w/...water...wine...sandwiches...would...would you like a glass of water...Would you like a glass of wine... Would you like a sandwich... what...where...what do you do...where are you from...we're from the west...

3 LISTENING (1)

NEVILLE: Jackie!
JACKIE: Mmm?
NEVILLE: It's coffee time.
JACKIE: Oh, is it? All right. Just a minute. Right. Coming. Where's the cafeteria?
NEVILLE: It's upstairs. I'll show you ... Here. This is the cafeteria.
JACKIE: Oh ... mmm ... it's nice and modern, isn't it?
NEVILLE: Yes, it's quite nice. Coffee? Would you like a cup of coffee?
JACKIE: Mmm. Yes please.
NEVILLE: And a biscuit?
JACKIE: A biscuit ... er ... no, no thanks. No biscuit. Just a coffee.
NEVILLE: Right ... Morning, Mrs Jenkins.
MRS JENKINS: Morning, Mr Johnson. What's it to be today?
NEVILLE: A cup of coffee, please. Oh no, sorry ... can I have two cups, please?
MRS JENKINS: Two cups of coffee. Here you are. That's 24p please.
NEVILLE: 20...22...24... There you are ... 24 pence.
MRS JENKINS: Thank you.
NEVILLE: Here you are, Jackie. Here's your coffee. It's white. I hope that's all right.
JACKIE: Oh, yes. That's fine, thanks. How much is it?
NEVILLE: What? Oh, it's 12p ... no, no, no! I'll pay ... yes, really ... you can pay tomorrow.
JACKIE: Oh, OK ... thanks very much, Neville. Cheers! Mmm, it's nice and strong!

LISTENING (2)

Listen to the tape and fill in the sentences in your book.

TESSA: Hello, Murray!
MURRAY: Oh, hello Tessa. Tessa, meet Peter. Peter's a friend from America.
TESSA: How do you do!
PETER: Pleased to meet you!
TESSA: Where are you from in America, Peter?
PETER: From New York City.
TESSA: Oh, yes. What do you do?
PETER: I'm an engineer.
MURRAY: Let's go and have a drink.
TESSA: Good idea.
MURRAY: Here we are Now what would you like to drink, you two? Tessa?
TESSA: A glass of wine, please.
MURRAY: Would you like white or red?
TESSA: White, please.
MURRAY: And what about you, Peter? Would you like a glass of wine?
PETER: No, thanks, not wine. A glass of beer, I think.
MURRAY: Good. I think I'd like beer, too ... Excuse me, can I have two beers and a glass of white wine?
BARMAN: Yes, sir ... that's 70p please ... thank you.
MURRAY: Here you are, Tessa. Your wine.
TESSA: Oh, good! It's nice and cold.
MURRAY: Well, cheers everyone!
PETER: Cheers!

Unit 10

4 OPEN DIALOGUE
Neville and his friend, Maria, meet you in a cafeteria.
NEVILLE: Oh, hello!
STUDENT: ....
NEVILLE: Meet Maria. Maria's a student too.
STUDENT: ....
MARIA: Hello.
NEVILLE: Listen, I must go now. It's late. I'll see you later, Maria. Goodbye, you two.
STUDENT: ....
MARIA: What's your name, by the way? Your first name?
STUDENT: ....
MARIA: Sorry, what?
STUDENT: ....
MARIA: Oh, are you English?
STUDENT: ....
MARIA: Oh, are you? Well, would you like a cup of coffee?
STUDENT: ....
MARIA: And a biscuit?
STUDENT: ....
MARIA: Right. And don't worry . . . I'll pay.
STUDENT: ....

Part B ORAL EXERCISES

Exercise 1 Offer people something to eat or drink.
Ah, here's Murray! Offer him a cup of coffee.
Would you like a cup of coffee, Murray?
Ah, here's Tessa! Offer her a cup of tea.
Would you like a cup of tea, Tessa? Now go on.
Ah, here's Sally! Offer her a glass of wine.
Would you like a glass of wine, Sally?
Ah, here's George! Offer him a sandwich.
Would you like a sandwich, George?
Ah, here's Neville! Offer him a glass of orange juice.
Would you like a glass of orange juice, Neville?
Ah, here's Sheila! Offer her a cup of coffee.
Would you like a cup of coffee, Sheila?

Exercise 2 Ask for something to eat or drink.
A cup of tea or a cup of coffee?
Can I have a cup of coffee, please?
A glass of milk or a glass of water?
Can I have a glass of water, please? Now go on.
A cup of coffee or a cup of chocolate?
Can I have a cup of chocolate, please?
A glass of milk or a glass of orange juice?
Can I have a glass of orange juice, please?
A cup of chocolate or a cup of tea?
Can I have a cup of tea, please?
A glass of orange juice or a glass of milk?
Can I have a glass of milk, please?

Exercise 3 Ask again – this time for yourself and a friend.
I think I'd like a cup of tea.
Right! Can I have two cups of tea, please?
I think I'd like a glass of milk.
Right! Can I have two glasses of milk, please? Now go on.
I think I'd like a cup of coffee.
Right! Can I have two cups of coffee, please?
I think I'd like a glass of orange juice.
Right! Can I have two glasses of orange juice, please?
I think I'd like a glass of water.
Right! Can I have two glasses of water, please?
I think I'd like a cup of chocolate.
Right! Can I have two cups of chocolate, please?

Exercise 4 Ask the price of things.
I think I'll have a cup of coffee.
How much is it?
I think I'll get some cakes.
How much are they? Now go on.
Mmm. This milk is nice and cold.
How much is it?
And what about some sandwiches?
How much are they?
I'll have a cup of tea.
How much is it?
Mmm. This orange juice is good.
How much is it?

Exercise 5 Say how much things cost. Look at page 57.
How much is a coffee?
It's 12 pence.
How much are the sandwiches?
They're 22 pence each. Now go on.
How much is a tea?
It's 10 pence.
I see. And orange juice?
It's 12 pence.
How much are the cakes?
They're 10 pence each.
How much is a cup of chocolate?
It's 15 pence.

Exercise 6 A Rhyme.

Tea for me
Coffee for you
Coffee and tea
For you and me
Coffee, tea and biscuits
Coffee, tea and biscuits
Coffee, tea and biscuits
And a cake for you and me.

UNIT 11 Do you like tea with lemon?

	Skills	Functions	Example Sentences	Main Structures
SET 1	1. Speaking 2. Speaking	Ask and say the time (hours, half and quarter hours)	*What's the time?* *It's four o'clock.*	*What's the time? It's* + time *Is it* + time? *Yes, it is.*
SET 2	1. Speaking 2. Speaking	Ask what people like Say what you like	*Do you like tea with lemon?* *Yes, I do/No, I don't/It's all* *right.*	
SET 3	1. Speaking 2. Speaking 3. Speaking 4. Speaking and Writing	Ask and say what people like Apologise Accept apologies	*Does he like tea with milk?* *Yes, he does/No, he doesn't/* *He thinks it's all right.* *Sorry!* *That's all right!*	*Does he like* + noun/gerund? *Yes, he/she does.* *No, he/she doesn't.* *He/She thinks it's/they're* etc. *all right.*
EXTENSION	1. Reading and Writing	Three job advertisements: students choose one and write an appropriate application letter, using given framework.		
	2. Listening and Writing	An au-pair is interviewed for a job. Students mark the au-pair's answers on a chart.		
	3. Reading	Reading Text: newspaper article.		

OPEN DIALOGUE

ORAL EXERCISES

1. Say the correct time

    Is it 3 o'clock? *Yes, it is.*
    Is it half-past five? *No, it isn't, it's half-past four.*

2. Ask Neville what he likes

    Ask him if he likes tea with lemon.
    Do you like tea with lemon?

3. Say what you like or don't like

    Do you like tea with lemon?
    Yes, I do.

4. Ask what other people like

    Ask if Maria likes sightseeing.
    Does she like sightseeing?

5. Say what Maria likes or doesn't like

    Does she like sunbathing?
    Yes, she does.

6. Say what you like or don't like

    Do you like sightseeing?

SPEECHWORK

A STRESS   half past four ● ● ●
           quarter past four ● . ● ●
           quarter to four ● . . ●

B INTONATION   Do you like sightseeing? ↗

C PRONUNCIATION   /ɒ/ hot, what

ACTIVE VOCABULARY

dog	sugar	like
spider	lemon	drink
detective story	whisky	drive
record	coca-cola	smoke
letter	classical	want
child(ren)	music	learn
watch	jazz	speak
clothes	all right	get
sightsee(ing)	That's all right!	ask
sunbathing	sorry	answer
cook(ing)	with	
write (writing)	black (coffee)	
read(ing)	past	What's the time
quarter	to	o'clock
half	wrong	

Unit 11

Do you like tea with lemon?

IN MARIA'S FLAT

NEVILLE: What's the time, Maria?
MARIA: It's four o'clock. Would you like a cup of tea?
NEVILLE: Mmm! Yes, please.
MARIA: Do you like tea with lemon?
NEVILLE: Yes, I do.
MARIA: Oh good. Here you are ———— Sugar?
NEVILLE: Yes please.
MARIA: Mind the cup!
NEVILLE: Oh, sorry!
MARIA: That's all right! I'll get a cloth. Let's have some music. Do you like Rita Hamilton?
NEVILLE: Yes, she's all right.
MARIA: Well, *I* like her. I think she's very good.

Set 1 Ask and say the time (1)

What's the time? It's four o'clock.

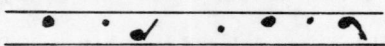

1. four o'clock
2. quarter past four
3. half past four
4. quarter to five

1. Look at these clocks. Ask and answer like this:
1. What's the time? It's three o'clock.
2. What's the time? It's half past four.
3. What's the time? It's ————

UNIT 11

Is it three o'clock? Yes, it is.

2. Look at the clocks again. Ask and answer like this:
1. Is it three o'clock? Yes, it is.
2. Is it ————? Yes, it is.

Set 2 Ask what people like / Say what you like

Do you like tea with lemon? Yes, I do.
Do you like sightseeing? No, I don't.

Do you like Frank Sinatra? — He's all right.
Do you like Elizabeth Taylor? — She's all right.
Do you like the Rolling Stones? — They're all right.
Do you like small dogs? — They're all right.
Do you like classical music? — It's all right.
Do you like whisky? — It's all right.

DO YOU LIKE:	YOU	YOUR PARTNER	DO YOU LIKE:	YOU	YOUR PARTNER
Tea with lemon			Small dogs		
Tea with milk			American films		
White coffee			Detective stories		
Black coffee			Spiders		
Coca-cola			Jazz		
Whisky			Classical music		
Sightseeing			....		
Sunbathing			....		
Writing letters			....		
Cooking					

1. Look at the chart. Write in your answers:
Yes/No/AR (it's all right — you like it but not very much)

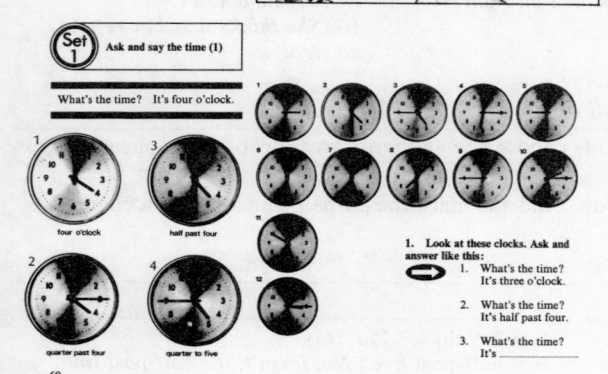

DIALOGUE

This dialogue brings together and contrasts *Would you like . . . ?* and *Do you like . . . ?* A common mistake made by foreigners is to use *Do you like . . . ?* invariably.
Revise the 'offering' function briefly (as in Unit 10); this should emphasise the difference.
Explain the apology *Oh, sorry* and the polite response *That's all right!*

SET 1 Ask and say the time

What's the time?   It's four o'clock.

Practise the hours, half hours and quarter hours separately first, using a toy clock or blackboard sketches.

Ex 1 Students work in pairs, taking turns to ask and answer.

Ex 2 Proceed as Ex 1.
Check students by asking them individually to form questions for which you give the repeated answer *Yes, it is*. If the actual time at the end of this practice coincides with a whole, half or quarter hour, ask a student what time it is now.

SET 2 Ask what people like / Say what you like

Use examples or pictures to explain the unfamiliar vocabulary in the chart of 'likes and dislikes'. Practise the pronunciation of all the items.
Space has been left in the final box for students to suggest both male and female singers, film stars, personalities and pop groups who are currently popular.
Give an example of the question with the various types of answer, showing by your facial expression the difference between *Yes!*, *No* and *It's/He's/She's/They're all right*.
Point out that the pronoun changes when you use *all right* with a male/female or plural subject.

Ex 1 Give an example. Explain *AR — it's all right*.
Students mark in their own answers before working orally on the questions and answers.

Ex 2 Do you like tea with lemon?

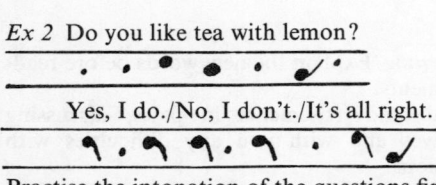

Yes, I do./No, I don't./It's all right.

Practise the intonation of the questions first.
Then practise the intonation of the different types of answers.
Students work in pairs asking each other if they like the various items listed, and note down their partner's answers as in Ex 1.
Students can either take turns and ask each other the same question, or work through a block of questions before changing parts.

SET 3 Ask and say what people like
Does he like tea with milk?   Yes, he does.

Ex 1 & 2 These two exercises give controlled practice in 3rd person singular forms, question and answer. Exercise 1 practises these forms with *he*, Exercise 2 with *she*.
In both exercises practise first: *Yes, he/she does* answers, next: *No, he/she doesn't*, and finally: *He/She thinks it's all right*.
The question and answer forms must be well mastered before students go on to Ex 3 and 4.

Ex 3 Students should have filled in their partner's answers in Set 2, Ex 2. This exercise practises talking about those answers to a third person.
Each student takes a new partner and asks the new partner about his previous partner's answers. In this way, all students can be active simultaneously.

Ex 4 The students ask you some questions, possibly taking turns to ask. All students write down your answers, transposing them to *he/she* as appropriate i.e. your answer *Yes, I do* should be written down by them as *Yes, he/she does* etc.

Unit 11

UNIT 11

2. Now ask your partner what he/she likes, like this:
   Do you like tea with lemon?
   Yes I do/No I don't/It's all right.

   Write in his/her answer also: (Yes/No/AR)

   When you answer about the people, remember to say:
   He's/She's/They're all right
   and when you answer about more than one thing, you say: *They're* all right

Set 3 Ask and say what people like

Does he like tea with milk?   Yes, he does.
         black coffee?   No, he doesn't.
         coca-cola?   He thinks it's all right.

Does she like jazz?   Yes, she does.
          classical music?   No, she doesn't.
          Frank Sinatra?   She thinks he's all right.

Yes.	No.	All right.
white coffee	black coffee	sunbathing
tea with lemon	coca-cola	whisky
detective stories	Frank Sinatra	cooking
Elizabeth Taylor	small dogs	pop-music
jazz	sightseeing	the Rolling Stones
spiders	writing letters	detective stories

1. Look at Neville's answers to the questions. Work with a partner. Ask and answer like this:
   Does he like tea with lemon?
   Yes he does.

   Does he like black coffee?
   No he doesn't.

   Does he like sunbathing?
   He thinks it's all right.

   First ask about the 'Yes list, then the 'No' list and then the 'All right' list.

62

UNIT 11

Yes.	No.	All right.
black coffee	white coffee	writing letters
sunbathing	whisky	coca-cola
cooking	Frank Sinatra	sightseeing
American films	jazz	Elizabeth Taylor
small dogs	spiders	detective stories
tea with lemon	tea with milk	

2. Look at Maria's answers to the questions. Work with a partner. Ask and answer like this:
   Does she like black coffee?
   Yes she does.

   Does she like spiders?
   No she doesn't.

   Does she like coca-cola?
   She thinks it's all right.

   Work as in Exercise 1

3. Look at your partner's answers to the questions on page 61. Work with a new partner (somebody else in the class). Ask and answer about your *first* partner's answers, like this:
   Does he/she like tea with lemon?
   Yes, he/she does
      or
   No, he/she doesn't
      or
   He/she thinks it's all right.

4. Ask your teacher what he/she likes. Write in the answers
   Does your teacher like white coffee? ....
   coca-cola? ....
   whisky? ....
   jazz? ....
   Frank Sinatra? ....
   spiders? ....
   cooking? ....

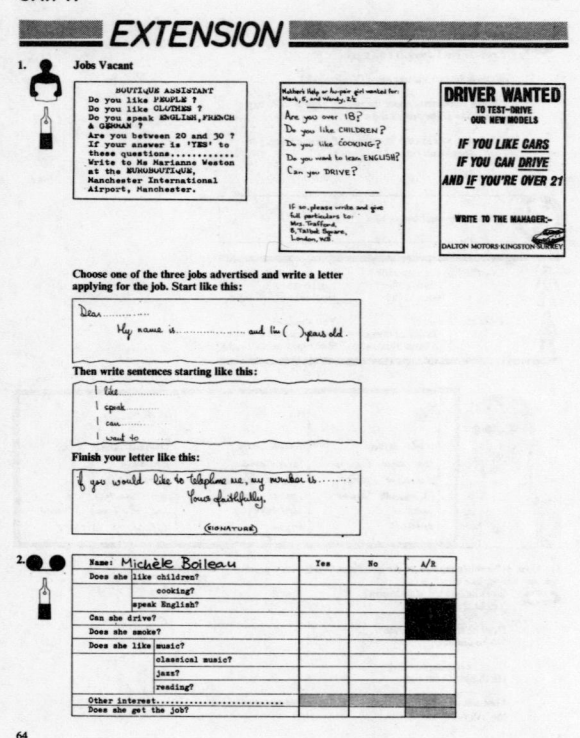

EXTENSION

1 *Reading and writing* Explain the new words before reading the advertisements.

Students read the advertisements in pairs, discussing between themselves and with you any difficulties with words or expressions.

Choose one of the advertisements. Write a specimen letter of application yourself, working within the framework suggested in the Students' Book. Do not elaborate your letter unnecessarily.

Students choose their own advertisement and write a similar letter, possibly for homework.

2 *Listening* Explain the context of the listening passage: a French girl is applying for the au-pair job in the second advertisement. This is an interview between the mother and her.

Go through the form first.

Play the tape through twice without stopping. Do not pause unless necessary.

Check the answers.

Open Dialogue See General Guide and tapescript (page 59).

Oral Exercises See General Guide and tapescript (page 60).

Speechwork See General Guide and tapescript (page 59).

Unit 11

Tapescript
Part A

1 DIALOGUE
NEVILLE: What's the time, Maria?
MARIA: It's four o'clock. Would you like a cup of tea?
NEVILLE: Mmm! Yes, please.
MARIA: Do you like tea with lemon?
NEVILLE: Yes, I do.
MARIA: Oh good. Here you are ... Sugar?
NEVILLE: Yes please. (leans over to get the sugar)
MARIA: Mind the cup!
NEVILLE: Oh, sorry!
MARIA: That's all right! I'll get a cloth. (goes out and returns) Let's have some music. Do you like Rita Hamilton?
NEVILLE: Yes, she's all right.
MARIA: Well, I like her. I think she's very good. (puts on record)

2 SPEECHWORK
Part A: Stress
Say after me:
one...two...three...four...
da da da...half past one...half past two...
half past three...half past four...
da di da da...quarter past one...quarter past two...
quarter past three...quarter past four...
da di di da...quarter to one...quarter to two...
quarter to three...quarter to four...

Part B: Intonation
Say after me:
tea...do you like tea...jazz...do you like jazz...
beer...do you like beer...coffee...do you like coffee...
whisky...do you like whisky...cooking...do you like cooking
...coca-cola...do you like coca-cola...Frank Sinatra...do
you like Frank Sinatra...writing letters...do you like
writing letters...

Part C: Pronunciation
Say after me:
/ɒ/.../ɒ/...what...what...o'clock...what's the time...
it's two o'clock...not...not...no, I'm not...hot...hot...
coffee...this coffee is hot...pop...do you like pop...
dogs...do you like dogs...Australia...do you like Australia
...I'm not Australian...

3 LISTENING
Mrs Trafford interviews a French girl Michele Boileau for a job as an au pair. Look at the form on page 64 in your books and mark the right answers. Now listen please.

Doorbell rings.
MRS TRAFFORD: Ah, hello, you must be Miss Boileau.
MICHELE: Yes, that's right. Michele Boileau.
MRS TRAFFORD: Come in, Michele, and sit down.
MICHELE: Thank you.
MRS TRAFFORD: Your English is good.
MICHELE: Oh thank you. Well, I want to learn more English, of course.
MRS TRAFFORD: Yes, of course. Well, you can go to English classes here. Ah, here are the children. This is Mark and this is Wendy.
MICHELE: Hello. And how old are you?
MARK: Five and a half.
MRS TRAFFORD: Do you like children?
MICHELE: Yes I do, very much. I have a little brother of four at home.
MRS TRAFFORD: Oh, that's good. Cigarette?
MICHELE: No thank you. I don't smoke.
MRS TRAFFORD: Now let's see ... you're eighteen ... by the way, can you cook?
MICHELE: Yes, I can. I cook at home a lot, I like cooking.
MRS TRAFFORD: Oh, that's good. Er ... I'm afraid we go out quite a lot in the evenings so we would like you to be here ...
MICHELE: Oh, that's all right. I like reading and I like music. I've got lots of records with me.
MRS TRAFFORD: Oh, what sort of music do you like?
MICHELE: I like jazz best but classical music is all right.
MRS TRAFFORD: Is there anything else apart from music that you like doing?
MICHELE: Er ... I like sightseeing.
MRS TRAFFORD: Oh well, there's a lot to see in London. You can take the car if you like sometimes.
MICHELE: But I can't drive.
MRS TRAFFORD: You can't drive?
MICHELE: No ... I'm sorry.
MRS TRAFFORD: Oh that's all right. It's not very important. Well, do you think you would like the job?
MICHELE: Oh yes. The children are sweet.
MRS TRAFFORD: Well, if you like, you can start on Monday.
MICHELE: Thank you very much. Yes, that's fine.

4 OPEN DIALOGUE
You go to see Neville in his flat.
NEVILLE: Hello.
STUDENT: ....
NEVILLE: Come in, please.
STUDENT: ....
NEVILLE: What's the time? My watch is wrong, I think.
STUDENT: ....
NEVILLE: Thank you. Well, would you like a cup of coffee?
STUDENT: ....
NEVILLE: Do you like white coffee?
STUDENT: ....
NEVILLE: Sugar?
STUDENT: ....
NEVILLE: Right ... Just one moment ... Here you are.
STUDENT: ....
NEVILLE: Mind the cup!
STUDENT: ....
NEVILLE: Oh, that's all right. I'll get a cloth. Let's have some music. Do you like pop music?
STUDENT: ....
NEVILLE: Oh, one moment. Here's an Eagles record. Do you like the Eagles?
STUDENT: ....
NEVILLE: Well, I think they're very good.

Unit 11

Part B ORAL EXERCISES

Exercise 1 Say the correct time
Look at the clocks on page 60.

Is it three o'clock?
Yes, it is.

Is it half past five?
No, it isn't, it's half past four. Now go on.

Is it quarter to four?
No, it isn't, it's quarter to five.

Is it quarter past six?
Yes, it is.

Is it ten o'clock?
No, it isn't. It's nine o'clock.

Is it half past ten?
No, it isn't, it's half past eleven.

Exercise 2 Ask Neville what he likes.

Ask him if he likes tea with lemon.
Do you like tea with lemon?

Ask him if he likes black coffee.
Do you like black coffee? Now go on.

Ask him if he likes whisky.
Do you like whisky?

Ask him if he likes white coffee.
Do you like white coffee?

Ask him if he likes cooking.
Do you like cooking?

Ask him if he likes Frank Sinatra.
Do you like Frank Sinatra?

Exercise 3 Say what you like or don't like.
You are Neville. Look at the chart on page 62.

Do you like tea with lemon?
Yes, I do.

Do you like black coffee?
No, I don't.

Do you like whisky?
It's all right. Now go on.

Do you like jazz?
Yes, I do.

Do you like pop music?
It's all right.

Do you like small dogs?
No, I don't.

Do you like Elizabeth Taylor?
Yes, I do.

Do you like coca cola?
No, I don't.

Do you like whisky?
It's all right.

Do you like writing letters?
No, I don't.

Do you like the Rolling Stones?
They're all right.

Exercise 4 Ask what other people like.

Ask if Maria likes sightseeing.
Does she like sightseeing?

Ask if Neville likes spiders.
Does he like spiders? Now go on.

Ask if Maria likes detective stories.
Does she like detective stories?

Ask if Neville likes writing letters.
Does he like writing letters?

Ask if Neville likes Frank Sinatra.
Does he like Frank Sinatra?

Ask if Maria likes sunbathing.
Does she like sunbathing?

Exercise 5 Say what Maria likes or doesn't like.
Look at the chart on page 63.

Does she like sunbathing?
Yes, she does.

Does she like white coffee?
No, she doesn't.

Does she like writing letters?
She thinks it's all right. Now go on.

Does she like spiders?
No, she doesn't.

Does she like sightseeing?
She thinks it's all right.

Does she like black coffee?
Yes, she does.

Does she like Elizabeth Taylor?
She thinks she's all right.

Does she like American films?
Yes, she does.

Does she like whisky?
No, she doesn't.

Exercise 6 Say what you like or don't like. Listen.

Do you like sightseeing?
Yes, it's all right.

Do you like small dogs?
No, I don't. Now go on.

Say what *you* like or don't like.
Do you like sightseeing?
....

Do you like small dogs?
....

Do you like cooking?
....

Do you like detective stories?
....

Do you like Frank Sinatra?
....

Do you like sunbathing?
....

Do you like writing letters?
....

UNIT 12 Consolidation Unit

	Skills	Activity	Functions Revised	See Units 7-11 tables.
DIALOGUE	Listening	Maria meets Joe at the Manchester International Club. The dialogue is a seven-part playlet, using language from the previous five units, and to a lesser extent, language from Units 1-6		
1.	Reading and Speaking	Students take the parts of the characters in the dialogue and read it in pairs.		
2.	Reading and Speaking	Students read the dialogue again, substituting personal facts and information.		
3.	Writing (fill-in exercise)	Sentences testing the use of positive, negative and interrogative forms of *to be*, including the auxiliary *do/does*.		
4.	Writing (fill-in dialogue)	Allan visits Maria's flat. Students fill in Maria's part of the dialogue. The exercise tests the functions practised in Units 7-11.		
5.	Reading	Letter from a foreign girl to an English friend. Passage for silent reading; comprehension questions from teacher follow.		
6.	Writing (fill-in exercise)	Test of possessive adjectives.		
7.	Crossword	Crossword using food and drinks vocabulary learnt in previous units.		

SPEECHWORK			ACTIVE VOCABULARY		
A Stress	it's nice and hot ● ● ●		club		soon
	it isn't very hot ● ● ● ●		drink	good	quickly
			university	lonely	again
			lesson	short	sleep
B Intonation	ˈWhere are you fromˈ in Italy?		class	little	dance
			town	Italian	
C Pronunciation	/dʒ/ George, jazz		place		Cheers!

Unit 12

Consolidation Unit

At the Manchester International Club

PART 1.
MARIA: Excuse me!
MAN: Yes?
MARIA: Where's the International Club?
MAN: It's over there, next to the cinema.
MARIA: Oh yes. Thank you.

PART 2.
GIRL: Name please.
MARIA: Maria Magnani.
GIRL: Are you a member?
MARIA: No, I'm not.
GIRL: Oh, well, it's 50p please.
MARIA: Sorry, how much is it?
GIRL: 50p... 50 pence.
MARIA: Oh, I see... here you are... Where's the cloakroom?
GIRL: It's here. This is the cloakroom, and that's the clubroom in there.
MARIA: Thank you.

PART 3
JOE: Hello! I'm Joe. What's your name?
MARIA: Maria.
JOE: Oh, are you English?
MARIA: No, I'm not. I'm Italian. And you?
JOE: I'm American.
MARIA: Oh. Do you speak Italian?
JOE: No, I don't. Sorry!
MARIA: Oh, that's all right.

PART 4
JOE: Would you like a drink, Maria?
MARIA: Yes, please.
JOE: Beer, wine or coca-cola?
MARIA: Wine please. White wine.
JOE: Can I have two glasses of white wine, please.
MARIA: Oh, thanks.
JOE: Cheers!
MARIA: Cheers!
JOE: Oh, it isn't very good.
MARIA: No, but it's nice and cold.

PART 5
JOE: Do you like Manchester, Maria?
MARIA: It's all right.
JOE: Where are you from in Italy?
MARIA: From the north. From Milan. Where are you from?
JOE: I'm from California. But I live in Manchester now, well, a suburb of Manchester. I'm a student at the University.

PART 6
JOE: Oh, this is a Breakaway record. Do you like Breakaway?
MARIA: Yes, I do. They're very good. Well, would you like a dance?
JOE: Yes, all right.

PART 7
MARIA: What's the time?
JOE: It's quarter past eleven.
MARIA: Oh, I must go.
JOE: Oh... what's your telephone number?
MARIA: It's 477 9372.
JOE: 4.7.7...9.3.7.2. Right! Well, can I telephone you soon? Is that all right?
MARIA: Yes, that's fine. Well, bye!... and thanks for a lovely evening.
JOE: Bye!

1. Read the dialogue with your partner. One of you can be Maria, the other can be the man in part 1, the girl in part 2, and Joe in parts 3–7.

UNIT 12

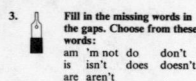

2. Read parts 3, 4, 5 and 7 again with your partner. This time say your own name and nationality; say what you would like to drink; say where you are from and where you live now; and say your own telephone number. Change parts afterwards.

3. Fill in the missing words in the gaps. Choose from these words:
am 'm not do don't
is isn't does doesn't
are aren't 's

1. Where _____ you live?
2. What _____ he do?
3. _____ you like tea? No, I _____.
4. _____ you English? No, I _____.
5. Where _____ Mr and Mrs Brown live?
6. _____ they from Manchester? Yes, they _____.
7. _____ you from London? Yes, I _____.
8. What _____ you do?
9. _____ he Australian? No, he _____.
10. _____ he like jazz? No, he _____.
11. _____ she like Mozart? Yes, she _____.
12. _____ you from London? No, we _____.
13. What _____ she do? She _____ a journalist.

4. Allan Simmons goes to see Maria in her flat. Write in what Maria says

MARIA: Come in, Allan
ALLAN: Mmm! It's nice and big. My flat is very small.
MARIA: _____
ALLAN: Yes, please. But no milk. I like black coffee.
MARIA: _____
ALLAN: Thank you. Mmm! It's nice and strong.
MARIA: _____
ALLAN: I live in a suburb south of Manchester. Where are you from, Maria?
MARIA: _____
ALLAN: Milan! That's nice.
MARIA: _____
ALLAN: Manchester? Yes, I do. I like big towns. Do you like it here?
MARIA: _____
ALLAN: Well, I must go soon. It's late.
MARIA: _____
ALLAN: It's half past four. I must telephone Focus Films. Where's the telephone?
MARIA: _____
ALLAN: Oh, where's the bedroom? Is this the bedroom?
MARIA: _____
ALLAN: Right – thanks.

Now read the dialogue with your partner

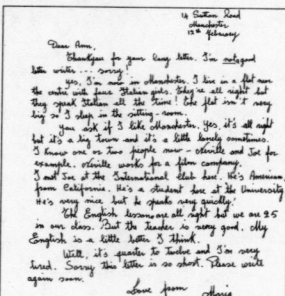

5. A letter from Maria to an English friend

DIALOGUE

Play each part separately. Between parts, introduce any new vocabulary.
Play the whole dialogue through again without stopping.

1 Students read the dialogue in pairs. One student reads Maria's role, the other reads all the other roles.
If there is enough time, have a 'public' reading; allot the four roles to individual students.

2 Give an example of how to change the personal information in the parts selected for re-reading.
Students work in pairs, changing parts afterwards.

3 Individual writing exercise for class or homework. Check answers afterwards.
Answers:
1 do 2 does 3 Do...don't 4 Are...I'm not 5 do 6 Are...are 7 Are...am 8 do 9 Is...isn't 10 Does...doesn't 11 Does...does 12 Are...aren't 13 does...is

4 Students work in pairs filling in Maria's part.
When they have finished, ask them to re-read the dialogue in pairs, possibly new pairs.
Key to what Maria says:
   This is my flat.
   Would you like a cup of coffee?
   Here you are.
   Where do you live?
   I'm from Milan.
   Do you like Manchester?
   Yes, I do./No, I don't./It's all right.
   What's the time?
   It's in the bedroom.
   Yes it is./No it isn't. That's the bedroom over there.

5 Go through the letter carefully explaining any new vocabulary.
Or, present the new vocabulary first, and ask students to read the letter silently.
Then ask some comprehension questions e.g. *Where is Maria now? Where does she live? Does she like the other girls? Where does she sleep? Does she like Manchester? Who is Joe? Does she like Joe? Does she like her English lessons? Maria is tired – why?*

Unit 12

6 A fill-in exercise to practise the use of possessive adjectives. Students work individually. Classwork or homework.

7 Individual or group work in class – or for homework. If possible, students should not look back to Units 10 and 11.
Answers:
ACROSS 4 *sugar* 5 *milk* 6 *whisky* 7 *tea* 9 *coffee* 10 *white*
DOWN 1 *drinks* 2 *like* 3 *am* 6 *water* 8 *do* 9 *cup*

UNIT 12

6. Fill in the right responses using these adjectives
my   her
your   our
his   their
e.g. Is that John's car? *No, that's his car over there.*
1. Is that Tessa's house? _____
2. Is that Murray's car? _____
3. Is that your car? _____
4. Is that the Freemans' house? _____
5. Is that my room? _____
6. Is that Tessa's and my office? _____
7. Is that Jackie's coffee? _____
8. Is that our bus, Allan? _____

7. A Food and Drink Crossword

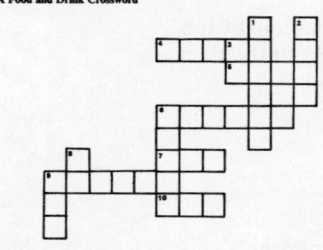

Clues
Across 4. Coffee? Yes, please. With _____? No, thanks, just milk. 5. A glass of _____, please. 6. A strong drink. 7. English people drink this at four o'clock. 9. This _____ is nice and strong. 10. _____ wine or white wine?

Down 1. Tea, orange-juice and coca-cola are _____ 2. Do you _____ tea with lemon? 3. I _____ English, not American. 6. Would you like a glass of beer or wine? No thanks. Just _____ please. 8. _____ you like coca-cola? Yes, I _____ 9. Would you like a _____ of coffee?

REMEMBER
Words and Phrases

a drink   good   soon   sleep
a university   lonely   quickly   dance
a lesson   short   again
a class   little
a town   Italian   cheers!
a place
a club

69

63

Unit 12

Tapescript
Part A

1 DIALOGUE
At the Manchester International Club

Part 1
MARIA: Excuse me!
MAN: Yes?
MARIA: Where's the International Club?
MAN: It's over there, next to the cinema.
MARIA: Oh yes. Thank you.

Part 2
GIRL: Name please.
MARIA: Maria Magnani.
GIRL: Are you a member?
MARIA: No, I'm not.
GIRL: Oh, well, it's 50p please.
MARIA: Sorry, how much is it?
GIRL: 50p . . . 50 pence.
MARIA: Oh I see . . . here you are . . . Where's the cloakroom?
GIRL: It's here. This is the cloakroom, and that's the clubroom in there.
MARIA: Thank you.

Part 3
JOE: Hello! I'm Joe. What's your name?
MARIA: Maria.
JOE: Oh, are you English?
MARIA: No, I'm not. I'm Italian. And you?
JOE: I'm American.
MARIA: Oh. Do you speak Italian?
JOE: No, I don't. Sorry!
MARIA: Oh, that's all right.

Part 4
JOE: Would you like a drink, Maria?
MARIA: Yes, please.
JOE: Beer, wine or coca-cola?
MARIA: Wine please. White wine.
JOE: Can I have two glasses of white wine, please?
MARIA: Oh, thanks.
JOE: Cheers!
MARIA: Cheers!
JOE: Oh, it isn't very good.
MARIA: No, but it's nice and cold.

Part 5
JOE: Do you like Manchester, Maria?
MARIA: It's all right.
JOE: Where are you from in Italy?
MARIA: From the north. From Milan. Where are you from?
JOE: I'm from California. But I live in Manchester now, well, a suburb of Manchester. I'm a student at the University.

Part 6
JOE: Oh, this is a Breakaway record. Do you like Breakaway?
MARIA: Yes, I do. They're very good. Well, would you like a dance?
JOE: Yes, all right.

Part 7
MARIA: What's the time?
JOE: It's quarter past eleven.
MARIA: Oh, I must go.
JOE: Oh . . . what's your telephone number?
MARIA: It's 477 9372.
JOE: 4.7.7. . . . 9.3.7.2. Right! Well, can I telephone you soon? Is that all right?
MARIA: Yes, that's fine. Well, bye! . . . and thanks for a lovely evening.
JOE: Bye!

2 SPEECHWORK
Part A: Stress
Say after me:
di da di da...it's nice and hot...it's nice and strong...
it's nice and big...it's nice and warm...it's nice and cold...
di da di da di da...it isn't very hot...it isn't very strong...
it isn't very big...it isn't very warm...it isn't very cold...

Part B: Intonation
Say after me:
in Italy...where are you from in Italy...in France..!where are you from in France...in England..!where are you from in England...in America..!where are you from in America...

Part C: Pronunciation
Say after me:
/dʒ/.../dʒ/...Joe...George...Jackie...John...do you like Joe...do you like George...do you like Jackie...do you like John...do you like jazz, Joe...do you like orange juice, Jackie...just a moment, George,...just a moment, John...

UNIT 13 Train to Coventry

	Skills	Functions	Example Sentences	Main Structures
SET 1	1. Speaking 2. Speaking and Writing	Ask and say the time (minutes)	*What's the time?* *It's ten past nine.*	*It's* (ten) *past/to* (nine)
SET 2	1. Speaking 2. Writing 3. Speaking/Writing 4. Writing and Speaking	Ask and talk about fixed times	*What time does the train leave?* *It leaves at twenty-past nine.*	What time does the bus leave? the film start? the shop open? *It* leaves/starts/opens *at*+time It arrives at four *in the morning* *in the afternoon* *in the evening*
EXTENSION	1. Roleplay	Situational dialogue: at a travel agent's. Students work from a printed timetable.		
	2. Reading and Writing	Tourist leaflet describing a town, its facilities, the opening and closing times of its public buildings. Students research information about their own town and write their own leaflet.		
	3. Listening	Railway station and airport announcements; students write down numbers, places and times.		
	4. Reading	Reading Text: Maureen's letter.		

OPEN DIALOGUE

ORAL EXERCISES		
	1. Ask what time things happen	The bus leaves soon. Hurry up! *What time does it leave?*
	2. Say what time things happen	What time does the bus arrive? *Let's see . . . it arrives at twenty past eleven.*
	3. Ask exactly what time things happen	The plane arrives at five o'clock. *Five in the morning or five in the evening?*
	4. Check information	The train leaves at six-hundred hours. *I see; it leaves at six a.m.*
	5. Correct information politely	I think the bus leaves at eleven o'clock. *No, it doesn't, it leaves at five past.*

SPEECHWORK			ACTIVE VOCABULARY		
A STRESS	it starts at five ● ● ● it opens at five ● ● ● ●		train	leave	a.m.
			plane	arrive	p.m.
			flight	start	morning
B INTONATION	ˈWhatˈtime does theˈbus leave?↘		match	finish	afternoon
C PRONUNCIATION	/s/ starts		platform	open	evening
	/z/ opens		shop	close	
	/ɪz/ closes		film	single	hurry up!
			a lot of	return	what time . . . ?
				late	let's see

Unit 13

Train to Coventry

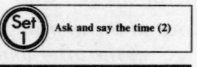

Murray, Neville and Jackie go to Coventry to do a film.

MURRAY: Three to Coventry, please.
MAN: Single or return?
MURRAY: Return please.
NEVILLE: Hurry up, Murray! It's late. It's ten past nine!

Set 1 Ask and say the time (2)

What's the time? It's ten past nine.

1. five past nine
2. ten past nine
3. twenty past nine
4. twenty-five past nine
5. twenty-five to ten
6. twenty to ten
7. ten to ten
8. five to ten

1. Ask and answer like this:
1. What's the time?
   It's five past two.
2. What's the time?
   It's twenty past four.

2. Say these times and write them

13.25 twenty-five past one
8.05
21.35
19.20
2.50

16.55
5.10
18.40
11.35
22.50

DIALOGUE

Show where the city of Coventry is on the map.
Explain that *three*, *single* and *return* refer to tickets.
This part of the dialogue is not actively practised in the Unit. If your students are resident in, or are intending to visit England in the near future, this short exchange could be extracted for practice with appropriate substitutions.
You should draw your students' attention to time: telling the numbers of minutes *past* or *to* the hour.

SET 1 Ask and say the time (2)

Ex 1 What's the time?   It's ten past nine.

Revise times from Unit 11 (hours, half and quarter hours) and numbers in multiples of 5 up to 60.
Notice that *minute* is not introduced in this Unit; the comparatively uncommon *It's ten minutes past nine* is intentionally avoided. The use of *minutes* with telling precise times e.g. *It's eleven minutes past four* is not introduced, but can be explained if necessary.
Use a toy clock, if available, for intensive practice of times before moving on to the exercise.
Practise minutes past the hour, then minutes to the hour, then a mixture of both.
Give two examples of the exercise T–S. Students then work in pairs, taking turns to ask and answer.

Ex 2 Go through the exercise orally first, more than once if necessary.
Write more times on the blackboard for extra practice.
Students then complete the written version of the times, either in class or for homework.

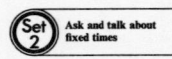

DIALOGUE

This dialogue can be combined with the first part (see above) to form a situational dialogue *At the Station*.
You could substitute different times and platform numbers. If you think this is useful, make an overhead stencil with the skeleton of the dialogue printed to show where substitutions are to be made. Add a list of possible substitutions below the dialogue.

SET 2 Ask and talk about fixed times

Introduce the new vocabulary in the chart. Practise the pronunciation. Go through the times orally.

Ex 1 What time does the train leave?

It leaves at twenty past nine.

Practise the intonation of the question chorally.
Students practise making the questions first.
Work through the exercise in three blocks: 1) *bus, train and plane* 2) *film, match* 3) *post office, bank*.
Students first say the full question *What time does the bus leave/arrive?* then the short question *What time does it leave/arrive?* Work like this through the three blocks.
Practise the intonation of the answer, then work through the chart again, asking the students to give full answers – *It leaves at . . .*, *It arrives at . . .* etc.
Give an example of the exercise, do a few examples T–S and S–T, then ask students to work in pairs, taking turns to ask and answer.

Ex 2 Explain the meaning of *Meet me*. The time of meeting need not be exactly the same as the time of arrival, or the time of starting/finishing. Students can choose simple sentences e.g. *The film starts at 7. Meet me at 6.55* or complex sentences e.g. *The plane leaves at 6 and arrives at 8. Meet me at 8* (or *8.05*). This will depend on the context.
Some sentences can be written in class, the rest can be done as homework.

Unit 13

67

Unit 13

UNIT 13

a.m. = morning
p.m. = afternoon (1 p.m.–6 p.m.)
       evening   (6 p.m.–12 a.m.)

3 a.m. = three o'clock in the morning
3 p.m. = three o'clock in the afternoon
8 p.m. = eight o'clock in the evening

3. Say all the times in a different way. Look at the example in sentence 1
   1. The train leaves at 6 a.m.
      The train leaves at six o'clock in the morning.
   2. The bus leaves at 7 p.m.
      The bus leaves at _____
   3. The plane arrives at 1.30 a.m.
      _____
   4. The film starts at 9 p.m.
      _____
   5. The film finishes at 10.45 p.m.
      _____
   6. The bank closes at 3.30 p.m.
      _____

4. Look at the information. Ask and answer like this:
   What time does the shop open? It opens at 9 o'clock.
   What time does the shop close? _____

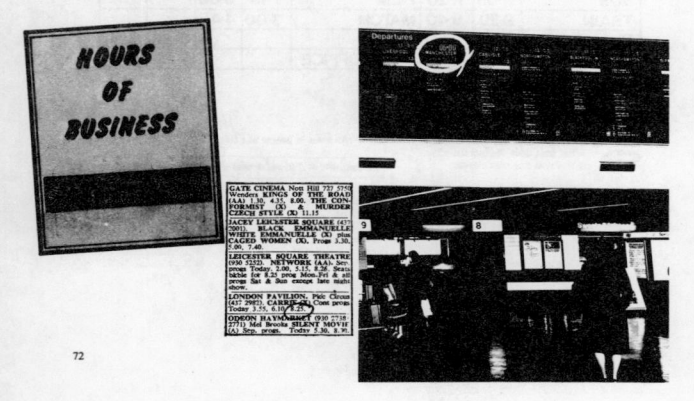

UNIT 13

EXTENSION

MANCHESTER INTERNATIONAL AIRPORT
Domestic Passenger Arrivals

	Airline	Flight No.	Day	Dep	Arr
Birmingham	DA	DA053	Daily	0900	0935
Bristol	DA	DA055	Daily	1845	2005
Edinburgh	BE	BE916	Daily	0840	0925
Edinburgh	BE	BE483	Daily	1835	1920
London	BE	BE4406	Daily	0800	0845
London	BE	BE4424	Daily	1415	1500
Newcastle	DA	DA052	Daily	0750	0835
Newcastle	DA	DA056	Daily	1800	1845

1. **Roleplay**
   You go into a travel agency in Manchester. You want to be in London at 10 a.m. Work with a partner. Find out:
   a) What time your plane leaves Manchester
   b) What time it arrives at London airport
   c) What your flight number is

   Now do the same for these situations:
   You want to be in Edinburgh at 8 p.m.
   You want to be in Birmingham at 10.30 a.m.
   You want to be in Newcastle at 9 a.m.

Tourist Information Board — July 14th–21st

WELCOME TO SLAXTON-ON-SEA

Here is some practical information about the town to help you make your stay as pleasant and enjoyable as possible.

BANKS
Lloyds   44 High St.   Hours 9.30 a.m. – 3.30 p.m.
                           (Thursday also
                           4.30 – 6.00 p.m.)
Barclays   31 High St.   Hours 9.30 a.m. – 3.30 p.m.
National Westminster
             14 George St. Hours 9.30 a.m. – 3.30 p.m.

POST OFFICE
             51 High St.   Hours 9.00 a.m. – 5.30 p.m.

DEPARTMENT STORES
Whitings   12 West St.   Hours 9.00 a.m. – 6.00 p.m.
                           Late night Monday 9.00 a.m. –
                           7.00 p.m.
                           Early closing Thursday
                           1.00 p.m.
John Hanns   46 High St.   Hours 9.00 a.m. – 6.00 p.m.
                           Early closing Thursday
                           1.00 p.m.

CINEMAS
The Odeon   High St.   Showing this week July 14 – 21
                           "Holiday Fun" Perf 7.00 – 8.45
The Rex   George St.   Showing this week until
                           Wednesday
                           "A Day in the Life"
                           Perf 7.15 – 9.00
                           From Wednesday
                           "Flight to Hong Kong"
                           Perf 7.00 – 8.45

ENJOY YOUR STAY IN SLAXTON-ON-SEA

2. Find out the same information for your town. Write the information for your brochure.

Ex 3 Check that the students have a rough idea of the difference between afternoon and evening. Call out a few times e.g. *9 a.m. . . . 3 p.m. . . . 6 p.m. . . .* etc, and get students to say the times in their full form i.e. *nine o'clock in the morning* etc.
If plenty of oral practice is done in class, the exercise can be set as written homework.
Or, either work T–S or let students work in pairs changing parts afterwards.

Ex 4 Students study the signs/notices in pairs and write down a list of questions which they can ask (see Students' Book for examples).
Then in the same pairs, or in different pairs, they write in answers to their questions.
Check orally.

EXTENSION

1 *Roleplay* Revise the pronunciation of the names of towns, the flight numbers and possibly the times of departure and arrival.
This will draw the students' attention to the chart which they use in the following roleplay.
Give an example of a typical conversation using a good student to give the answers. Keep it simple e.g. *I want to be in London at 10 a.m. tomorrow. What time does the plane leave Manchester? . . . What time does it arrive at London airport?* etc.
Students work in pairs, each taking one situation.
If there is enough time, ask one pair to perform in front of the class.

2 Explain *department store* and *early closing*.
Ask a few questions like *What time does the bank close on Wednesday/Thursday?* (Days of the week are presented for active learning in Unit 15.)
Students work in pairs. The information will probably need to be researched for homework. The student can divide the research between them.
Allow some time in the following lesson for students to put the information together in the form of a tourist leaflet.

3 *Listening* Students should be able to extract the relevant information after hearing the tape only once.
While playing the tape, do not pause to explain the 'padding' of the announcement at the airport.
Check answers afterwards.

Open Dialogue See General Guide and tapescript (page 69).

Oral Exercises See General Guide and tapescript (page 69).

Speechwork See General Guide and tapescript (page 69).

Unit 13

Tapescript
Part A
1 DIALOGUE
Murray, Neville and Jackie go to Coventry to do a film.
MURRAY:	Three to Coventry, please.
TICKET SELLER:	Single or return?
MURRAY:	Return please.
NEVILLE:	Hurry up, Murray! It's late. It's ten past nine!
MURRAY:	What time does the train leave?
JACKIE:	It leaves at twenty past nine.
MURRAY:	Which platform does it leave from?
JACKIE:	Platform Nine. It's over there.
MURRAY:	All right, let's go!

2 SPEECHWORK
Part A: Stress
Say after me:
di da di da...it starts at five...it starts at six...it starts at two...it leaves at four...it leaves at one...it leaves at three...
di da di di da...it opens at one...it opens at three...it opens at nine...it closes at three...it closes at six...it closes at five...

Part B: Intonation
Say after me:
what time does the train leave...what time does the bus leave...
what time does the plane leave...what time does the film start...
what time does the match start...what time does the bank close...

Part C: Pronunciation
Say after me:
/s/.../s/...glass...cups...cakes...biscuits...starts...works...
/z/.../z/...trains...planes...films...leaves...arrives...opens...
/ɪz/.../ɪz/...glasses...sandwiches...matches...finishes...closes...
it starts at three and finishes at five...it opens at nine and closes at six...it leaves at eight and arrives at ten...

3 LISTENING
Listen to these announcements at a railway station and answer the questions in your book.
Your attention please.
The train now leaving from platform six is the nine fifteen to London.
Your attention please.
The train now arriving at platform ten is the six forty from Liverpool.
Now listen to this announcement at Manchester International Airport and answer the questions.
Your attention please. Passengers on flight DAO52 to Newcastle are requested to proceed to the Departure Lounge. We regret that owing to weather conditions the flight has been delayed and is now due to take off at eight fifty. We regret any inconvenience caused to passengers. Thank you.

4 OPEN DIALOGUE
Look at the flight timetable on page 73. You want to go to London tomorrow. Choose a flight and write down the times and the flight number. Now talk to Allan.
ALLAN:	Hello.
STUDENT:	....
ALLAN:	You're going to London tomorrow, aren't you?
STUDENT	....
ALLAN:	What time does the flight leave Manchester?
STUDENT:	....
ALLAN:	Is that in the morning or in the evening?
STUDENT:	....
ALLAN:	Oh, well, I'll take you to the airport in my van.
STUDENT:	....
ALLAN:	That's all right. What time does the flight arrive in London?
STUDENT:	....
ALLAN:	Oh, that's nice and quick. Well, I'll see you tomorrow then. Goodbye for now!
STUDENT:	....

Part B ORAL EXERCISES
Exercise 1 Ask what time things happen.
The bus leaves soon. Hurry up!
What time does it leave?

The film starts soon. Hurry up!
What time does it start? Now go on.

The bank closes soon. Hurry up!
What time does it close?

The train leaves soon. Hurry up!
What time does it leave?

The post office closes soon. Hurry up!
What time does it close?

The lesson starts soon. Hurry up!
What time does it start?

Exercise 2 Say what time things happen. Look at the chart on page 71.

What time does the bus arrive?
Let's see . . . it arrives at twenty past eleven.

What time does the film start?
Let's see . . . it starts at quarter past seven. Now go on.

What time does the plane leave?
Let's see . . . it leaves at quarter past one.

What time does the match finish?
Let's see . . . it finishes at quarter to five.

What time does the bank close?
Let's see . . . it closes at half past three.

What time does the post office open?
Let's see . . . it opens at nine o'clock.

Unit 13

Exercise 3 Ask exactly what time things happen.
Talk to the travel agent.

The plane arrives at five o'clock.
Five in the morning or five in the evening?

The bus leaves at one o'clock.
One in the morning or one in the afternoon? Now go on.

The boat leaves at four o'clock.
Four in the morning or four in the afternoon?

The plane leaves at six o'clock.
Six in the morning or six in the evening?

The plane arrives at two o'clock.
Two in the morning or two in the afternoon?

The train arrives at seven o'clock.
Seven in the morning or seven in the evening?

Exercise 4 Check the information.
The train leaves at six-hundred hours.
I see, it leaves at 6.00 a.m.

The bus leaves at nineteen-hundred hours.
I see, it leaves at 7.00 p.m. Now go on.

The boat leaves at eighteen-hundred hours.
I see, it leaves at 6.00 p.m.

The bus arrives at nine-hundred hours.
I see, it arrives at 9.00 a.m.

The plane leaves at nineteen-hundred hours.
I see, it leaves at 7.00 p.m.

The train arrives at fifteen-hundred hours.
I see, it arrives at 3.00 p.m.

Exercise 5 Correct the information politely.
Look at the chart on page 71.
I think the bus leaves at eleven o'clock.
No, it doesn't, it leaves at five past.

I think the train leaves at nine o'clock.
No, it doesn't, it leaves at twenty past. Now go on.

I think the plane arrives at four o'clock.
No, it doesn't, it arrives at ten to.

I think the film starts at seven o'clock.
No, it doesn't, it starts at quarter past.

I think the post office closes at five o'clock.
No, it doesn't, it closes at half past.

I think the match finishes at five o'clock.
No, it doesn't, it finishes at quarter to.

UNIT 14 Shopping in Coventry

	Skills	Functions	Example Sentences	Main Structures

SET 1	1. Speaking
	2. Speaking
	3. Speaking
	4. Writing
		Ask people to do things
		Agree to do things
		Say you can't do things
			Can you buy some fruit?
			Yes, of course/Yes, OK.
			Can you open the door?
			I'm sorry, I can't just now.
				Can you buy some
				  + plural noun
				  + collective noun
				Can you open/close + noun
				Can you meet + personal pronoun

SET 2	1. Speaking
	2. Speaking
	3. Speaking
		Ask what people would like
		Say what you would like
			What would you like?
			I'd like some oranges, please.
			I'd like some oranges, please.
			How many would you like?
				I'd like some
				  + plural noun
				  + collective noun
				How many + plural noun
				  + would you like?

SET 3	1. Speaking 2. Speaking	Ask for and give specific information	*Can I have an orange, please?* *Yes, which one would you like?* *This one.*	*Which one/ones would you like?* *This/that one* *These/those ones*
SET 4	1. Speaking	Talk about the weather	*Lovely day, isn't it?* *Yes, beautiful.*	*Lovely/beautiful/awful day, isn't it?*
EXTENSION	1. Reading and Writing 2. Speaking 3. Listening and Writing		Write a note based on the framework of a model example, telling a friend what shopping to do. Group work: asking questions about the items in a menu. Conversation in the restaurant car of a train. Students select information about food and drink.	

OPEN DIALOGUE

ORAL EXERCISES		
	1. Ask people what they would like	*What would you like? Would you like some fruit?* *Yes, please.*
	2. Offer people things and Ask them to buy them	*Would you like some fruit for lunch?* *Yes, please.* *Well, can you buy some?*
	3. Say what you would like	*What sort of fruit would you like, apples or oranges?* *I think I'd like some apples* and *some oranges.*
	4. Ask somebody to meet you and your friends	*Your train arrives at 10.* *Can you meet me at the station?*
	5. Ask for specific information	*Can I have an apple?* *Yes, which one would you like?*
	6. Give specific information	*Which apples would you like? These ones?* *No, those ones over there.*

SPEECHWORK

		ACTIVE VOCABULARY			
A STRESS	I'd like some fruit and some cheese ••●•●	apple	fruit	lunch	open
B INTONATION	Lovely day, isn't it?	orange	bread	supper	closed
C PRONUNCIATION	/ʃ/ shop, Sheila	egg	meat	dinner	lovely
		potato	fish		beautiful
		tomato	cheese	buy	awful
		vegetable	soap	do some	terrible
		stamp	toothpaste	shopping	
		cigarette	shampoo	eat	ready?
		envelope		pack up	how many?
		ticket	door	open	which
		pen	window	close	thanks
		menu	suitcase	drink	all right!
			bottle		then
			day		at

71

Unit 14

Shopping in Coventry

At the factory, after filming.
MURRAY: Are we ready to go?
JACKIE: Yes, I think so.
SECRETARY: Focus Films? Yes, one moment. Mr Freeman, can you speak to Tessa Richards?
MURRAY: I'm sorry, I can't just now. We're in a hurry. It's late. The train leaves at ten past.
SECRETARY: All right. I'll tell her.
MURRAY: Thank you very much. Well, Neville and I will pack up. Can you buy some fruit for the journey, Jackie?
JACKIE: Yes, of course.
MURRAY: Can you meet us at the station afterwards?
JACKIE: Yes, O.K.

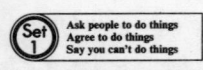

(speech bubbles) "Well, Neville and I will pack up. Can you buy some fruit for the journey, Jackie?" "Yes, of course."

Set 1 Ask people to do things
Agree to do things
Say you can't do things

Can you buy some fruit?
Yes, of course.

1. **Look at the pictures. Ask and answer like this:**
   Can you buy some fruit?
   Yes, of course.

   Can you buy some ...?
   Yes, of course.

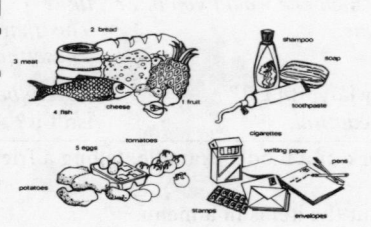

(pictures: 1 fruit, 2 bread, 3 meat, 4 fish, cheese, shampoo, soap, toothpaste, 5 eggs, tomatoes, cigarettes, writing paper, pens, potatoes, stamps, envelopes)

Can you open the window?   Yes, O.K.
Can you close the door?   I'm sorry, I can't just now.

2. **Ask and answer like this:**
   Can you open the door?
   Yes, O.K.   or I'm sorry, I can't just now.

Can you meet us at the station?
Yes, O.K.   or I'm sorry, I can't.

I'm at the station. Can you meet me?
He's at the station. Can you meet him?
She's at the station. Can you meet her?
We're at the station. Can you meet us?
They're at the staion. Can you meet them?

(speech bubbles)
1. "I'm at the station"
2. "We're at the hotel"
3. "She's at the bank"
4. "They're at the cinema"
5. "He's at the post office"
6. "We're at the station"
7. "She's at the hotel"
8. "I'm at the cinema"
9. "They're at the post office"
10. "He's at the bank"

3. **Ask and answer like this:**
   Can you meet me at the station?
   Yes, O.K. or Yes, of course.   or I'm sorry, I can't.

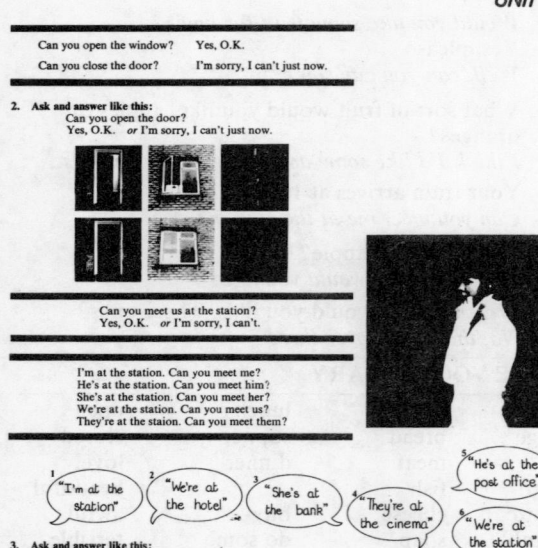

   The door is open. Can you close it?

4. **Make the right requests**
   1. The window is open. _____
   2. The door is closed. _____
   3. Here's a bottle of wine. _____
   4. The window is closed. _____
   5. Here's my suitcase. _____
   6. The door is open. _____

DIALOGUE

Set the scene for the dialogue. Murray, Neville and Jackie have been in Coventry making a film. It's now time to go back to Manchester. Tessa rings from Manchester just when they are going to leave for the train.
Draw the students' attention to the requests *Can you . . . ?* and the replies *Yes, of course/Yes, OK/ I'm sorry, I can't*.

SET 1 Ask people to do things
Agree to do things/Say you can't do things

Ex 1 Can you buy some fruit?   Yes, of course.

Use the wall picture/OHP (6) or real pictures to introduce and practise the new vocabulary.
Practise the intonation of the exchange chorally.
Give an example of the exercise using a few items from the list. Students work in a chain round the class S1-S2, S2–S3 etc.
This will give you a chance to correct pronunciation and to see that the students say *some* (weakly stressed /səm/) before each item.

Ex 2 Can you open the window?

Yes, OK.   I'm sorry, I can't just now.

Introduce the new vocabulary using the classroom door and window, and sketches of a bottle and suitcase. Demonstrate the meaning of open and close.
Practise the intonation of the question and answers.
Demonstrate the meaning of *Yes, OK* by carrying out the request, and *I'm sorry, I can't just now*, by showing that you are temporarily occupied (e.g. busy writing, washing your hair, etc.).
Give an example of the exercise.
Students work in pairs, either saying *Yes, OK* to all the requests first, and *I'm sorry, I can't just now* the second time, or choosing how they want to answer.

Ex 3 Can you meet us at the station?   Yes, OK.

Present and practise the object pronouns. Use other familiar sentence forms to illustrate their use e.g. *Do you like Frank Sinatra/Elizabeth Taylor/The Rolling Stones?* Answer: *Yes, I like him/her/them very much.*
Give an example of the exercise.
Work S–T round the class to make sure that the students understand how the exercise works. Vary your own answer so that they get the idea that they can choose what to say in reply.
Students then work in pairs.

Ex 4 Students work individually or in pairs and fill in the right requests.
Check orally.

Unit 14

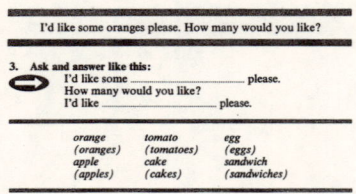

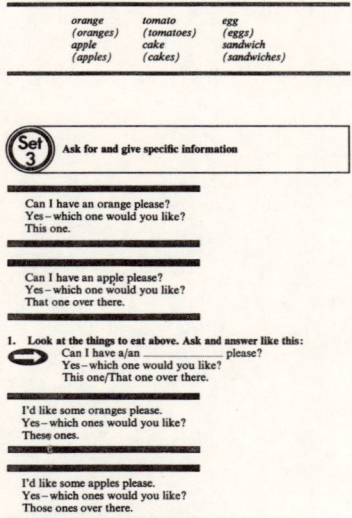

DIALOGUE

The dialogue is best presented in two parts.
Read as far as Jackie's reply *Three please*, then proceed with Set 2. The rest of the dialogue can be presented before Sets 3 and 4.

SET 2 Ask what people would like
Say what you would like

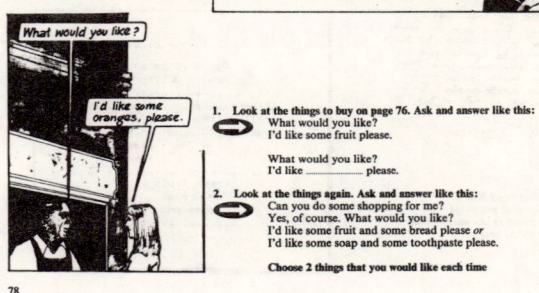

What would you like?   I'd like some oranges please.

Ex 1 Practise the intonation of the question and answer. Refer students to the list of items in Set 1 or use the wall picture/OHP (6).
Students work in a chain or in groups where one member is the shopkeeper and the others are customers.

Ex 2 Give an example of the exercise, showing that the students are to ask for two things from the list.

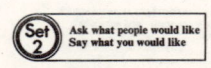

Ex 3 I'd like some oranges please.

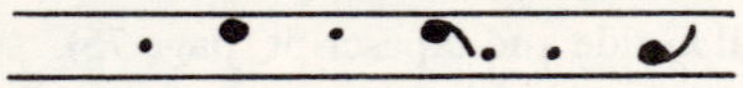

How many would you like?

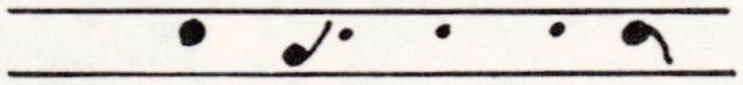

Practise the intonation of the question *How many . . . ?*
Ask one student to be the shopkeeper and give one or two examples of the exercise, choosing from the list on the page.

SET 3 Ask for and give specific information

Play the second half of the dialogue.
Can I have an orange please?

Yes—which one would you like?   This one.

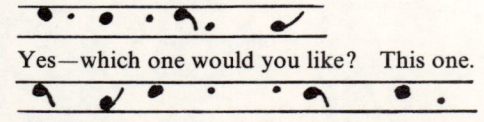

Ex 1 If possible, bring some apples and oranges of different sorts and sizes into the classroom so that the students can make a realistic choice.
Demonstrate the meaning of *this one* and *that one over there* by picking up *this one* and pointing to *that one over there*.
Students work in pairs and practise both answers.

Ex 2 Proceed as Ex 1. The situation is more obviously in a shop as opposed to a home or a restaurant.

Unit 14

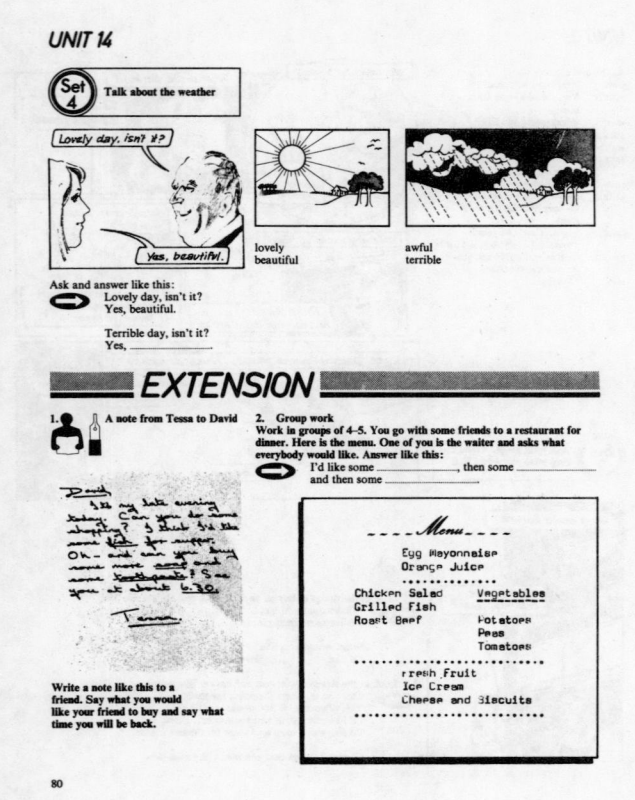

SET 4 Talk about the weather

Lovely day, isn't it?   Yes, beautiful.

Practise the pronunciation of the weather words, showing the meaning by your facial expression and a picture of a sunny/rainy day.
Students repeat the exchange chorally.
Check that they sound enthusiastic or depressed as appropriate.
Work T–S, then S–S round the class.

EXTENSION

1 *Reading and Writing* Students read the note silently, possibly consulting each other in pairs. Write a framework for a note on the blackboard and ask them to write a similar note to a friend, in class or for homework.
Students should choose items from the list in Set 1.

2 *Group work* Go through the menu with the students.
Practise the pronunciation of the names of dishes.
Give an example of your choice. One student asks you *What would you like?* You answer according to the pattern *I'd like some . . . , then some . . . and then some . . .*
Students form groups and choose one of their group to be a waiter and take all the orders.

3 *Listening* The menu on the train is the same as the menu printed in the book. Play the tape through first without stopping, then again, pausing at the relevant places if necessary.
Check afterwards.

Open Dialogue See General Guide and tapescript (page 75).

Oral Exercises See General Guide and tapescript (page 76).

Speechwork See General Guide and tapescript (page 75).

Unit 14

Tapescript
Part A

1 DIALOGUE

At the factory after filming

MURRAY:	Are we ready to go?
JACKIE:	Yes, I think so. (Phone rings)
SECRETARY:	Focus Films? Yes, one moment. Mr Freeman, can you speak to Tessa Richards?
MURRAY:	I'm sorry, I can't just now. We're in a hurry. It's late. The train leaves at ten past.
SECRETARY:	All right. I'll tell her.
MURRAY:	Thank you very much. Well, Neville and I will pack up. Can you buy some fruit for the journey, Jackie?
JACKIE:	Yes, of course.
MURRAY:	Can you meet us at the station afterwards?
JACKIE:	Yes, O.K.

At the greengrocer's

MAN:	Yes, can I help you?
JACKIE:	Yes, I'd like some fruit, please.
MAN:	What would you like?
JACKIE:	I'd like some oranges, please.
MAN:	How many would you like?
JACKIE:	Three please. And some of those apples.
MAN:	Which ones would you like?
JACKIE:	Those ones over there – the Granny Smiths. Three of them.
MAN:	Right. That's 44 pence please . . . Lovely day, isn't it?
JACKIE:	Yes, beautiful. Thank you very much. Goodbye.
MAN:	Goodbye.

2 SPEECHWORK

Part A: Stress

Say after me:

di di di da di di da...I'd like some fruit and some cheese... I'd like some bread and some cheese...I'd like some meat and some fish...I'd like some bread and some fish...I'd like some eggs and some cheese...

Part B: Intonation

Say after me:

isn't it...isn't it..lovely day, isn't it...beautiful day, isn't it... awful day, isn't it..terrible day, isn't it...good food, isn't it... good film, isn't it..strong coffee, isn't it...

Part C: Pronunciation

Say after me:

/ʃ/.../ʃ/... she...Yes she is...no she isn't...Sheila... here's Sheila...English...Sheila's English...finishes...it finishes at six...shop...shopping...can you do some shopping...I'd like some fish...some fresh fruit...some shampoo...some sugar...sugar please, Sheila...

3 LISTENING

Murray, Neville and Jackie are in the restaurant car on the train going back to Manchester. Listen to them talking and write down in your books what each of them has to eat and drink.

(Sound up on train moving, clinking of cutlery etc.)

NEVILLE:	Wow, I'm hungry. Where's the menu? Ah here. Mmm.
JACKIE:	Let's have a look. Are you having something to start with?
NEVILLE:	I don't know. Are you Murray?
MURRAY:	Don't know. What is there?
NEVILLE:	Egg mayonnaise and orange juice. I'm going to have egg mayonnaise.
MURRAY:	Nothing for me, thanks.
JACKIE:	Can I have an orange juice?
MURRAY:	Yes, of course. What's the main course?
JACKIE:	Er . . . chicken salad . . . grilled fish . . .
MURRAY:	Mmm . . . fish . . . sounds all right.
NEVILLE:	And roast beef.
MURRAY:	Oh . . . roast beef . . . oh well . . .
NEVILLE:	Well, I'm going to have roast beef.
MURRAY:	O.K. I'll join you. Jackie?
JACKIE:	Fish for me . . . oh, wait a moment . . . no . . . no, I think I'll have the chicken.
NEVILLE:	The chicken salad?
JACKIE:	Yes, that sounds nice.
NEVILLE:	Anything with it? Any vegetables?
JACKIE:	No, not for me.
MURRAY:	I'll have some potatoes and some peas.
NEVILLE:	Peas . . . no, I don't like peas. Tomatoes . . . yes, I'll have tomatoes.
MURRAY:	No potatoes?
NEVILLE:	No thanks. And to drink?
JACKIE:	Just water for me, please.
NEVILLE:	I'd like a beer, I think. Murray?
MURRAY:	Er . . . a glass of red wine would be nice.
	(later in the meal)
MURRAY:	Well, that was good. Any pudding, you two? There's ice-cream, fresh fruit or cheese and biscuits.
NEVILLE:	No thanks, just coffee.
JACKIE:	Same for me.
MURRAY:	Well, I shall have some cheese and biscuits. Jackie, can you catch the waiter's eye?

4 OPEN DIALOGUE

You are having dinner with Murray. Look at the menu on page 80.

MURRAY:	Well, here's the menu . . . Let's see . . . there's chicken, fish and roast beef. Do you like fish?
STUDENT:	....
MURRAY:	Or what about chicken? Would you like some chicken salad?
STUDENT:	....
MURRAY:	All right. And what about vegetables?
STUDENT:	....
MURRAY:	Fine. And what would you like after that – fresh fruit, or ice-cream, or cheese and biscuits?
STUDENT:	....
MURRAY:	And to drink?
STUDENT:	....
MURRAY:	Right. I'll order.

Unit 14

Part B ORAL EXERCISES

Exercise 1 Ask people what they would like. Look at the food on page 76.

What would you like? Would you like some fruit?
Yes, please.

What would you like? Would you like some bread?
No, thank you. Now go on.

What would you like? Would you like some meat?
No thanks, I don't like meat.

What would you like? Would you like some fish?
Yes, please, that sounds nice.

What would you like? Would you like some eggs?
No, thanks, nothing for me.

Exercise 2 Offer people things and ask them to buy them. Look at the food again.

Would you like some fruit for lunch?
Yes, please.
Well, can you buy some?

Would you like some bread for lunch?
Yes, please.
Well, can you buy some? Now go on.

Would you like some meat for lunch?
Yes, please.
Well, can you buy some?

Would you like some fish for lunch?
Yes, please.
Well, can you buy some?

Would you like some eggs for lunch?
Yes, please.
Well, can you buy some?

Exercise 3 Say what you would like. Jackie is going to the shops.

What sort of fruit would you like, apples or oranges?
I'd like some apples and *some oranges*.

And would you like meat or fish?
I'd like some meat and *some fish*. Now go on.

Cheese or eggs?
I'd like some cheese and *some eggs*.

Do you want soap or shampoo?
I'd like some soap and *some shampoo*.

Do you need stamps or envelopes?
I'd like some stamps and *some envelopes*.

What about toothpaste? Or do you want soap?
I'd like some toothpaste and *some soap*.

Exercise 4 Ask somebody to meet you and your friends.

Your train arrives at 10.
Can you meet me at the station?

Her plane arrives at 9.
Can you meet her at the airport? Now go on.

His train arrives at 5.
Can you meet him at the station?

Your planes arrive at 8.
Can you meet us at the airport?

Their train arrives at 4.
Can you meet them at the station?

Her train arrives at 7.
Can you meet her at the station?

Exercise 5 Ask for specific information.

Can I have an apple?
Yes, which one would you like?

I'd like some eggs.
Yes, which ones would you like? Now go on.

I'd like some tomatoes.
Yes, which ones would you like?

Can I have an orange?
Yes, which one would you like?

Can I have a pen?
Yes, which one would you like?

I'd like some envelopes.
Yes, which ones would you like?

Exercise 6 Give specific information.

Which apples would you like? These ones?
No, those ones over there.

Which cake would you like? That one?
No, this one. Now go on.

Which oranges would you like? Those ones?
No, these ones.

Which envelopes would you like? These ones?
No, those ones over there.

Which book would you like? This one?
No, that one over there.

Which sandwich would you like? That one?
No, this one.

Which eggs would you like? Those ones?
No, these ones.

Which cakes would you like? These ones?
No, those ones over there.

UNIT 15 Happy Birthday!

	Skills	Functions	Example Sentences	Main Structures
SET 1	1. Speaking 2. Speaking and Writing 3. Speaking 4. Speaking 5. Writing	Ask and talk about dates	*When's Tessa's birthday?* *It's on January 10th.* *January 10th is a Monday.* *Tessa's birthday is on Monday.*	Tessa's *birthday is on* January 10th Murray's *birthday is on* Monday January 10th *is a* Monday/Tuesday *It's/That's on* Monday/Tuesday etc. *When's Tessa's/your/his* birthday?
SET 2	1. Speaking 2. Writing and speaking 3. Speaking 4. Speaking	Ask for and make suggestions Agree and disagree with suggestions	*What shall we give her?* *Let's give her some chocolates.* *Yes, that's a good idea.* *No, not chocolates.*	*What shall we give* him/her? *What shall we do?* *Let's give* him/her *a book/some flowers* *Let's go to the cinema.*
SET 3	1. Speaking 2. Speaking	Express pleasure Thank people for things	*What a beautiful room!* *What beautiful flowers!* *Thank you for the beautiful flowers.*	*What* a beautiful book! an interesting book! beautiful posters! interesting posters!
EXTENSION	1. Reading and Writing	A 'thank you' letter. Students use a model letter to write sentences thanking a friend for presents.		
	2. Reading	Newspaper advertisement for a concert tour by Nana Mouskouri, with the dates of her tour.		
	3. Listening	Conversation between David and Tessa about his mother's birthday present and outing; students extract important facts.		
	4. Reading	Reading Text: Festivals, Parties and Presents.		

OPEN DIALOGUE

ORAL EXERCISES		
	1. Say when people's birthdays are	When's Tessa's birthday? *It's on January 10th.*
	2. Say what month people's birthdays are in	Is Tessa's birthday in March? *No, it's in January.*
	3. Agree with suggestions	What shall we give him? A record? *Yes, that's a good idea. Let's give him a record.*
	4. Suggest things to do	What shall we do? Shall we go to the cinema? *Yes, that's a good idea.*
	5. Express pleasure when people give or show you things	Do you like the flowers? *Yes, I do. They're beautiful.*
	6. Disagree with suggestions	Let's go to the cinema tonight. *No, not the cinema!*

SPEECHWORK		ACTIVE VOCABULARY		
A STRESS	What a beautiful room! ● ● ● ● ● What beautiful flowers! ● ● ● ●	January, February etc. (months) Monday, Tuesday etc. (days) 1st, 2nd etc. (Ordinal numbers)		
B INTONATION	What shall we do?	flower	people	different
C PRONUNCIATION	/dʒ/ /j/ Jackie Young	book	chocolate	interesting
		plate	perfume	That's a good idea!
		poster	aftershave	Happy Birthday!
		T-shirt	date	go to ...
			birthday	go out for ...
		meal		give
		walk	today	watch TV
		party	tomorrow	television
		man	next	stay at home
		year	also	try
		television		
		family		

77

Unit 15

Happy Birthday

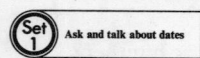

Oh, when is it?
It's Tessa's birthday soon.
It's on January the tenth.

In the cafeteria at Focus Films
MURRAY: It's Tessa's birthday soon.
ALLAN: Oh, when is it?
MURRAY: It's on January the tenth.
JACKIE: That's on Monday!
MURRAY: Yes, that's right.

Set 1 Ask and talk about dates

Days of the week	Months of the year		Dates			
Monday	January	July	1st	= first	16th	= sixteenth
Tuesday	February	August	2nd	= second	17th	= seventeenth, etc.
Wednesday	March	September	3rd	= third		
Thursday	April	October	4th	= fourth	20th	= twentieth
Friday	May	November	5th	= fifth	21st	= twenty-first, etc.
Saturday	June	December	6th	= sixth		
Sunday			7th	= seventh	30th	= thirtieth
			8th	= eighth	31st	= thirty-first, etc.
			9th	= ninth		
			10th	= tenth		
			11th	= eleventh		
			12th	= twelfth		
			13th	= thirteenth		
			14th	= fourteenth		
			15th	= fifteenth		

When's Tessa's birthday? It's on January the tenth (January 10th)

1. Ask and answer like this:
   When's Tessa's birthday?
   It's on January the tenth.

   When's Murray's birthday?
   It's on _____

   Focus Films – Birthdays
   Tessa – January 10th
   Jackie – April 1st
   Murray – November 11th
   George – July 3rd
   Neville – February 27th
   Allan – May 2nd
   Sheila – December 5th

83

DIALOGUE

Refer the students to the months of the year and the days of the week before you play the tape and read the dialogue. Note that the date *January the tenth* is written here as it is spoken, not in its correct form *January 10th*.

The dialogue should be presented in three parts: the first, up to *Yes, that's right,* followed by Set 1 exercises; the second up to *Yes, that's a good idea* followed by Set 2 exercises; the third, up to the end followed by Set 3 exercises.

SET 1 Ask and talk about dates

Spend some time introducing and reading the months of the year and the dates. It is enough if the students can say the months and dates at this stage; they can be memorised later on.

The students should however be able to read abbreviated dates *(Feb 3rd = February the third)* before doing the exercises.

Ex 1 When's Tessa's birthday?   It's on January the tenth.

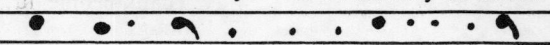

Give one or two examples of the exercise.
Work T–S through all the dates. Students then repeat the exercise working in pairs.

Ex 2 January the tenth is a Monday.

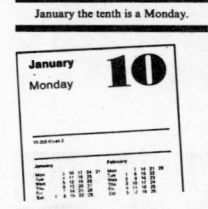

Present and practise the days of the week; these should be actively memorised.
If enough students have diaries with them, they can work in pairs or groups and check what days of the week the various Focus birthdays fall on, and write down the answers.
Or, use a large calendar in front of the whole class and ask the students to say the day e.g. *November the fourteenth is a ....day* as you come to it in the calendar. Then all students write the day down.

Ex 3 Tessa's birthday is on January 10th.

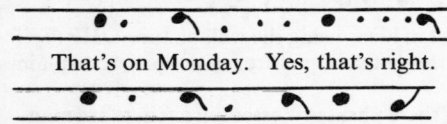

That's on Monday.   Yes, that's right.

Students use the answers from the previous exercise.
Give an example. Then students work in pairs.
Check with individual students.

Ex 4 Ask a student when his birthday is, then tell the class e.g. *Peter's birthday is on August 4th.*
Tell the students to find out each other's birthdays, write down the date and then tell the class.

Ex 5 Students work in pairs to fill in the answers together. This exercise could be set as individual homework.
N.B. The answer to Question 7 requires that the students know when your birthday is.

SET 2 Ask for and make suggestions
            Agree and disagree with suggestions
What shall we give her?   Let's give her some chocolates.

Yes, that's a good idea!/No, not chocolates.

Ex 1 Use pictures from a magazine to present the new vocabulary. Practise the pronunciation.
Practise the intonation of the exchange.
Give some examples of the exercise, playing both parts yourself.
Show the students that they must say *What shall we give him?* or *What shall we give her?* depending on the sex of the person whose birthday it is.
Students work in pairs, suggesting one or two things each for Tessa and Murray's birthdays.

Unit 15

Unit 15

UNIT 15

2. Decide what to give these people for their birthdays

TESSA: _____
MURRAY: _____
ALLAN: _____
NEVILLE: _____
JACKIE: _____

Now practise making the suggestions with a partner, like this:

○ It's _____'s birthday tomorrow.
Let's give him/her _____
That's a good idea./No, not _____ Let's give him/her _____

IDEAS

go to a cafe — 1 go to the cinema
go to the beach — 2 go to the club
go out for a meal — 3 go out for a walk
go home — 4 have a party
watch TV — 5 stay at home

What shall we do?
Let's go to the cinema.
Yes, that's a good idea./No, let's go to the cafe

3. Ask and answer like this:

○ What shall we do?
Let's go to the cinema.
Yes, that's a good idea./No, let's _____

What shall we do?
Let's _____
Yes, that's a good idea./No, let's _____

What shall we do on Friday evening? Let's go out for a meal.

4. Work with a partner. Make suggestions for the times below. Ask and answer like this:

○ What shall we do on _____
Let's _____
Yes, that's a _____/No, let's _____

Tuesday evening   Saturday afternoon   Sunday morning
Friday evening   Saturday evening

85

Ex 2 Individual work. Students look at the list of presents and choose one present for each of the people listed, writing the name of the present next to the name of the person. Students work in pairs as in Ex 1.

They should only need one 'conversation' for each person on the list; if their partner's suggestion is not the same as their own, they say *No, not . . . Let's give him/her a . . .* But they should take turns to introduce the conversation.

Ex 3 What shall we do?   Let's go to the cinema.

Yes, that's a good idea./ No, let's go to the club.

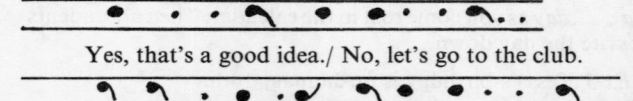

Go through the list of ideas using the wall picture/OHP (7) if available, otherwise sketches, pictures or actions, to explain them.

Practice in saying these phrases is essential as there are many small words which tend to be omitted e.g. *go out for a . . .* (Note that in the first four examples the stress falls on the verb *go*, but in the fifth and sixth examples it falls on *out*.)

Give an example then work T–S; all students should have the chance to read something from the list, while you correct them if necessary.

At this stage agree with their suggestions, i.e. say *Yes, that's a good idea*.

After this practice, give another example showing how to disagree with the suggestion while suggesting something else at the same time i.e. say *No, let's go . . .* etc.

Work with one student T–S and S–T for a couple of examples.

Then students work in pairs. Go round and listen.

Ex 4 What shall we do on Friday evening?

Let's go out for a meal.

Practise the questions first to revise the pronunciation of the days of the week and parts of the day.

Choose a student and work through one or two examples. Students work in pairs as in Ex 3.

SET 3 Express pleasure

Ex 1 What a beautiful room!

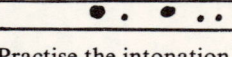

Practise the intonation.
Substitute *lovely* and *interesting*; students repeat chorally after you.
Write *What a beautiful . . .* on the blackboard. Ask students to look at the list of things and people in their books. Choose one or two to suit *What a beautiful . . .* (e.g. *house, girl*) then go round the class asking individual students to complete the exclamation, choosing something from the list.
Repeat with other adjectives in the same way.
(The adjectives can go with all of the nouns; one or two are rather unusual but quite acceptable e.g. *interesting garden, beautiful man*.)

Ex 2 What beautiful flowers!

Practise the intonation.
Proceed as in Ex 1. (The choice of appropriate adjectives to correspond with the noun is more limited here.)

EXTENSION

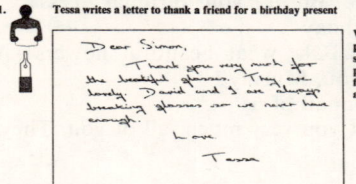

1 Read the opening of the letter together with students.
Give an example of the substitution possibilities and of other changes which have to be made e.g. *Thank you very much for the lovely record. It is very beautiful.*
Explain other possible variations e.g. omitting the adjective in the first sentence.
Point out that we often say *very interesting* and *very nice*, but rarely say *very lovely* and *very beautiful*.

2 Students read and study the programme for the Nana Mouskouri concert.
Ask simple questions to elicit dates and ticket prices e.g. *When is she in Leeds? How much are the tickets? Where is she on Nov. 28th?*

3 *Listening* Play the tape through twice, pausing the second time so that the students can fill in their answers.

Open Dialogue See General Guide and tapescript (page 82).

Oral Exercises See General Guide and tapescript (page 83).

Speechwork See General Guide and tapescript (page 82).

Unit 15

Tapescript
Part A

1 DIALOGUE
In the cafeteria at Focus Films
MURRAY: It's Tessa's birthday soon.
ALLAN: Oh, when is it?
MURRAY: It's on January the tenth.
JACKIE: That's on Monday!
MURRAY: Yes, that's right.

ALLAN: What shall we give her?
MURRAY: Let's give her some chocolates.
JACKIE: No, not chocolates. Let's give her some flowers.
MURRAY: Yes, that's a good idea.

On January 10th
TESSA: Good morning, everyone! Awful day, isn't it?
MURRAY: Yes, terrible! But it's your birthday, Tessa. Happy Birthday!
TESSA: Oh, thanks. Oh, what beautiful flowers! Are they from you, Murray?
MURRAY: They're from all of us.
TESSA: Well, thank you very much, all of you. They're lovely!

2 SPEECHWORK
Part A: Stress
Say after me:
di di da di di da...what a beautiful house...what a beautiful room...what a beautiful book...what a beautiful film... what a beautiful day...
di da di di da...what beautiful rooms...what beautiful books ...what beautiful plates...what beautiful flowers.

Part B: Intonation
Say after me:
what shall we do...what shall we buy...what shall we have...where shall we go...where shall we eat...where shall we stay...when shall we go...when shall we eat... when shall we leave...

Part C: Pronunciation
Say after me:
/j/.../j/...yes...you...yes, you are...
/dʒ/.../dʒ/...Jackie...January...June...July...
/dʒ/.../j/...Jackie Young...Yes, this is Jackie Young... are you Jackie Young...university...are you at university... is John at university...John's birthday is in June... is your birthday in July...Yes, July...

3 LISTENING
It's Mrs Richards's birthday. Not Tessa Richards, but old Mrs Richards, David's mother. Tessa and David are trying to think what to give her for a birthday present, and also what to do on her birthday, Listen to them talking and write down the date of her birthday, what they decide to give her and what they decide to do.

TESSA: What day is it today, David?
DAVID: Tuesday. Why?
TESSA: No, I mean, what date is it?
DAVID: Er... January 12th.
TESSA: January 12th... it's your mother's birthday soon, isn't it?
DAVID: Good heavens! Yes, you're right. It's next week, on January 17th.
TESSA: That's next Monday. Well, what shall we give her this year?
DAVID: Oh, you decide. I want to watch a programme on TV.
TESSA: Oh come on, David. She's *your* mother.
DAVID: Oh, all right. Flowers?
TESSA: Oh, not flowers! And not chocolates either. It's so boring. Anyway you don't give your mother flowers, not on her birthday. Let's think... what about a record?
DAVID: No, not a record. She doesn't play records.
TESSA: Perfume?
DAVID: Mmm, no. No, I don't think she likes perfume. She's 65 anyway.
TESSA: So? Oh well, you know her, I suppose. What about a book?
DAVID: (doubtfully) Yes... but what about? She doesn't read very much.
TESSA: Well, what *does* she like?
DAVID: She likes her garden and her flowers!
TESSA: That's it! Let's give her a book about flowers!
DAVID: Yes, Yes, that's a good idea.
TESSA: In fact, I saw a book the other day called 'English Gardens and Flowers' – lots of pictures. I think it cost about four or five pounds.
DAVID: That sounds fine. Let's get her that.
TESSA: You say she's 65 this year?
DAVID: Yes... why?
TESSA: Well, we must do something, take her out somewhere or do something.
DAVID: Yes, you're right. What shall we do? Shall we have a party?
TESSA: No, not a party. She gets tired easily. Perhaps the theatre.
DAVID: I'm not sure.
TESSA: Well, look, let's invite her to supper on her birthday. Just her and your father.
DAVID: But it's a Monday, after work. No, let's go out for a meal instead.
TESSA: Mmm, all right. Where?
DAVID: What about the new Italian restaurant? They say it's very good.
TESSA: Yes, all right. Let's try that. Good idea. Let's hope she likes Italian food!

4 OPEN DIALOGUE
It's Saturday afternoon. You meet Tessa.
TESSA: Beautiful day, isn't it?
STUDENT: ....
TESSA: What shall we do?
STUDENT: ....

TESSA:	Good idea. Come on then. When's your birthday, by the way?
STUDENT:	....
TESSA:	Oh, is it? What shall we do on your birthday?
STUDENT:	....
TESSA:	Mmm, all right. Oh, it's Murray's birthday on November 14th. What shall we give him?
STUDENT:	....
TESSA:	Yes, that's a good idea. Let's give him that. I'll tell the others.

Part B ORAL EXERCISES

Exercise 1 Say when people's birthdays are.

Look at page 83.

When's Tessa's birthday?
It's on January 10th.
When's Jackie's birthday?
It's on April 1st. Now go on.
When's Murray's birthday?
It's on November 14th.
When's George's birthday?
It's on July 3rd.
When's Neville's birthday?
It's on February 27th.
When's Allan's birthday?
It's on May 2nd.
When's Sheila's birthday?
It's on December 5th.

Exercise 2 Say what month people's birthday's are.

Look at the list of birthdays again.

Is Tessa's birthday in March?
No, it's in January.
Is Jackie's birthday in May?
No, it's in April. Now go on.
Is Murray's birthday in December?
No, it's in November.
Is George's birthday in September?
No, it's in July.
Is Neville's birthday in June?
No, it's in February.
Is Allan's birthday in July?
No, it's in May.
And is Sheila's birthday in October?
No, it's in December.

Exercise 3 Agree with suggestions.

What shall we give him? A record?
Yes, that's a good idea. Let's give him a record.
What shall we give her? Some flowers?
Yes, that's a good idea. Let's give her some flowers.
Now go on.
What shall we give her? Some perfume?
Yes, that's a good idea. Let's give her some perfume.
What shall we give them? Some books?
Yes, that's a good idea. Let's give them some books.
What shall we give him? Some chocolates?
Yes, that's a good idea. Let's give him some chocolates.
What shall we give her? Some whisky?
Yes, that's a good idea. Let's give her some whisky.
What shall we give Neville? A record?
Yes, that's a good idea. Let's give him a record.
What shall we give Tessa and her husband? Some glasses?
Yes, that's a good idea. Let's give them some glasses.

Exercise 4 Suggest things to do.

Look at page 85

What shall we do? Shall we go to the cinema?
Yes, that's a good idea.
What shall we do? Shall we go to the club?
Yes, that's a good idea. Now go on.
What shall we do? Shall we go out for a walk?
Yes, that's a good idea.
What shall we do? Shall we have a party?
Yes, that's a good idea.
What shall we do? Shall we stay at home?
Yes, that's a good idea.

Exercise 5 Express pleasure when people give or show you things.

Do you like the flowers?
Yes, I do. They're beautiful!
Do you like my room?
Yes, I do. It's beautiful! Now go on.
Do you like the garden?
Yes, I do. It's beautiful!
Do you like the chocolates?
Yes, I do. They're beautiful!
Do you like the kitchen?
Yes, I do. It's beautiful!
Do you like the glasses?
Yes, I do. They're beautiful!

Exercise 6 Disagree with these suggestions.

Let's go to the cinema tonight.
No, not the cinema!
Well, shall we go to London?
No, not London! Now go on.
Let's have a party.
No, not a party!
Shall we go to the club?
No, not the club!
Let's go out for a walk.
No, not a walk!
Shall we go out for a meal?
No, not a meal!
Well, I don't know. What *do* you want to do?
....

UNIT 16 A nice weekend

	Skills	Functions	Example Sentences	Main Structures
SET 1	1. Speaking 2. Speaking 3. Speaking 4. Speaking	Ask people what they want to do Say what you want to do	*What do you want to do?* *I want to go home.*	*What do you/does he want to do?* *I want/He wants to go home.* 　　　　　　　go to bed. 　　　　　　　go to the cinema. *I'm bored/tired.*
SET 2	1. Speaking 2. Speaking 3. Speaking 4. Speaking 5. Speaking 6. Speaking 7. Speaking	Ask and talk about the past	*Where were you yesterday?* *I was at home.* *What did you do?* *I did the washing.* *Where did you go?* *I went to the theatre.* *What did you see?* *I saw the Mousetrap.* *What was it like?* *It was quite good.* *What did you have to eat?* *I had fish and chips.*	*What did* { *you do? I did my home- 　　　　　 work. 　　　　　 he see? He saw a film. 　　　　　 she have? She had a 　　　　　 sandwich.* *Where did they go? They went to London.* *Where* { *was John? He was at home.* 　　　　 *were you? We were at home.* *What was the book like?* *It was quite good/very interesting.*
EXTENSION	1. Reading and Writing 2. Reading 3. Listening and Writing		Students read Jackie's diary for the weekend and write a similar diary entry for their own weekends. Holiday postcard. Conversation about Murray and Anna Freeman's holiday in Rome. Students extract facts about the holiday and write a postcard about the holiday, as if from Rome.	

OPEN DIALOGUE

ORAL EXERCISES		
	1. Ask people about the past (1)	Ask Murray if he had a nice weekend. *Did you have a nice weekend, Murray?*
	2. Ask people about the past (2)	Ask Murray what he did yesterday. *What did you do yesterday, Murray?*
	3. Ask people to repeat statements	I went to the cinema last night. *Sorry! Where did you go?*
	4. Say what people did in the past	Where did Murray and Anna go on Saturday (which town)? *They went to London.*
	5. Ask what people want to do	I'm bored. *Do you want to go to the club?*
	6. Say what you want to do	What's the matter? *I'm tired. I want to go home.*

SPEECHWORK

		ACTIVE VOCABULARY		
A STRESS	What do you want to do? ●∙∙●∙●	theatre	yesterday	see (saw)
B INTONATION	ˈDid youˈhave aˈnice daˈy? ↗	musical	last night	yawn(ed)
C PRONUNCIATION	/aʊ/ out, down, house.	the news	last week	want(ed)
		variety programme		invite(d)
		documentary film	quite	sit (sat) down
		postcard	ill	go (went) home
		holiday	bored	go to sleep
		church	tired	stop (stopped)
		washing	old	say (said)
		shopping		find (found)
		chips		
		butter		What's the matter?
		toast		Don't laugh!
		weekend		Who?

Unit 16

N.B. Unit 16 introduces the past tense for the first time. Both teacher and students *need* to be able to use at least a few of the most common verbs in the past tense at an early stage. The verbs selected here will enable the students to talk in a simple way about what they did e.g. at the weekend.
The main exchange practised here is the question *What/Where did you . . . ?* and its corresponding answer.
Unit 16 does not provide systematic practice of all forms in the past tense. The past tense will be treated thoroughly in the next book of the Strategies series, *Building Strategies*.
In the following units however, reference will be made to the past tense; all verbs in the vocabulary lists will show both base and past tense forms.

DIALOGUE

Present the reading text first.
The dialogue can be presented as a whole or in two parts. The first part relates to Set 1 and goes up to *Tessa: But it's only a quarter past nine.*
Demonstrate the situation by acting yourself, showing that you are tired by yawning, and saying that you want to go back to bed.

A nice weekend

It's Friday night. Murray and Anna Freeman decide to go to London for the weekend. They drive down to London on Saturday morning and they stop for lunch in a pub on the way. In the afternoon they do some shopping and go and see some friends who live in West London. They decide to go to the theatre in the evening. Their friends say the musical, Evita, is very good, but the tickets are very expensive. In the end, they go to see The Mousetrap, an old Agatha Christie play. They stay the night with their friends and on Sunday morning they go for a walk in Hyde Park. In the afternoon they go to an exhibition at the Tate Gallery. Then after tea with their friends, they drive back to Manchester and get back home late on Sunday evening. On Monday morning Murray is very tired and is a little late for work.

Monday morning at work.
(*Murray yawns*)
TESSA: What's the matter Murray? Are you tired?
MURRAY: Yes, I am. Do you know what I want to do—I want to go home, go to bed and go back to sleep.
TESSA: But it's only a quarter past nine. Did you have a nice weekend?
MURRAY: Yes thanks, we did.
TESSA: What did you do?
MURRAY: We went to London and saw some friends—and we went to the theatre on Saturday night.
TESSA: Oh, what did you see?
MURRAY: Don't laugh—but we saw the Mousetrap!
TESSA: The Agatha Christie play? Did you? What was it like?
MURRAY: It was quite good. Just a detective story. We wanted to see the musical about Eva Peron, but the tickets cost £5 each! So we didn't go.
TESSA: Oh, what a pity! I want to see that too. Well, I did nothing all weekend. I was ill in bed. We went to a fish and chip bar on Friday night. I expect it was that.
MURRAY: Oh, what did you have to eat?
TESSA: Fish and chips, of course! Well, Murray, it's half-past nine. It's time . . .
MURRAY: . . . for a cup of strong, black coffee. I'll make it!

Unit 16

UNIT 16

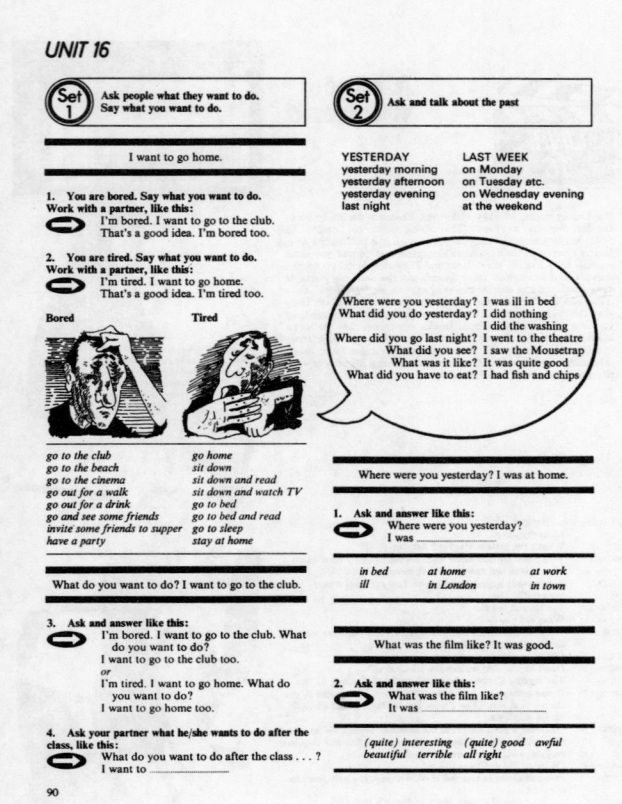

Set 1 — Ask people what they want to do. Say what you want to do.

I want to go home.

1. You are bored. Say what you want to do. Work with a partner, like this:
   - I'm bored. I want to go to the club.
   - That's a good idea. I'm bored too.

2. You are tired. Say what you want to do. Work with a partner, like this:
   - I'm tired. I want to go home.
   - That's a good idea. I'm tired too.

Bored
- go to the club
- go to the beach
- go to the cinema
- go out for a walk
- go out for a drink
- go and see some friends
- invite some friends to supper
- have a party

Tired
- go home
- sit down
- sit down and read
- sit down and watch TV
- go to bed
- go to bed and read
- go to sleep
- stay at home

What do you want to do? I want to go to the club.

3. Ask and answer like this:
   - I'm bored. I want to go to the club. What do you want to do?
   - I want to go to the club too.

   or
   - I'm tired. I want to go home. What do you want to do?
   - I want to go home too.

4. Ask your partner what he/she wants to do after the class, like this:
   - What do you want to do after the class . . . ?
   - I want to _____

90

Set 2 — Ask and talk about the past

YESTERDAY
- yesterday morning
- yesterday afternoon
- yesterday evening
- last night

LAST WEEK
- on Monday
- on Tuesday etc.
- on Wednesday evening
- at the weekend

Where were you yesterday? I was ill in bed
What did you do yesterday? I did nothing
Where did you go last night? I did the washing
What did you see? I went to the theatre
What was it like? I saw the Mousetrap
What did you have to eat? It was quite good
I had fish and chips

Where were you yesterday? I was at home.

1. Ask and answer like this:
   - Where were you yesterday?
   - I was _____

| in bed | at home | at work |
| ill | in London | in town |

What was the film like? It was good.

2. Ask and answer like this:
   - What was the film like?
   - It was _____

| (quite) interesting | (quite) good | awful |
| beautiful | terrible | all right |

SET 1 Ask people what they want to do
Say what you want to do

I want to invite some friends to dinner.

• • •• • • • •↘

Ex 1 Act out the meaning of *bored*. Introduce any new vocabulary from the BORED list and practise the pronunciation.
Give an example of the exercise.
Students work in pairs, taking the items on the list in turn or at random.

Ex 2 Act out the meaning of *tired*. Introduce the new vocabulary from the TIRED list and practise the pronunciation.
Proceed as in Ex 1.

Ex 3 What do you want to do?   I want to go to the club.

• • • • • • • • • •↘

Proceed as in Ex 1 and 2.
The *you* of What do *you* want to do? should be stressed.
Practise the two sentences together, chorally: *I want to go to the club. What do you want to do?*
Students work in pairs.

Ex 4 Students ask each other. This exercise can be done in a chain round the class so that everyone can hear the individual answers.

DIALOGUE

Before presenting the second part of the dialogue (from *Did you have a nice weekend?* to the end) write on the blackboard in large letters the words *Yesterday*, *Last weekend* and *Last night*, showing with dates or days of the week that you are referring to the past.
Some teachers may like to list the verbs as they occur in the dialogue with the past tense equivalents beside them.
The Mousetrap is a very old Agatha Christie play which has been in performance in London's West End (where many theatres are situated) for at least 25 years.
The musical about Eva Peron is a musical by Rice and Webber (famous through Jesus Christ Superstar) about the life of the young Argentinian woman dictator, Eva Peron.

SET 2 Ask and talk about the past

Where were you yesterday?

• ↘ • • •

The adverbial phrases of time and the sentences listed here draw the students' attention to the use of the past tense in the dialogue.
Practise the intonation of all the questions chorally, making sure that the questions are all spoken with a falling intonation at the end.

Ex 1–6 The same instructions apply to all these exercises.
Introduce the new vocabulary from the items for substitution and practise the pronunciation.
Practise the intonation of the question and answer chorally.
Work through one or two examples of each exercise T–S and S–T.
Students work in pairs or in a chain round the class.

Ex 7 Students ask each other similar questions.
If you show that the verbs stay the same for all personal pronouns (*I did, you did, he did* etc.) students can report their partner's answer to the rest of the class e.g.
S1: *What did you have for breakfast yesterday (Mary)?*
S2 (Mary): *I had a cup of coffee.*
S1 (to other students): *Mary had a cup of coffee for breakfast.*

UNIT 16

What did you do yesterday? I did the washing.

3. Ask and answer like this:
What did you do yesterday?
I did ....

| my homework | the ironing | the shopping |
| the housework | the washing | the garden |

Where did you go yesterday? I went to the cinema.

4. Ask and answer like this:
Where did you go yesterday?
I went to ....

the cinema	a friend's house	work
the beach		college
the club		town

What did you see? I saw The Mousetrap.

5. Ask and answer like this:
What did you see?
I saw ....

The Carlton Affair	the news	a documentary film about people at work
King Kong	a French film	
The Tower of London	Big Ben	a variety programme

What did you have for breakfast?
I had a cup of coffee.

6. Ask and answer like this:
What did you have for breakfast?
I had a .... and ....

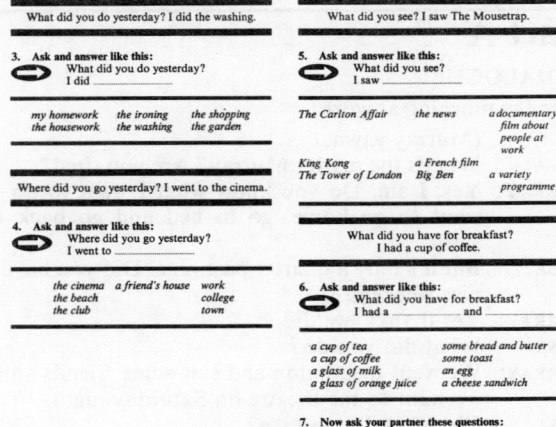

a cup of tea	some bread and butter
a cup of coffee	some toast
a glass of milk	an egg
a glass of orange juice	a cheese sandwich

7. Now ask your partner these questions:
What did you have for breakfast yesterday?
What did you have for lunch yesterday?
What did you do last night?
What did you see on television?
What was it like?
When did you go to bed?

EXTENSION

1 *Reading and writing* Students read the diary extract to themselves.
Ask a few comprehension questions e.g. *What did Jackie do in the morning? Who did she see?* etc.
Students write their own diaries in class.
Go round and help them with any new words which they may want to use.
Or, ask them to spend a few minutes preparing what they are going to write, and ask them to write the diary for homework.

2 *Reading* Explain the meaning of the new words. Show that *Wed.* is short for *Wednesday*.
Point out that when writing postcards, we often omit the subject *I* or *We*.

3 *Listening* (see tapescript page 88). Play the tape through a few times and ask the students to take notes about e.g. the weather, what the hotel was like, what Anna and Murray did on Monday night, and on Tuesday, and what Anna bought in Rome.
Students then use their notes to write a postcard modelled on the one in their books.

Open Dialogue See General Guide and tapescript (page 88).

Oral Exercises See General Guide and tapescript (page 89).

Speechwork See General Guide and tapescript (page 88).

UNIT 16

EXTENSION

1. Jackie writes her diary for last weekend

Saturday 8th — Went shopping in the morning. Saw Neville and Maria. Had lunch at an old pub outside Manchester. Did some housework in the afternoon. Went to see King Kong with Allan in the evening. Went to his flat after the film and had coffee. Back home at 1 a.m.! Allan wants to go to Madeira with me in July. Don't want to go — What shall I say to him?

Sunday 9th — Got up late. Went out for a walk. Washed my hair after lunch and did some ironing. Watched an old Hitchcock film on TV in the evening — it was very good. Went to bed early.

Now write your own diary for last weekend. Say what you did, where you went, what you saw, what time you got up or went to bed

2. George and Doris Blake went to Madeira for a holiday in January. Doris wrote this post-card to some friends

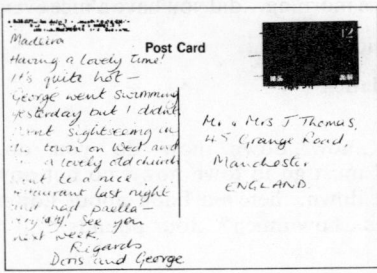

Post Card

Madeira
Having a lovely time!
It's quite hot.
George went swimming yesterday but I didn't. Went sightseeing in the town on Wed and a lovely old church. Went to a nice restaurant last night and had paella — my first. See you next week.
Regards
Doris and George

Mr. & Mrs J Thomas,
45 Grange Road,
Manchester,
ENGLAND

Unit 16

Tapescript
Part A

1 DIALOGUE
Monday morning at work
(Murray yawns)

TESSA: What's the matter Murray? Are you tired?
MURRAY: Yes, I am. Do you know what I want to do – I want to go home, go to bed and go back to sleep.
TESSA: But it's only a quarter past nine. Did you have a nice weekend?
MURRAY: Yes thanks, we did.
TESSA: What did you do?
MURRAY: We went to London and saw some friends – and we went to the theatre on Saturday night.
TESSA: Oh, what did you see?
MURRAY: Don't laugh – but we saw the Mousetrap!
TESSA: The Agatha Christie play? Did you? What was it like?
MURRAY: It was quite good. Just a detective story. We wanted to see the musical about Eva Peron, but the tickets cost £5 each! So we didn't go.
TESSA: Oh, what a pity! I want to see that too. Well, I did nothing all weekend. I was ill in bed. We went to a fish and chip bar on Friday night. I expect it was that.
MURRAY: Oh, what did you have to eat?
TESSA: Fish and chips, of course? Well, Murray, it's half past nine. It's time . . .
MURRAY: . . . for a cup of strong, black coffee. I'll make it.

2 SPEECHWORK
Part A: Stress
Say after me:

da di di da di da…what do you want to do…what do you want to see…what do you want to eat…where do you want to go…where do you want to sit…where do you want to eat…when do you want to leave…when do you want to go….

Part B: Intonation
Say after me:

¹nice day… ¹nice party… ¹nice evening… ¹nice holiday…

¹did you ¹have a ¹nice day… did you ¹have a ¹nice party…

¹did you ¹have a ¹nice morning… did you ¹have a ¹nice evening…

¹did you ¹have a ¹nice holiday…

Part C: Pronunciation
Say after me:

/aʊ/…/aʊ/…how…now…down…how do you do, Mr Brown…town…I must go to town now…no not now…sit down…please sit down…here's a book about flowers…it costs four pounds…how much?…four pounds….

3 LISTENING
Anna and Murray Freeman went to Rome for their holiday in January. Sue, a friend of Anna's comes to see her when she gets back from the holiday. Listen to their conversation, make some notes, and then write the postcard which Anna and Murray sent to Tessa and David on the last day of their holiday.

SUE: Anna! Hello – you're back!
ANNA: Sue! Come in and sit down! Yes, we got back on Sunday.
SUE: Well, what was Rome like? Hot?
ANNA: No, not hot. Not in January. But the weather was quite good. Nice and sunny but not very warm.
SUE: What was your hotel like?
ANNA: Oh, it was quite nice. Very comfortable. It was just outside the centre of Rome. Would you like some coffee?
SUE: Mmm. Please. Did you do some sightseeing?
ANNA: Oh yes. We arrived on Sunday night – Monday we didn't do much, just looked around, but on the Tuesday we spent the whole day sightseeing. We saw the Coliseum and St Peter's. What else – oh yes, an old Roman theatre.
SUE: Mmm. That sounds interesting.
ANNA: Sugar? Milk?
SUE: Just milk please. And you ate a lot of spaghetti did you?
ANNA: No. We had spaghetti the first night. That was Monday night. We went to a little restaurant, a trattoria, in a small street near the Coliseum and had a large plate of spaghetti each.
SUE: And?
ANNA: And Murray was ill all night!
SUE: Oh no!
ANNA: Yes, I don't know why. But he was all right on the Tuesday. So – it was no more spaghetti for us!
SUE: Did you buy anything nice?
ANNA: Mmm. Look, I bought this suitcase. Beautiful, isn't it?
SUE: Mmm, yes, it's lovely, Anna.
ANNA: More coffee?
SUE: No thanks. I must go. Well, it was nice to hear all about the holiday. Love to Murray.
ANNA: Yes, OK. See you, Sue. Bye!
SUE: Bye.

4 OPEN DIALOGUE
Talk to Jackie.

JACKIE: Hello! How are you?
STUDENT: ....
JACKIE: Oh, fine thanks. Did you have a nice weekend?
STUDENT: ....
JACKIE: What did you do? Where did you go?
STUDENT: ....
JACKIE: What did you see on TV – a film? The news?
STUDENT: ....
JACKIE: You sound tired. What time did you go to bed last night?
STUDENT: ....
JACKIE: Well, I went to bed at two, and I didn't have any breakfast this morning. What did you have?
STUDENT: ....
JACKIE: Mmm, that sounds good! Well, I must go and get a cup of coffee. Bye!
STUDENT: ....

Unit 16

Part B ORAL EXERCISES

Exercise 1 Ask people about the past.
Ask Murray if he had a nice weekend.
Did you have a nice weekend, Murray?
Ask Tessa if she had a nice evening.
Did you have a nice evening Tessa? Now go on.
Ask Neville if he had a nice lunch.
Did you have a nice lunch, Neville?
Ask Anna if she had a nice holiday.
Did you have a nice holiday, Anna?
Ask Jackie if she had a nice party.
Did you have a nice party, Jackie?
Ask Sally if she had a nice walk.
Did you have a nice walk, Sally?

Exercise 2 Ask people about the past again.
Ask Murray what he did yesterday.
What did you do yesterday, Murray?
Ask Tessa where she went yesterday.
Where did you go yesterday, Tessa? Now go on.
Ask Neville what he saw on television last night.
What did you see on television last night, Neville?
Ask Jackie what she had for breakfast.
What did you have for breakfast, Jackie?
Ask George where he was last night.
Where were you last night, George?
Ask Murray what the film was like.
What was the film like, Murray?

Exercise 3 Ask people to repeat statements.
I went to the cinema last night.
Sorry! Where did you go?
I did my homework yesterday.
Sorry! What did you do? Now go on.
I saw a documentary film on television last night.
Sorry! What did you see?
I had a cup of tea and an egg for breakfast this morning.
Sorry! What did you have?
I went to London at the weekend.
Sorry! Where did you go?
I had fish and chips for lunch today.
Sorry! What did you have?

Exercise 4 Say what people did in the past.
Answer these questions from the dialogue.
Where did Murray and Anna go on Saturday (which town)?
They went to London.
Who did they see?
They saw some friends. Now go on.
Where did they go on Saturday night?
They went to the theatre.
What play did they see?
They saw The Mousetrap.
What did Tessa do all weekend?
She did nothing.
Why did she do nothing?
She was ill in bed.
Where did she and David go on Friday?
They went to a fish and chip bar.
What did they have to eat?
They had fish and chips.

Exercise 5 Ask what people want to do. Look at page 90.
I'm bored.
Do you want to go to the club?
She's bored.
Does she want to go to the beach? Now go on.
He's bored.
Does he want to go to the cinema?
I'm bored.
Do you want to go out for a walk?
We're bored.
Do you want to go out for a drink?
They're bored.
Do they want to go and see some friends?
I'm bored.
Do you want to invite some friends to supper?
She's bored.
Does she want to have a party?

Exercise 6 Say what you want to do. Look at page 90.
What's the matter?
I'm tired. I want to go home.
What's the matter?
I'm tired. I want to sit down and read. Now go on.
What's the matter?
I'm tired. I want to sit down and watch television.
What's the matter?
I'm tired. I want to go to bed.
What's the matter?
I'm tired. I want to go to bed and read.
What's the matter?
I'm tired. I want to go to sleep.
What's the matter?
I'm tired. I want to stay at home.

UNIT 17 An invitation

	Skills	Functions	Example Sentences	Main Structures	
SET 1	1. Roleplay 2. Speaking 3. Speaking	Answer the telephone Say your name on the telephone Start a conversation	872 4679. Hello?/Is that Jackie?/ Yes, speaking. It's Allan here./How are you?/Fine thanks. And you?/Oh, all right.		
SET 2	1. Speaking 2. Writing 3. Speaking	Arrange to meet somebody	Are you free this evening? Yes, I am/No, I'm afraid I'm not.	On Monday/Tuesday etc. This Tomorrow	morning afternoon evening
SET 3	1. Speaking 2. Writing 3. Roleplay 4. Speaking	Invite people to do things Accept and refuse to do things Say you are pleased Say you are disappointed Make parting remarks	Would you like to go to the cinema? Yes, I'd love to. Sorry, I'm afraid I can't. Oh, good! Oh, what a pity! Bye! See you later/on Friday.	Would you like to I'd/I would love to.	go to the cinema? go out for a meal? come to lunch?
EXTENSION	1. Listening 2. Reading and Writing 3. Listening	Record telephone announcement about cinema programmes in Manchester. Students fill in times of the performances. Invitation card: letter of reply (accepting the invitation). Students write their own reply, accepting or refusing. College announcement about a coming event. Students write down the important facts.			

OPEN DIALOGUE

ORAL EXERCISES	1. Ask people if they are free	Ask Murray if he's free on Wednesday morning *Are you free on Wednesday morning, Murray?*
	2. Say when you are free	Are you free on Monday evening? *Monday evening? Yes, I am.*
	3. Invite people to do things	I'm free this evening. *Oh, would you like to go to the cinema?*
	4. Accept or refuse invitations	Would you like to go to the cinema tonight? *Yes, I'd love to/No, I'm afraid I can't.*
	5. Respond to these remarks	How are you? *Fine thanks. And you?* I'm sorry. I can't come to the cinema tonight. *Oh, what a pity!*

SPEECHWORK			ACTIVE VOCABULARY		
A STRESS	Monday afternoon ●·●·●		night diary invitation football tonight this (evening) lunchtime before after	well free ring (rang) come (came) bring (brought)	why? speaking how are you? Fine, thanks! What a pity! Oh good! I'd love to See you (on Friday) wait a moment
B INTONATION	Are you free on Monday? I'm free on Monday, but not Tuesday.				
C PRONUNCIATION	/ɑː/ can't, afternoon.				

Unit 17

DIALOGUE

The dialogue can be presented in two parts, breaking at *Jackie: Oh, all right.*
Telephone conversations are often difficult for foreigners. Answering the phone, saying your name etc. involve a slightly different use of structures that are otherwise familiar e.g. *Is that Jackie?* and *It's Allan here.*

SET 1 Answer the telephone
   Say your name on the telephone
   Start a conversation

Ex 1 872 4679 Hello? Is that Jackie?

Yes, speaking. Hello, it's Allan here.

Go through the exercise in sections.
Students repeat chorally and individually.
First practise saying all the telephone numbers; then the question *Is that Tessa?/Maria?/Murray?*; and finally *Hello, it's Murray/Neville/George here.*
Choose a student to take the part of Tessa. You are Murray. Give an example of the first telephone call.
Students work in pairs. Both partners should have the opportunity to be the caller and the 'called' in turn.

Ex 2 How are you? Fine, thanks! And you? Oh, all right.

Practise each phrase chorally and individually.
Practise T-S round the class (or with as many students as possible), then S-T, and finally S-S in pairs or in a chain around the class.

Ex 3 Ask one student to telephone you. You start by saying your number. The student can read the original dialogue from the book but must substitute your name and his name where appropriate.
Students telephone each other, changing parts afterwards.

An Invitation

UNIT 17

JACKIE:	872 4679. Hello?
ALLAN:	Is that Jackie?
JACKIE:	Yes, speaking.
ALLAN:	Hello, it's Allan here.
JACKIE:	Oh, hello Allan! How are you?
ALLAN:	Fine thanks! And you?
JACKIE:	Oh, all right.
ALLAN:	I didn't see you at work today.
JACKIE:	No, I wasn't well. I was at home but I'm all right now.
ALLAN:	Oh good. Listen, are you free on Thursday evening?
JACKIE:	No, I'm afraid I'm not.
ALLAN:	Oh, what a pity! What about this evening? Are you free this evening?
JACKIE:	Yes, I am. Why?

Set 1 Answer the telephone
Say your name on the telephone
Start a conversation

872 4679 Hello?   Is that Jackie?
Yes, speaking.   Hello, it's Allan here.

1. Roleplaying
Work in pairs. Take both parts in turn.

Murray rings Tessa. Tessa's telephone number is 354 5223.
Neville rings Maria. Maria's telephone number is 477 9372.
George rings Murray. Murray's telephone number is 678 1013.

How are you?
Fine thanks! And you?
Oh, all right.

2. Practise this exchange with your partner

3. Telephone your partner: remember what you practised in Exercises 1 and 2

Unit 17

UNIT 17

Set 2 Arrange to meet somebody

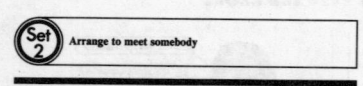

| Are you free on Thursday evening? | No, I'm afraid I'm not. |
| Are you free this evening? | Yes, I am. |

Today	Tomorrow	Thursday
this morning	tomorrow morning	on Thursday morning
this afternoon	tomorrow afternoon	on Thursday afternoon
this evening	tomorrow evening	on Thursday evening
tonight	tomorrow night	on Thursday night

Martha is a doctor. She works in a hospital.
This is her diary for the week.

Diary
- Monday: Hospital 8 a.m. – 4 p.m.
- Tuesday: night duty 8 p.m. – 8 a.m.
- Wednesday: free / 7 p.m. see Ann
- Thursday: hospital 8 a.m. – 4 p.m.
- Friday: hospital 8 a.m. – 4 p.m. / cinema 7.15 p.m. – Peter
- Saturday: shopping in morning / hospital 6 p.m. – 1 a.m.
- Sunday: lunch with Mother

1. Work in pairs. One of you is Martha. Ask Martha if she is free at these times:

   Monday evening
   Tuesday evening
   Wednesday afternoon
   Wednesday evening
   Thursday morning
   Friday evening
   Saturday afternoon
   Sunday at lunchtime
   Sunday evening

   Ask and answer like this:
   - Are you free on Monday evening?
   - Yes, I am.
   - Oh good! Are you free on Tuesday evening?
   - No, I'm afraid I'm not.
   - What a pity!
   - Are you free on _____

2. Write a diary like Martha's for yourself

3. Work in pairs, with your diaries. Ask your partner if he/she is free at these times:

   1. this evening
   2. tomorrow morning
   3. tomorrow afternoon
   4. tomorrow night
   5. on Saturday afternoon
   6. on Saturday evening
   7. on Sunday evening

96

UNIT 17

ALLAN: Well, would you like to go to the cinema tonight?
JACKIE: Yes, I'd love to. What a lovely idea!
ALLAN: What would you like to see? The Carlton Affair? Single Ticket to Death?
JACKIE: No, not Single Ticket to Death. I saw that last year. It's an old film. Let's go and see The Carlton Affair. What time does it start?
ALLAN: Let's see... er... it starts at 8.30. It's at the Odeon cinema.
JACKIE: Well, where shall we meet and when?
ALLAN: Let's meet outside the cinema just before eight thirty.
JACKIE: All right. See you then. Thanks for ringing. Bye!
ALLAN: Bye! See you later.

(Speech bubble: Well, would you like to go to the cinema tonight? / Yes, I'd love to)

**Set 3 Invite people to do things
Accept invitations to do things
Refuse invitations to do things**

Would you like to go to the cinema tonight?
Yes, I'd love to. or
Sorry, I'm afraid I can't.

1. Ask and answer like this:
   - Would you like to go to the cinema tomorrow?
   - Yes, I'd love to. or Sorry, I'm afraid I can't.
   - Would you like to _____?

go to the cinema	go out for a meal	come to lunch
go to the beach	go out for a drink	come to dinner
go to the club	go out for a walk	come to my house
go to a disco		

2. Joe telephones Maria, but she's out. So he writes her a note. Write invitations to three friends inviting them to:

   1. The cinema/Friday evening/King Kong
   2. Dinner/Saturday evening
   3. A meal/tomorrow evening

(Handwritten note: Dear Maria, Would you like to meet me for a drink on Saturday at lunchtime? Please ring me if you are free. My number is 456 0207. Yours, Joe.)

97

DIALOGUE

Play second part of dialogue from *Allan: I didn't see you at work today* to *Jackie: Yes I am*.

SET 2 Arrange to meet somebody

Look at the adverbial phrases of time. Indicate with real dates the meaning of *today, tomorrow* and *Thursday*.
Explain that *evening* and *night*, in terms of fixing dates and appointments, usually mean the same e.g. *Are you free this evening/tonight?* But point out that you say *tonight* and not *this night*.
Look at Martha's diary with the students.
Ask simple *yes/no* questions like *Is she free on Monday morning?* so that the students have a chance to sort out the information before doing the exercise in pairs.

Ex 1 Are you free on Thursday evening?

No, I'm afraid I'm not.

Are you free this evening?   Yes, I am.

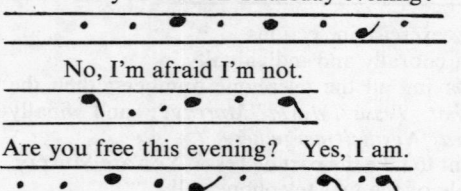

Practise the intonation of the question and answers.
Give one or two examples of the exercise using Martha's diary as the basis for the answers.
Practise the two phrases *Oh good!* and *What a pity!*
Students work in pairs changing parts perhaps halfway through the exercise.

Ex 2 Students write their own diaries for the week.
Do not be too particular about how accurately or in what language they write down their engagements.
An alternative is for them to mark *FREE* or *NOT FREE* in the different parts of the day for each day of the week.

Ex 3 Students work in pairs as in Ex 1, using their own diaries as a basis for their answers.

DIALOGUE

Help to set the context of this conversation (from *Allan: Well, would you like to go to the cinema tonight?* to the end) by writing on the blackboard the names of two cinemas and the names of the two films mentioned, and the starting times.
Students often get confused by the change from *Would you like to . . . ?* to *Yes, I'd love to* and tend to say *Yes, I'd like to* instead.
Explain that *love to* is a polite response and not in fact very strong. *I'd like to* is not polite enough (unless spoken very sincerely).

SET 3 Invite people to do things
Accept and refuse invitations to do things

Ex 1 Would you like to go to the cinema tonight?

Yes, I'd love to./Sorry, I'm afraid I can't.

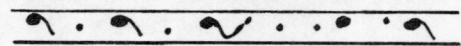

Unit 17

Go through the lists of 'invitations' and practise the pronunciation and especially the stress of the phrases. (Teachers should feel free to change or add to this list e.g. the beach, the club and the disco could be replaced by other places which are more relevant to the students' interests.

Practise the intonation of the question and the responses. Give a few examples of invitations varying the time e.g. *tonight/tomorrow/on Friday* and giving alternative responses.

Students work in pairs, inviting each other to do things at certain times.

Their answers should be as true as possible – they can refer to their diaries.

Ex 2 Read the note from Joe to Maria with the students. Together with the class, compose a note for Example 1 (an invitation to the cinema on Friday evening) and write it on the blackboard.

Write your own telephone number and name.

Students write their own notes for Examples 2 and 3 in class or for homework.

Ex 3 Choose a good student and act out the roleplay as simply as possible. Students do the same in pairs.

Ex 4 Students spend a few minutes preparing their conversation. All the students should be prepared to be the 'inviter'.

Students work in pairs. Afterwards ask one pair to give a 'public' performance.

EXTENSION

1 *Listening* Play the tape once or twice, pausing at relevant places so that the students can fill in the times.
Check their times afterwards.

2 *Writing* The invitation: explain *R.S.V.P.* and *Please bring a bottle*.
The letter: explain *very informal*.
Ask the students to suggest ways of refusing the invitation e.g. *I'm afraid I can't/I'm sorry I can't come* plus a simple excuse e.g. *I'm going to London that evening*.
Students write their own letters in class or for homework.

3 *Listening* This is an announcement made in a noisy students' common room. There is a lot of background noise and interruptions which may make it difficult for the students to extract the message. Play once through without stopping so that the students can feel the atmosphere. Ask the questions orally; if few students are able to answer, play the passage once again, stopping at the relevant places.

Open Dialogue See General Guide and tapescript (page 94).

Oral Exercises See General Guide and tapescript (page 95).

Speechwork See General Guide and tapescript (page 94).

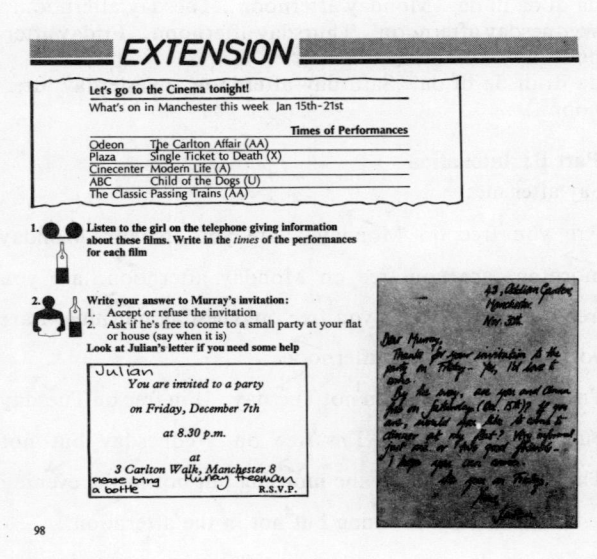

Unit 17

Tapescript
Part A

1 DIALOGUE
JACKIE: 872 4679. Hello?
ALLAN: Is that Jackie?
JACKIE: Yes, speaking.
ALLAN: Hello, it's Allan here.
JACKIE: Oh, hello Allan! How are you?
ALLAN: Fine thanks! And you?
JACKIE: Oh, all right.
ALLAN: I didn't see you at work today.
JACKIE: No, I wasn't well. I was at home but I'm all right now.
ALLAN: Oh good. Listen, are you free on Thursday evening?
JACKIE: No, I'm afraid I'm not.
ALLAN: Oh, what a pity! What about this evening? Are you free this evening?
JACKIE: Yes, I am. Why?
ALLAN: Well, would you like to go to the cinema tonight?
JACKIE: Yes, I'd love to. What a lovely idea!
ALLAN: What would you like to see? The Carlton Affair? Single Ticket to Death?
JACKIE: No, not Single Ticket to Death. I saw that last year. It's an old film.
Let's go and see The Carlton Affair. What time does it start?
ALLAN: Let's see . . . er . . . it starts at 8.30. It's at the Odeon cinema.
JACKIE: Well, where shall we meet and when?
ALLAN: Let's meet outside the cinema just before eight-thirty.
JACKIE: All right. See you then. Thanks for ringing. Bye!
ALLAN: Bye! See you later.

2 SPEECHWORK
Part A: Stress
Say after me:
da di da di da...Monday afternoon...Tuesday afternoon...Wednesday afternoon...Thursday afternoon...Friday afternoon...
da di di da di da...Saturday afternoon... yesterday afternoon...

Part B: Intonation
Say after me:
Are you 'free on Monday... are you 'free on 'Monday morning...are you 'free on 'Monday afternoon...are you 'free on Tuesday...are you 'free on 'Tuesday morning... are you 'free on 'Tuesday afternoon.
I'm 'free on Monday but 'not Tuesday... I'm 'free on Tuesday but 'not Wednesday...I'm 'free on Wednesday but 'not Thursday...I'm 'free in the morning but 'not in the evening ...I'm free in the morning but 'not in the 'afternoon...

Part C: Pronunciation
Say after me:
/ɑː/.../ɑː/...are...car...Father...this is my father's car... Martin...how are you, Martin...this afternoon... are you free this afternoon...a party...come to a party...it starts at half past four...Karin...ask Karin too...See you this afternoon...

3 LISTENING (1)
Listen to the information and write the times of the performances in your books.

(Pip)...this is a recorded message...cinema programmes in Manchester this week.
The Odeon is showing *The Carlton Affair,* certificate AA. There are three performances starting at two-thirty, five-thirty and eight-thirty. The Plaza is showing *Single Ticket to Death,* certificate X. There are two performances, starting at five-thirty and at eight-fifteen. The Cinecenter is showing *Modern Life,* certificate A: one performance only, starting at seven-thirty. The ABC is showing *Child of the Dogs,* certificate AA: two performances, starting at five-thirty and eight-thirty. The Classic is showing *Passing Trains,* certificate AA: two performances, starting at two-thirty and at seven-thirty. (Pip)...This is a recorded message...cinema programmes in Manchester this week...

LISTENING (2)
Listen to the students' meeting and answer the questions in your book.

Voice: (clears throat)...er...hello...can you listen please... I want to make an announcement...(chatter continues)... can you *listen* please, I want to say something...thank you ...it's just to announce that there is going to be a pop concert...(what?)...a pop concert here at the college on Friday at lunchtime from 12.30 to 1.30 (when?) sshh can I have a bit of hush please...I'll say that again...on Friday at 12.30...(you mean lunch time?) yes, during the lunch-break from 12.30-1.30...the tickets are 40 pence each... (Booh...40p...too much...) come on that's not very much ...in London it would be 80p...so 40p a ticket...if you're free on Friday at lunchtime please come to the concert, you can eat your sandwiches while you listen to the music... (who's playing?)...*The City Slickers* and *Rae Rowland*.... (mutters of surprise)...if you would like to buy a ticket can you please see Sally, the secretary... (chatter increases) sshhh...I'll say that again...can you please see Sally the secretary *before* Thursday...get that?...*before* Thursday. Thank you...

4 OPEN DIALOGUE
Look at the cinema programme on page 98.
Your telephone is ringing. Answer it. Brrr! Brrr! Brrr!

STUDENT: ....
MURRAY: Hello! It's Murray here.
STUDENT: ....
MURRAY: How are you?
STUDENT: ....
MURRAY: Oh, I'm all right. Did you have a nice weekend?
STUDENT: ....
MURRAY: Look, are you free this week on Friday or Saturday evening?

STUDENT: ....
MURRAY: Oh, good! Well, would you like to go to the cinema?
STUDENT: ....
MURRAY: Well, have a look at the programmes. What would you like to see?
STUDENT: ....
MURRAY: Mmm! All right. That sounds good. What time would you like to go?
STUDENT: ....
MURRAY: All right. Shall I meet you at your house?
STUDENT: ....
MURRAY: Oh, wait a moment! Where do you live? I don't remember.
STUDENT: ....
MURRAY: Oh, yes, of course. What time shall I come?
STUDENT: ....
MURRAY: All right. I'll see you then. Bye!
STUDENT: ....

I'm free on Saturday afternoon.
....
What shall we do this afternoon?
....
I'd like to meet your mother and father.
....
Isn't it a beautiful day!
....
I'd like something to eat. I'm hungry.
....
Phew! The weather is hot!
....
I don't want to go home just now.
....
What shall we do tomorrow?
....

Part B ORAL EXERCISES

Exercise 1 Ask people if they are free.
Ask Murray if he's free on Wednesday morning.
Are you free on Wednesday morning, Murray?
See if Sally is free tomorrow evening.
Are you free tomorrow evening, Sally? Now go on.
And check with Martha about Saturday night.
Are you free on Saturday night, Martha?
Also, see if Neville is free on Friday evening.
Are you free on Friday evening, Neville?
And ask if Tessa is free tomorrow afternoon.
Are you free tomorrow afternoon, Tessa?
And check with George about the same time.
Are you free tomorrow afternoon, George?

Exercise 2 Say when you are free. Look at Martha's diary.
Are you free on Monday evening?
Monday evening? Yes, I am.
Are you free on Tuesday evening?
Tuesday evening, No, I'm afraid I'm not. Now go on.
What about Wednesday afternoon? Are you free then?
Wednesday afternoon? Yes, I am.
And in the evening?
The evening? No, I'm afraid I'm not.
Are you free on Friday morning?
Friday morning? No, I'm afraid I'm not.
What about Sunday afternoon? I hope you're free then.
Sunday afternoon? Yes, I am.

Exercise 3 Invite people to do things. Look at page 97. and choose something suitable.
I'm free this evening.
Oh, would you like to go to the cinema?
What shall we do on Saturday afternoon?
Would you like to go to the theatre? Now go on.
I'm free this evening.
....

Exercise 4 Refuse or accept invitations.
Accept or refuse the invitations as *you* wish.
Would you like to go to the cinema tonight?
Yes, I'd love to.
Would you like to go to the cinema tonight?
No, I'm afraid I can't. Now go on.
Would you like to come to Tessa's birthday party on Saturday?
....
Would you like to come out for a walk this afternoon?
....
Would you like to come out for a meal with me tomorrow evening?
....
Would you like to come to the theatre on Saturday afternoon?
....
Would you like to come to supper with us this evening?
....

Exercise 5 Respond to these remarks.
What would you say?
How are you?
Fine thanks, And you?
I'm sorry I can't come to the cinema with you tonight.
Oh, what a pity! Now go on.
But I can come to your birthday party.
....
And I wondered if you would like to come to the football match with me on Saturday?
....
And are you free for lunch someday next week?
....
O.K. – let's meet then, but anyway I'll see you at your birthday party on Sunday.

UNIT 18   Going to work

	Skills	Functions	Example Sentences	Main Structures
SET 1	1. Roleplay 2. Speaking 3. Speaking 4. Speaking	Ask and say how people get to work Say how you get to work	*How do you get to work?* *I go by bus.*	*How do you get* to work? *does he travel* to college? to school? *I go/he goes* etc by car by bus by train

SET 2	1. Speaking
	    Speaking and
	    Writing
	3. Speaking
	4–7. Speaking
		Ask and say how often people do things
		Say how often you do things
			Do you ever go by bus?
			No, never.
			He usually goes by car.
				I walk/he walks
				I cycle/he cycles
				*I always/usually/often/sometimes/
				never go by car.*

SET 3	1. Speaking 2. Speaking	Ask and say how far places are	*How far is it to work?* *It's about seven miles.*	*How long does the journey/it take you/him* etc?
SET 4	1. Speaking 2. Speaking	Ask and say how long journeys take	*How long does it take?* *It takes about 25 minutes.*	*It takes me/him* etc. *about 20 minutes.*
SET 5	1. Speaking 2. Speaking	Ask and say how much things cost	*How much does it cost?* *It costs about £1.*	*Half a mile one and a half miles.* *an hour two and a half miles* etc.

EXTENSION	1. Listening,
	   Speaking and
	   Writing
		Interview with people, on how they get to work. Students mark in information about method, distance, cost and time as they listen to the interviews. They interview partners and note the same information.		

	2. Graph
	   Reading and
	   Writing
		Group work to interpret graphs and write generalised report (a few statements) about them.		

	3. Listening	Game. Sound effects of different types of transport.		
	4. Reading	Two Reading Texts: Newspaper article on traffic. Press Release from C.R.A.G.		

OPEN DIALOGUE

ORAL EXERCISES		
	1. Ask people at Focus how they get to work	*How do you get to work, Murray? By car?* *Yes, that's right.*
	2. Say how you get to work	*How do you get to work, Murray?* *I go by car.*
	3. Say how people usually get to work (1)	*How does Murray get to work?* *He always goes by car.*
	4. Say how people usually get to work (2)	*Does Murray ever go by car?* *Yes, he always does.*
	5. Ask how long it takes people to get to work	*Murray lives about seven miles away.* *How long does his journey take by car?*
	6. Talk about distance and time to get to work	*How far is it to work, Murray?* *It's about 7 miles. It takes about 25 minutes by car.*

SPEECHWORK

A STRESS	How long did it take? ● ● .. ●
B INTONATION	I usually go by bus.
C PRONUNCIATION	/h/ How much, hello.

ACTIVE VOCABULARY

article	kilometre	always	ask
journey	question	usually	travel
tax	per cent	often	get to
insurance	traffic	sometimes	take
rush-hour	accident	never	cost
bicycle			walk
petrol	how?	about	cycle
	how far?	however	
minute	how long?	whereas	by (by bus)
hour	nothing		
mile			angry

Unit 18

Going to work

DIALOGUE
This dialogue should be presented initially as a whole for the sake of continuity. It can be divided into parts for intensive practice subsequently.

Explain the new Traffic vocabulary: *rush-hour, petrol,* and *car tax and insurance.*

Students may find it interesting to convert *miles* into *kilometres,* and English money into their own national currency, and thus compare the costs of travel.

And how long does it take?

Er... let's see... it usually takes about twenty-five minutes. That's in the rush-hour, of course.

(from the Manchester News)
Manchester Traffic Problem Increases
An accident in the centre of Manchester on Friday night brought traffic to a standstill for one hour. One motorist left his office at 6 o'clock and got home at half-past eight. He lives seven miles away. Asked why he did not turn around and try another route, he answered: 'There is only one route through the centre of Manchester. It's all one way now!'

The traffic problem is the same in the rush hour. 'The only people who get to work on time are cyclists,' said another angry motorist. 'If Manchester Council doesn't improve the traffic system I shall buy a bicycle.'

Mr J. H. Jones, from the Manchester Council made this comment: 'The one-way system is all right; it's the number of motorists that's wrong. It's a mystery to me why more people don't leave their cars at home and travel by train or cycle to work.'

Sally Baker is writing an article on car pollution. She asks some people at Focus Films about their journey to work.

MURRAY: Hello Sally. I saw your article yesterday in the Manchester News. It was very good.
SALLY: Oh thanks. Well, I'm writing another one now. Can you answer some questions?
MURRAY: Er... Yes... What about?
SALLY: About your journey to work, how you travel, how far it is and that sort of thing.
MURRAY: Oh... Oh yes of course.
SALLY: Oh good! Well, how do you get to work?
MURRAY: I go by car.
SALLY: By car... Mmm... and how far is it?
MURRAY: It's about seven miles.
SALLY: And how long does it take?
MURRAY: Er... let's see... it usually takes about twenty-five minutes. That's in the rush-hour, of course.
SALLY: Yes . . . and how much does it cost you?
MURRAY: Cost? Nothing! Oh, I see—you mean in petrol?
SALLY: Yes—and in tax and insurance.
MURRAY: Oh, well, about 50p in petrol and about another 50p in tax and insurance, I suppose. About a pound altogether.
SALLY: And how much does it cost by bus, do you know?
MURRAY: By bus? Er... about 50p.
SALLY: Do you ever go by bus?
MURRAY: No, never. I went by bus once and I was an hour late for work.
SALLY: I see. Thank you.

SET 1 Ask and say how people get to work
Say how you get to work

The chart in Unit 18 is the basis for work in all the sets. Copy the chart on to an overhead stencil and block out with a piece of paper the parts of the chart which are not relevant to the Set. As each Set progresses, uncover the next part of the chart.

Ex 1 How do you get to work? I go by bus/I walk.

• • • • • • • • • • • •

Direct the students' attention to the first line of the chart. Practise the intonation of the question and answer chorally. Point out that you say *go by bus/car/train* but *walk* and not *go by foot.* (It is possible to say *go on foot* but this is relatively uncommon.)

Give an example of the exercise.

Students work in pairs, taking turns to ask and answer.

Ex 2 Students ask each other how they get to *work/school/college.*

Give an example first, choosing a student in the class to answer your question.

Ex 3 How does Murray get to work? He goes by car.

• • • • • • • • • • •

Practise the pronunciation and intonation of the question and answer.
Give an example of the exercise. Students work in pairs.

Ex 4 Students ask, about somebody in the class *How does (Mary) get to work, (Peter)?* Give an example first.

UNIT 18

Set 1 Ask and say how people get to work
Say how you get to work

How do you get to work? I go by car/bus/train
                         I walk

1. Roleplaying
Work with your partner. Look at the chart. One of you answers for the people at Focus Films, like this:
  How do you get to work, Murray?
  I go by car.

  How do you get to work, George?
  I _____

Name	Murray Freeman	George Blake	Jackie Young	Allan Simmons	Tessa Richards
Method of transport	car	bus	walks	train and bus	car
Distance to work in miles	7	2	½	8	5½
Time	25 mins	15 mins	10 mins	45 mins	20 mins
Cost of journey (single)	75p	20p	—	55p	60p

2. Ask your partner how he gets to work/school/college, like this:
  How do you get to work/school/college, _____ ?
  I _____

How does Murray get to work? He goes by car.

3. Ask and answer about the people at Focus Films, like this:
  How does Murray get to work?
  He goes by car.

  How does George get to work?
  He _____

4. Ask somebody in the class about their partner, like this:
  How does _____ get to work/school/college?
  He/she _____

Unit 18

Set 2 — Ask and say how often people do things
Say how often you do things

Getting to work

MURRAY:	always by car — never by bus
GEORGE:	usually by bus — sometimes cycles
JACKIE:	often walks — sometimes by bus
ALLAN:	usually by train and bus — sometimes by car
TESSA:	always by car — never by bus

Do you ever go by bus? No, never.

1. Ask the people at Focus about their journeys to work again. Ask and answer like this:

    Do you ever go by bus, Murray?
    No, never.

    Do you ever cycle, George?
    Yes, sometimes.

2. Ask your partner if he/she ever goes by car
    goes by bus
    goes by train
    walks
    cycles
    Write down what he/she says. Then tell the class

    How does Murray get to work? He always goes by car.

3. Ask and answer about the Focus people like this:
    How does George get to work?   He usually goes by bus but he sometimes cycles.
    How does _____ get to work?   He/she _____

4. Ask your partner like this:
    How do you get to work _____? I _____ (but _____)

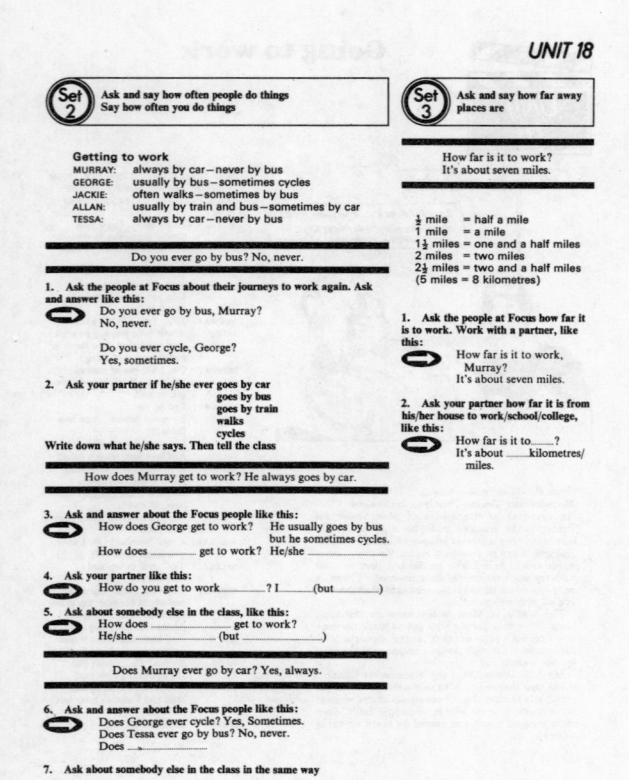

5. Ask about somebody else in the class, like this:
    How does _____ get to work?
    He/she _____ (but _____)

    Does Murray ever go by car? Yes, always.

6. Ask and answer about the Focus people like this:
    Does George ever cycle? Yes, Sometimes.
    Does Tessa ever go by bus? No, never.
    Does _____

7. Ask about somebody else in the class in the same way

Set 3 — Ask and say how far away places are

How far is it to work?
It's about seven miles.

½ mile = half a mile
1 mile = a mile
1½ miles = one and a half miles
2 miles = two miles
2½ miles = two and a half miles
(5 miles = 8 kilometres)

1. Ask the people at Focus how far it is to work. Work with a partner, like this:

    How far is it to work, Murray?
    It's about seven miles.

2. Ask your partner how far it is from his/her house to work/school/college, like this:

    How far is it to _____?
    It's about _____ kilometres/miles.

103

SET 2 Ask and say how often people do things
Say how often you do things

Present the adverbs of frequency in a decreasing order of frequency: *always; usually; often; sometimes; never.*
This can be indicated on a frequency chart with ticks (perhaps a class register showing how often people attend classes).
Practise the pronunciation of the adverbs.

Ex 1 Do you ever go by bus?   No, never.

Practise the intonation of the question and answer.
Give an example using the chart 'Getting to work'.
Two questions can be asked about each person.
Students work in pairs, or in a chain round the class.

Ex 2 Students ask each other similar questions and note down the answers.
Give an example and write down the answer on the blackboard e.g. *Mary – usually by train; sometimes by bus.*

Ex 3 How does Murray get to work?   He always goes by car.

Point out the position of the frequency adverbs: they always go before the main verb. It might help here to do a substitution drill e.g.

Mary always goes by bus.   train
Mary always goes by train.   sometimes
Mary sometimes goes by train.   John   etc.

Change the names, the adverbs and the method of transport.
Practise the intonation of the question and answer.
Give some examples of the exercise using the chart again, showing how to combine sentences where necessary.
Work T-S through the exercise once, and then possibly S-S.

Ex 4 Students ask each other how they get to work/school. Answers can be simple e.g. *I always go by train* or complex e.g. *I usually go by train but I sometimes go by bus.*

Ex 5 Students ask students from other pairs about how their partners get to work. The student who is answering can refer to his notes from Ex 2.

Ex 6 The questions about how Focus people get to work require only brief answers.

Ex 7 As in Ex 6.

SET 3 Ask and say how far away places are
How far is it to work?   It's about seven miles.

Some teachers may prefer to talk in terms of *kilometres*. In this case practise also *half a kilometre, one and a half kilometres* etc. (But when the students answer for the people at Focus, they should express the distance in *miles*.)

Ex 1 Proceed as in Set 1 Ex 1.

Ex 2 Proceed as in Set 1 Ex 2.

SET 4 Ask and say how long journeys take

How long does it take?   It takes about 25 minutes.

Ex 1 Practise saying times before doing this exercise (see note in Students Book).
Proceed as in Set 1 Ex 1.

Ex 2 Proceed as in Set 1 Ex 2.

SET 5 Ask and say how much things cost

How much does it cost?   It costs about one pound.

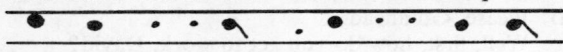

Ex 1 Proceed as in Set 1 Ex 1.

Ex 2 Students can give the cost of their own journeys in their own currency if they are not resident in England.

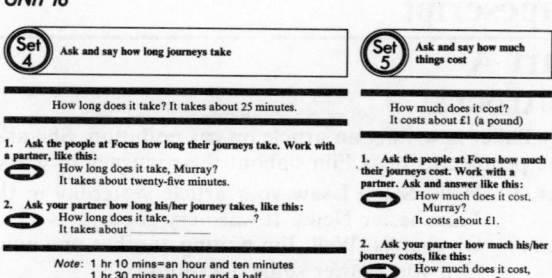

EXTENSION

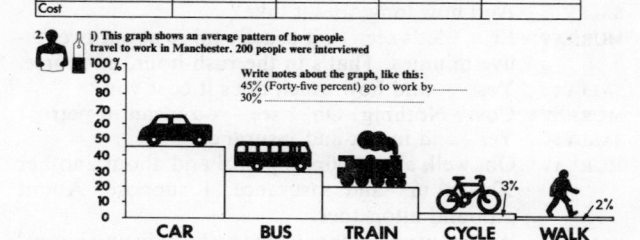

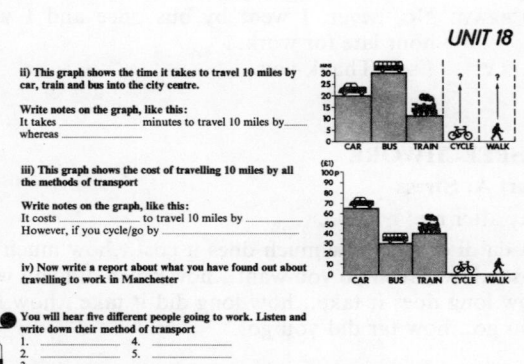

1 *Listening* The students listen to the interviews with three other people and fill in the information as they listen.
Check the answers after each of the interviews.
Students in pairs interview each other. It may help to ask them to write down first what questions they are going to ask so that the interview runs more smoothly.
As they interview their partner, they write in the answers in the spare column on the chart.

2 These graphs can be studied in groups. All members of each group write notes on the graphs.
When the three graphs have been studied and notes taken, the groups re-form so that the new groups consist of a representative from each of the original groups (see Introduction: General Teaching Notes (page vii).
In the new groups the answers are compared and general conclusions about travelling in Manchester can be discussed in preparation for a written report (for homework).

3 *Listening* Recognition of the method of transport is based on sound effects. This is a fairly easy game and can be saved for the last five minutes of class time as a form of relaxation.

Open Dialogue See General Guide and tapescript (page 101).

Oral Exercises See General Guide and tapescript (page 101).

Speechwork See General Guide and tapescript (page 100).

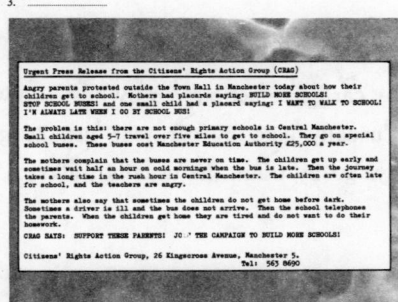

Unit 18

Tapescript
Part A

1 DIALOGUE
Sally Baker is writing an article on car pollution. She asks some people at Focus Films about their journey to work.

MURRAY: Hello Sally, I saw your article yesterday in the Manchester News. It was very good.
SALLY: Oh thanks. Well, I'm writing another one now. Can you answer some questions?
MURRAY: Er... Yes... What about?
SALLY: About your journey to work, how you travel, how far it is and that sort of thing.
MURRAY: Oh... Oh yes of course.
SALLY: Oh good! Well, how do you get to work?
MURRAY: I go by car.
SALLY: By car... Mmm... and how far is it?
MURRAY: It's about seven miles.
SALLY: And how long does it take?
MURRAY: Er... let's see... it usually takes about twenty-five minutes. That's in the rush-hour, of course.
SALLY: Yes... and how much does it cost you?
MURRAY: Cost? Nothing! Oh, I see – you mean in petrol?
SALLY: Yes – and in tax and insurance.
MURRAY: Oh, well, about 50p in petrol and about another 50p in tax and insurance, I suppose. About a pound altogether.
SALLY: And how much does it cost by bus, do you know?
MURRAY: By bus? Er... about 50p.
SALLY: Do you ever go by bus?
MURRAY: No, never. I went by bus once and I was an hour late for work.
SALLY: I see. Thank you.

2 SPEECHWORK
Part A: Stress
Say after me:
da da di di da...how much does it cost...how much did it cost...how much do you want...how much did you want...how long does it take...how long did it take...how far do you go...how far did you go...

Part B: Intonation
Say after me:
I usually go by car...I sometimes go by bus...I always go by train...he usually goes by car...she usually goes by bus...we always go by train...he usually walks...I always walk...

Part C: Pronunciation
Say after me:
/h/.../h/...how...how much...how far...how long...how many...how much is it...how far is it...how long does it take...how many would you like...how hot is it...hello...how do you do...Hello, I'm Helen...Helen who?...Helen Hunter...

3 LISTENING (1)
Listen to Sally Baker interviewing some other people about their journeys to work. Fill in the information in the survey in your books.

SALLY: Hello! You're David, aren't you? Tessa has talked a lot about you.
DAVID: Oh yes. You must be Sally Baker, from the Manchester News.
SALLY: That's right. As you know, I'm doing a survey on people's journeys to work and I thought I might ask you a few questions.
DAVID: Please. Go ahead.
SALLY: Well, first, how do you get to work, David?
DAVID: By train usually. Then I walk the rest.
SALLY: Train and then you walk. Mmm. How far is it to your school? You are a teacher, aren't you?
DAVID: Yes, that's right. Well, I suppose it's... let's see... it's about ten miles in all.
SALLY: Ten miles... and that takes you how long?
DAVID: Oh, let's see... fifteen minutes by train and then a ten minute walk. That's what?... twenty-five minutes. Yes, about twenty-five minutes.
SALLY: I see. And how much does it cost you – the train ticket, that is?
DAVID: Er... a single ticket costs 45 pence.
SALLY: 45... right, thank you, David. That's all.
DAVID: Oh, right. Thanks.

SALLY: Martha, you're a doctor, aren't you?
MARTHA: Yes, that's right. At the Manchester Royal Hospital.
SALLY: And you live near the hospital?
MARTHA: Quite near, yes. About four miles away.
SALLY: And how do you get to the hospital every day? By bus?
MARTHA: No, I go by car. It's a very old car but it's all right. The petrol costs are high though, and the insurance.
SALLY: Oh, how much do you reckon it costs you to make the journey from your home to the hospital then?
MARTHA: Tax and insurance included?
SALLY: Yes.
MARTHA: About 70p.
SALLY: And how long does it take you to get there?
MARTHA: Oh... usually about fifteen minutes, I suppose.
SALLY: Great. That's fine. Thanks very much. I won't keep you any longer, Martha.
MARTHA: Oh, it's a pleasure. When can I see the article?
SALLY: Next week, I hope.
MARTHA: O.K., I'll look out for it. Bye!

SALLY: Paul, what do you do?
PAUL: I'm a student. At the technical college.
SALLY: Do you have a car?
PAUL: A car? Me? No... I have a bicycle. A very old bicycle. It doesn't go very fast.
SALLY: And that's how you get to college each day, is it?
PAUL: That's right. I cycle. It's not far – about a mile.
SALLY: And how long does that usually take you?

Unit 18

PAUL: Let's see . . . I usually leave five minutes before the first lesson . . . yes, about five minutes.
SALLY: You never go by bus?
PAUL: No, why should I? It doesn't cost anything to cycle!
SALLY: O.K., thanks, Paul. I'd better leave you now to get to your class.
PAUL: O.K., Bye!

4 OPEN DIALOGUE

Talk to Sally about your journey to work, school or college.

SALLY: Hello. Can you answer some questions?
STUDENT: ....
SALLY: They're about your journey to work every day – or to school or college. My first question is: how do you get there – by car, by bicycle, or how?
STUDENT: ....
SALLY: I see. How far is it from your home?
STUDENT: ....
SALLY: Can you tell me how long it takes you?
STUDENT: ....
SALLY: And how much does that cost you?
STUDENT: ....
SALLY: Where do you live? I don't remember.
STUDENT: ....
SALLY: And where do you work or go to school?
STUDENT: ....
SALLY: Oh yes. That's right. Well, thank you. That's very interesting. Oh, one more question – do you always travel this way?
STUDENT: ....
SALLY: I see. Thank you.

Part B ORAL EXERCISES

Exercise 1 Ask the people at Focus how they get to work. Look at page 102.

How do you get to work, Murray? By car?
Yes, that's right.
How do you get to work, George? By bus?
Yes, that's right. Now go on.
How do you get to work, Jackie? Do you walk?
Yes, that's right.
How do you get to work Allan? By train and bus?
Yes, that's right.
How do you get to work, Tessa? By car?
Yes, that's right.

Exercise 2 Say how you get to work. Answer for the people at Focus.

How do you get to work, Murray?
I go by car.
How do you get to work, George?
I go by bus. Now go on.
How do you get to work, Jackie?
I walk.
How do you get to work, Allan?
I go by train and bus.
How do you get to work, Tessa?
I go by car.

Exercise 3 Say how people usually get to work. Look at page 103.

How does Murray get to work?
He always goes by car.
How does George get to work?
He usually goes by bus. Now go on.
How does Jackie get to work?
She often walks.
How does Allan get to work?
He usually goes by train and bus.
How does Tessa get to work?
She always goes by car.

Exercise 4 Say how people usually get to work.

Does Murray ever go by car?
Yes, he always does.
Does George ever go by bus?
Yes, he usually does.
Does Tessa ever go by bus?
No, she never does. Now go on.
Does Jackie ever go by bus?
Yes, she sometimes does.
Does Allan ever go by train and bus?
Yes, he usually does.
Does Jackie ever walk?
Yes, she often does.
Does Allan ever go by car?
Yes, he sometimes does.
Does George ever cycle?
Yes, he sometimes does.
Does Murray ever go by bus?
No, he never does.

Exercise 5 Ask how long it takes people to get to work. Look at page 102 again.

Murray lives about 7 miles away.
How long does his journey take if he goes by car?
George lives about 2 miles away.
How long does his journey take if he goes by bus?
Now go on.
Jackie lives half a mile away.
How long does her journey take if she walks?
Allan lives 8 miles away.
How long does his journey take if he goes by train and bus?
Tessa lives about $5\frac{1}{2}$ miles away.
How long does her journey take if she goes by car?

Unit 18

Exercise 6 Talk about the distance and time to get to work. Answer for the people at Focus again.

How far is it to work, Murray?
It's about 7 miles. It takes about 25 minutes by car.
How far is it to work, George?
It's about 2 miles. It takes about 15 minutes by bus. Now go on.
How far is it to work, Jackie?
It's about half a mile. It takes about ten minutes if I walk.
How far is it to work, Allan?
It's about 8 miles. It takes about 45 minutes by train and bus.
How far is it to work, Tessa?
It's about 5½ miles. It takes about 20 minutes by car.

UNIT 19 Focus on People at Work

	Skills	Functions	Example Sentences	Main Structures
SET 1	1. Speaking 2. Speaking 3. Reading and Writing 4. Writing 5. Speaking 6. Speaking 7. Speaking 8. Writing	Ask and say what people do every day Say what you do every day	*What time does Walter get up?* *He gets up at seven o'clock.* *I get up at seven-thirty.*	What time *do you* get up? *does she* start work? go to bed? *I get up/She gets up* at 7.00. Where *do you* work? *does he* have lunch? *I usually have* lunch in the canteen. *He sometimes has.* What *do you* do after supper? *does he* *I watch/He watches* television.
SET 2	1. Speaking 2. Speaking	Ask people about their jobs	*What do you do?/What does he do?* *He works for Ford. He works in a car factory in Coventry.* *I work for Focus Films.* *I work in a studio at the Focus Film Centre.*	*I work for* Ford. *He/She works for* *I work/He–She works* in an office in Manchester.
EXTENSION	1. Listening 2. Reading and Writing	The interview with Walter Moaney, on which the introductory text is based. Newspaper article: a well-known actor describes a typical day. Students prepare questions about the text, then rewrite it in the past tense.		

OPEN DIALOGUE

ORAL EXERCISES

1. Ask where people work

   Walter's an engineer.
   Oh, yes. Where does he work?

2. Say what people do every day

   What time does Walter get up?
   He gets up at seven.

3. Say what you do every day

   What time do you get up, Doris?
   I get up at quarter past seven.

4. Ask what other people do every day

   What time does he get up?
   At seven.

5. Ask people what they do every day

   What time do you get up, Sally?
   I get up at seven-thirty.

6. Answer questions about people's daily routine

   Does Walter have lunch in the canteen?
   Yes, that's right, he does.

SPEECHWORK

A STRESS	he gets up at six •●●•●
B INTONATION	What time do you get up?
C PRONUNCIATION	/tʃ/ Richards, watch

ACTIVE VOCABULARY

factory
canteen
hospital
studio
radio
pub
pint
breakfast
wife
husband

at work
at school
at college

early

get (got) up
go to work
go to bed
go home
have (had) breakfast
work(ed) for
read (read) the paper
do (did) the housework
do the ironing
mark(ed) homework
study (studied)
listen(ed) to the radio
play(ed) records
prefer (preferred)

Unit 19

Focus on people at work

1. Meet Walter Moaney. Walter is an engineer. He works for Ford in a factory in Coventry.
2. Here is a typical day for Walter. He gets up at 7 o'clock and has breakfast.
3. Then he goes to work. He goes to work by bus. He starts work at 8 o'clock.
4. He usually has lunch in the factory canteen.
5. He finishes work at 5.30. Then he goes home and has supper.
6. After supper he usually reads the paper and watches television.
7. He sometimes goes out to the pub and has a pint of beer.
8. He goes to bed at about 10.30.
9. Walter lives in a small house in Coventry. He's married with four children.
10. He and his wife are Irish. They like Coventry but they prefer Ireland. Walter says: "I like my job here but Ireland is my home".

PICTURES AND TEXT

The text beneath the pictures is not recorded.
Use the wall picture/OHP (8) of Walter's Day to present the text. Students look at the pictures as you point to them and listen as you read the text for each picture.
Students can repeat the text chorally.
Direct the students' attention to the text and pictures in their books. Go through the pictures again asking indivdual students to read the appropriate sentence(s) as a commentary.
Ask a few comprehension questions e.g. *What does Walter do? Who does he work for? Where does he work?* etc.

UNIT 19

Set 1
- Ask what people do every day
- Say what people do every day
- Say what you do every day

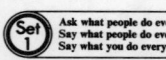

Focus on daily routine

Name & Job	gets up at	starts work at	has lunch	finishes work at	after supper	goes to bed at
Walter Moaney (engineer)	7.00	8.00	in the canteen	5.30	reads the paper and watches TV	about 10.30
Sally Baker (journalist)	7.30	9.00	at work	5.00	goes to see friends or does the housework	about 11.30
David Richards (teacher)	8.00	9.15	at school	4.30	marks homework and reads the paper	about 11.00
Martha Hunt (doctor)	6.30	8.00	in the hospital canteen	4.00	reads, plays records, listens to the radio	about 10.30
Doris Blake (housewife)	7.15	8.00	at home	9.00	watches TV and does the ironing	about 11.00
Paul Blake (student)	8.45	10.00	in the student canteen at college	4.00	studies, or goes to see friends, or goes out for a beer	12.00

1. Ask and answer like this:

    a) What time does Walter get up?
    He gets up at seven o'clock.

    What time does Sally get up?
    She gets up at _____ etc.

    b) What time does Walter start work?
    He starts work at eight o'clock.

    What time does Sally start work?
    She starts work at _____ etc.

    c) Where does Walter have lunch?
    He has lunch in the canteen.

    Where does Sally have lunch?
    She has lunch _____ etc.

SET 1 Ask and say what people do every day
Say what you do every day

Students study the chart. Explain any new vocabulary, especially words from the section entitled *after supper*.

Ex 1 The students should work down the vertical columns of the chart, in order to practise each verb intensively.
Give an example of the question and answer before each section; the answer should be given in full form at this stage.
Practise the intonation.
Work T-S for a few examples and then students work in pairs.
One student asks the questions in the first section i.e. *gets up at* . . . , the other in the next i.e. *starts work at* . . . and so on.

Unit 19

Ex 2 Choose a good student and work S-T through the printed questions about Walter; the student asks and you answer.
Then work T-S for one of the other characters.
Students ask and answer in pairs about the other four characters, changing parts after each character.

Ex 3 Students read the programme notes.
Point out the use of *Then* and *After supper* which act as links.
Students write similar notes in class for one of the other suggested characters; they do the other two for homework.

Ex 4 Students fill in the questionnaire individually in class. Fill in a model questionnaire, if necessary, for yourself on the blackboard.

Ex 5 Students work in pairs and ask each other questions about their daily routine.
Give an example and show the students how to write notes e.g.
Mary gets up – 7 a.m.
    starts work – 8.30 etc.

Ex 6 Demonstrate from your blackboard notes how to read the notes in spoken form e.g. *Mary gets up at seven o'clock. She starts work at half past eight* etc.
Point out the use of *at*, but do not stress it.

Ex 7 Go through the list and explain any new vocabulary. Practise the pronunciation.
Students form groups of 5-6 and appoint a 'secretary' to take notes.
Give each of the groups a ready-made stencil so that the secretary simply has to fill in the information from the group members and make a generalisation in the final column (the stencil saves time and ensures that the exercise runs smoothly). e.g.

Student 1 gets up at 7.30
Student 2   8.00
Student 3   8.00
Student 4   7.00
Average about 7.30 – 8.00

The groups should contain at least five students to be able to make a reasonable generalisation.

Ex 8 Students work in the groups formed for Ex 7 and write a few sentences stating their conclusions.

UNIT 19

d) What time does Walter finish work?
He finishes work at half-past five.

What time does Sally finish work?
She finishes work at .... etc.

e) What does Walter do after supper?
He reads the paper and watches television.

What does Sally do after supper?
She .... etc.

f) What time does Walter go to bed?
He goes to bed at about half-past ten.

What time does Sally go to bed?
She goes to bed at about .... etc.

2. Now ask and answer all the questions about each of the people in turn, like this:
What time does Walter get up?
What time does he start work?
Where does he have lunch?
What time does he finish work?
What does he do after supper?
What time does he go to bed?

3. Here are Murray's notes for the programme about Walter Mooney

> This is a typical day for Walter Mooney, an engineer. He gets up at 7.00 and has breakfast. Then he goes to work. He starts at 8.00. He usually has lunch in the canteen. He finishes work at 5.30. Then he goes home and has supper. After supper he usually reads the paper and watches T.V. He goes to bed at about 10.30.

Now write programme notes for
i) Sally Baker
ii) David Richards
iii) Martha Hunt

UNIT 19

4. Complete the questionnaire about your daily routine

QUESTIONNAIRE

Name:
Address:
Name of School or College or Institution:
Time you get up:
Time you start work or school or college:
Time you finish work or school or college:
What you usually do after supper:
Time you go to bed:

5. Now ask your partner about his/her typical day, like this:
What time do you get up? I get up at ....
What time do you start work (school or college)?
What time do you finish work (school or college)?
What do you usually do after supper?
What time do you go to bed?

Make notes on what your partner says

6. Now tell the class about your partner's daily routine, like this:
He/she gets up at .... He/she starts work at

7. Group Activity
i) Find out the time most people get up
                                  start school or work or college
                                  finish school or work or college
                                  go to bed
ii) Find out what most people do after supper

8. Now write a few lines about your group. Write like this:

> DAILY ROUTINE – REPORT
> In our group most people get up at ....
> They start ....

105

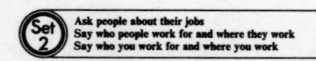

Unit 19

UNIT 19

Set 2
Ask people about their jobs
Say who people work for and where they work
Say who you work for and where you work

What does Walter do? He's an engineer.
He works for Ford.
He works in a car factory in Coventry.

Name	Job	Company/Authority	Place of work
Walter Moaney	an engineer	Ford	car factory in Coventry
David Richards	a teacher	Manchester Council	school outside Manchester
Martha Hunt	a doctor	National Health Service	hospital in Manchester
Sally Baker	a journalist	The Manchester News	office in the centre of Manchester
Doris Blake	a housewife		at home
Paul Blake	a student	Focus Films	studio at the Focus Film Centre

1. Ask and answer like this:
   What does David do? He's a _____
   He works for _____
   He works in a _____

2. Now ask your partner what he/she does, like this:
   What do you do?
   I'm a/an _____
   (I work for _____)
   (I work in a/an _____)
   (study at _____)

112

UNIT 19

EXTENSION

1. Listen to the interview with Walter Mooney and follow the pictures and text on page 108.

2. [article excerpt]

FACE TO FACE

This week with *Barry Miles* from the Royal Exchange Theatre.

Barry Miles is an actor from the Royal Exchange Theatre in Manchester. Just now you can see him in Shakespeare's 'Othello' where he plays the leading role.

Our reporter, Sally Baker, asked him about his typical day. He says: "I get up at ten, have breakfast - orange juice, an egg and a cup of black coffee - and read the paper. Then at eleven I go to the theatre and rehearse. Not Othello but our next production. Then what? A late lunch at the pub with the others. Then we're free in the afternoon. Sometimes I go to the cinema, go shopping or see friends. Tea at five, then I go back to the theatre. The evening performance starts at seven thirty. After the performance? We all go to the theatre bar, have drinks and talk I usually have some sandwiches then. I go to bed late, about one o'clock. Yes, that's quite a typical day for me".

Now write an article for the Manchester News and say what Barry did yesterday.

113

SET 2 Ask people about their jobs
Say who people/you work for and where they/you work

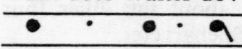

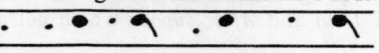

What does Walter do?

He's an engineer. He works for Ford.

He works in a car factory in Coventry.

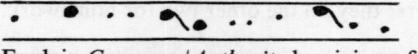

Explain *Company/Authority* by giving a few local examples; say who you work for, ask one or two students (whom you know to have jobs) what company/authority they work for etc.
Explain *Manchester Council* and *National Health Service* by comparing them to similar authorities in the students' own country.

Ex 1 Practise the pronunciation of the companies and authorities.
Give an example of the exercise.
Work through a few examples orally T-S.
Students complete the exercise in pairs.

Ex 2 Students ask each other what they do and who they work for, if applicable. If they are full-time students, they simply answer:
I'm a student. I study at _____

EXTENSION

1 *Listening* The listening passage is an interview with Walter Moaney.
The content is the same as that in the text beneath the pictures at the beginning of the Unit, but it is slightly extended and in the form of a dialogue.
Students listen and follow the pictures and text.

2 *Reading and writing* Explain the new theatre vocabulary: *actor, leading role, rehearse* and *performance*. The passage is recorded.
Students read the article. Then in pairs they make up 6-8 questions about the second paragraph and write them down.
Each pair takes turns to ask another pair a question.
Give one or two examples of the questions the students can ask.
Write on the blackboard the verb phrases from the second paragraph of Face to Face e.g. *get up at ten, have breakfast, read the paper* etc.
Demonstrate how the past tenses of these verbs are formed.
Write *Yesterday* in large letters beside the list. Go through the list saying: *Yesterday, I got up at ten* etc. Write the past form beside the base form of the verbs.
Students should be able to supply some of the past tense forms themselves.
Students copy the list and then write a paragraph relating what Barry Miles did yesterday.

Open Dialogue See General Guide and tapescript (page 107).

Oral Exercises See General Guide and tapescript (page 107).

Speechwork See General Guide and tapescript (page 107).

Unit 19

Tapescript
Part A

1 SPEECHWORK
Part A Stress

Say after me:

di da da di da...he gets up at six...he leaves home at nine... he starts work at ten...he has lunch at one...he leaves work at six... he gets home at seven...he goes out at nine... he gets back at ten...

Part B: Intonation

Say after me:

what time do you get up...what time do you start work... what time do you have lunch...what time do you get home ...where do you have lunch...what do you do in the evening ...what do you do after supper...

Part C: Pronunciation

Say after me:

/tʃ/ ... /tʃ/ ... Richards ... Mrs Richards ... Manchester ... Mrs Richards lives in Manchester...the children are in Manchester...lunch...they have lunch at school...I had sandwiches for lunch...chicken sandwiches...a chocolate... would you like a chocolate?...watch...watch TV...do you often watch TV?...no, but the children watch it...

2 LISTENING

INTERVIEWER: And your name is...?
WALTER: Moaney, Walter Moaney, Mr Walter Moaney.
INTERVIEWER: Ah, yes, that's right, Mr Moaney, or can I call you Walter?
WALTER: Please do.
INTERVIEWER: Now Mr. Moaney ... sorry ... Walter, I'd like to ask you a few details about your life. Questions about your work and your daily routine. Now first of all. What do you do and where do you work?
WALTER: I'm an engineer and I work in a car factory in Coventry.
INTERVIEWER: Oh, a car factory?
WALTER: That's right. It's a big factory. I work for Ford.
INTERVIEWER: Tell me about the job, Walter.
WALTER: Well, I start work at 8.00. Of course I get up fairly early at about 7.00, and have breakfast. I go to work by bus – it's not far, about 3 miles. It takes me about 20 minutes. I usually have lunch in the factory canteen but sometimes I have sandwiches. I finish work at 5.30. Then I go home and have supper.
INTERVIEWER: What do you do in the evenings, Walter. I mean after supper?
WALTER: Well, I read the paper usually, watch TV and sometimes I go out and have a beer with my friends. I go to bed at about 10.30.
INTERVIEWER: And what does your wife do after supper, Walter?
WALTER: The children go to bed – we have four children – at about nine o'clock. Then she watches TV. She likes detective films. Sometimes she does some housework – you know, ironing and things like that. But usually she reads and watches TV.
INTERVIEWER: Have you got a big house, Walter?
WALTER: No, we live in a small house, not really big enough for us and the four kids. It's in Coventry, not outside. I like Coventry but I'm ...
INTERVIEWER: Of course, you're not English, are you, Walter?
WALTER: No I'm not. I'm Irish and so is my wife. I like Coventry you know, but I prefer Ireland. Ireland's my home.
INTERVIEWER: I understand, Walter. Ireland's your home. Anyway, thank you for your answers to my questions.

3 OPEN DIALOGUE

Talk to Sally about what you do every day.

SALLY: Hallo! Well, as you know, I'm a journalist for the Manchester News. What do you do?
STUDENT: ....
SALLY: Oh yes ... where?
STUDENT: ....
SALLY: What time do you get up in the morning?
STUDENT: ....
SALLY: And go to bed?
STUDENT: ....
SALLY: That's a long day. What do you usually do after supper?
STUDENT: ....
SALLY: Oh, do you? I usually go out and see friends. Well, I must go back to the office now. Bye!
STUDENT: ....

Part B ORAL EXERCISES

Exercise 1 Ask where people work.

Walter's an engineer.
Oh, yes, where does he work?

Jackie's a secretary.
Oh, yes, where does she work? Now go on.

Helen and Sheila are typists.
Oh, yes, where do they work?

I'm a technician.
Oh, yes, where do you work?

We're both teachers.
Oh, yes, where do you work?

Allan's a van driver.
Oh, yes, where does he work?

Unit 19

Exercise 2 Say what people do every day. Look at page 109.

What time does Walter get up?
He gets up at seven.

And what time does he start work?
He starts work at eight.

What time does Sally get up?
She gets up at seven-thirty. Now go on.

And at what time does she start work?
She starts work at nine.

And what time does she finish work?
She finishes work at five.

What time does Doris go to bed?
She goes to bed at eleven.

And what time does she get up in the morning?
She gets up at quarter past seven.

What time does Martha Hunt get up?
She gets up at six-thirty.

Exercise 3 Say what you do every day. You are Doris Blake. Look at page 109.

What time do you get up, Doris?
I get up at quarter past seven.

And what time do you start work round the house?
I start work at eight o'clock. Now go on.

Where do you have lunch?
I have lunch at home.

When do you finish work?
I finish work at nine o'clock.

And after supper? What do you do after supper?
I watch TV and do the ironing.

What time do you go to bed?
I go to bed at about eleven o'clock.

Exercise 4 Ask what people do every day. Look at page 109. and ask about Walter.

What time does he get up?
At seven.

What time does he start work?
At eight. Now go on.

Where does he have lunch?
In the canteen.

What time does he finish work?
At half past five.

What does he do after supper?
He reads the paper and watches TV.

What time does he go to bed?
At about half past ten.

Exercise 5 Ask what people do every day. Look at page 109. Ask Sally.

What time do you get up, Sally?
I get up at seven-thirty.

What time do you start work?
I start work at nine. Now go on.

Where do you have lunch?
I have lunch at work.

What time do you finish work?
I finish work at five.

What do you do after supper?
I go and see friends.

What time do you go to bed?
I go to bed about eleven-thirty.

Exercise 6 Answer the questions. Look at page 109.

Does Walter have lunch in the canteen?
Yes, that's right, he does.

Does he finish work at six?
No, he doesn't. He finishes work at half past five. Now go on.

Does Sally have lunch at home?
No, she doesn't. She has lunch at work.

Does she finish work at five?
Yes, that's right, she does.

Does David get up at eight?
Yes, that's right, he does.

Does he go and see friends after supper?
No, he doesn't. He marks homework and reads the paper.

Does Martha get up at seven?
No, she doesn't. She gets up at half past six.

Does she have lunch in the hospital canteen?
Yes, that's right, she does.

UNIT 20 Consolidation

	Skills	Activity
PART 1	Reading	Information leaflet about the Manchester Film Festival, and a circular letter inviting people to send in their entries.
1.	Reading and Speaking	Information form contains personal details about three visitors to the Festival. Students follow the printed interview as a model for their interviews with two visitors.
2.	Writing (fill-in form)	Students fill in similar personal details about themselves in the last column of the form.
3.	Speaking	Students interview each other, using the printed interview as a model.
4.	Listening	Conversation between two visitors to the Festival.
5.	Roleplay	Students act out a similar conversation, using their own names, using a variety of functions.
6.	Listening, Reading and Speaking	Murray's opening speech at the Festival. Students listen to and read the speech, then practise delivering the first part of it.
PART 2		
1.	Sorting	Rearranging activities from a day's routine into the logical time sequence.
2.	Vocabulary	Opposite meanings of words.
3.	Grouping	Words to be grouped into groups of similar meaning/concept.
4.	Transformation	Spoken/written transformation of times printed in figures to their spoken (fully spelt) form.
5.	Fill-in	Correct prepositions to be filled in.
6.	Fill-in	Correct forms of present tense of verbs to be filled in.
7.	Fill-in	Correct object pronouns to be filled in.
8.	Fill-in	Correct forms of past tense of verbs to be filled in.
9.	Fill-in Dialogue	Short exchanges in different situations; one speaker's part is to be filled in (this is quite a long exercise).
	Games	(not referred to in Students' Book) to practise 1) Present Simple 2) food and drink vocabulary 3) Past Simple.
	Speaking	Flight timetable. Students discuss the flying times for different destinations, using question and answer forms.
	Discussion	Facts from a survey about leisure activities in Britain. To be discussed in groups. The printed facts are a basis for comparison with the students' own countries.

ACTIVE VOCABULARY

language	foreign	fly
world	vegetarian	
art		
photography	abroad	

Unit 20

UNIT 20

PART 1.

Welcome to Manchester for the *Fifth International Festival of Documentary Films*.
November 15th to November 23rd.
This year it's in Manchester!
At the Palace Theatre and Cinema, Oxford Street, Manchester
Films from the U.S.S.R., the People's Republic of China, Hungary, U.S.A.
Canada, and many, many more!

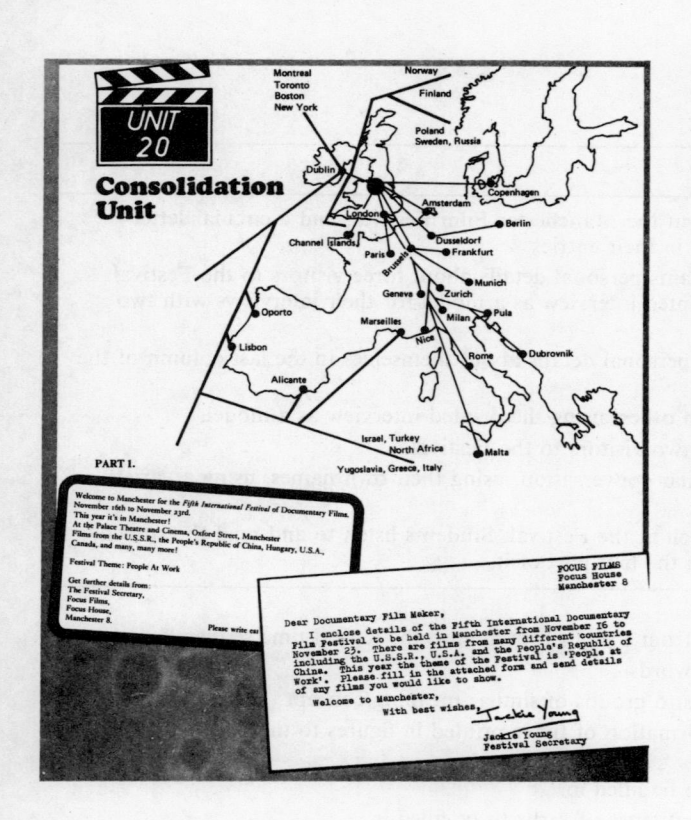

Festival Theme: People At Work

Get further details from:
The Festival Secretary,
Focus Films,
Focus House,
Manchester 8.

Please write ear...

FOCUS FILMS
Focus House
Manchester 8

Dear Documentary Film Maker,
I enclose details of the Fifth International Documentary Film Festival to be held in Manchester from November 16 to November 23. There are films from many different countries including the U.S.S.R., U.S.A. and the People's Republic of China. This year the theme of the Festival is 'People at Work'. Please fill in the attached form and send details of any films you would like to show.
Welcome to Manchester,
With best wishes,
Jackie Young
Jackie Young
Festival Secretary

CONSOLIDATION

This Unit is divided into two parts.
Part 1 contains extension activities based on the language introduced in the last 7 Units and also some from earlier units. The activities include reading, listening, interviews and roleplay.
Part 2 is a type of test, with a series of different kinds of self-assessment exercises.
Suggestions for a few games are included in the teacher's notes but not in the Students' Book.
This Unit ends with two short oral activities which are optional, depending on how much time is available.
Teachers can decide whether to do the test before or after the extension activities.

Part 1 Information leaflet and letter

Students study the information leaflet and the letter in pairs. This is not for intensive study, but to serve as an introduction for the subsequent activities in the Unit.

Festival Administration Office—Manchester Airport
Please fill in this form to help make your stay in Manchester a pleasant one.

Name	Mizuki Brown	Buzz Anderson	Gina Colbert
Nationality	American	Australian	French
Domicile	San Francisco	Sydney	Montreal
Occupation	Journalist	Cameraman	Student at University
Professional Interests	the history of the cinema	underwater photography	films about ordinary people
Personal Interests	modern art, photography	sport, stamps	reading, music, foreign languages
Type of Accommodation required	Hotel (full board)	Guest House (bed and breakfast)	Hostel (bed and breakfast)
Food/drink	Vegetarian	I like everything	I don't drink or smoke
Other interests while in Manchester	I would like to visit the Manchester News office	I would like to see a football match with Manchester United	I would like to see Manchester University
Signed	Mizuki Brown	Buzz Anderson	Gina Colbert

A reporter from Manchester Radio interviews Mizuki Brown

JOHN MENZIES: Hello, my name is John Menzies. I am a reporter for Manchester Radio. You are a visitor to the Fifth International Festival of Documentary Films?
MIZUKI: That's right.
JOHN MENZIES: May I ask you some questions?
MIZUKI: Yes, of course.
JOHN MENZIES: Your name is _____?
MIZUKI: Mizuki Brown.
JOHN MENZIES: And what nationality are you, Mizuki?
MIZUKI: American.
JOHN MENZIES: Where in the U.S.A. are you from, Mizuki?
MIZUKI: I'm from San Francisco.
JOHN MENZIES: And, what do you do?
MIZUKI: I'm a journalist.
JOHN MENZIES: What are your professional interests, Mizuki?
MIZUKI: I'm interested in the history of the camera.
JOHN MENZIES: And your personal interests?
MIZUKI: Modern art and photography.

Information form

Look at the information form with the students and explain any unfamiliar vocabulary.
Practise the pronunciation of the more difficult words: *photography, foreign languages, vegetarian*.

Unit 20

1 Ask one student to take the part of Mizuki Brown in the printed interview; you read the part of the reporter John Menzies.
The other students follow the information from the application form.
Students work in pairs. One is the reporter; the other is Buzz Anderson or Gina Colbert.
The printed interview should serve as a framework for their own interviews.

2 Students fill in similar information about themselves in the empty column in the chart. (They need not fill in the section *Type of accommodation required*) The last section can be changed to *Interests while in England/London*.

3 Give an example of an interview with yourself as the person who is being interviewed.
Ask a student to be the reporter; tell him to start with the question *May I ask you some questions?*
Students work in pairs and interview each other.

4 *Listening* Students listen to the conversation between Mizuki and Buzz.
Inform them that they are going to act a similar conversation afterwards, so they should listen closely to the language used.

5 *Roleplay* Students work freely in pairs. You go round and listen.
If there is enough time, one pair can give a 'public' performance.

6 Introduce the new vocabulary. Play the tape of the speech, then go through the speech in more detail.
Ask a few comprehension questions to elicit the past tense e.g. *Where did they go to make the film?*
Do some choral reading practice on the first half of the speech.
Ask students to practise reading this part of the speech to themselves, as if they were going to make a speech.
Choose one student to read the first paragraph in front of the class.

UNIT 20

JOHN MENZIES: I see. And where are you staying in Manchester?
MIZUKI: In a hotel.
JOHN MENZIES: Finally, what would you like to do or see in Manchester – apart from the Film Festival?
MIZUKI: Oh, I would like to visit the Manchester News office.
JOHN MENZIES: Thank you very much.

1. Work with a partner. Interview Buzz Anderson and Gina Colbert.
2. Fill in your own name and personal information in the empty column on page 117. Your professional interests can be about anything, not necessarily films or photography.
3. Interview your partner as in Exercise 1.
4. Listen to the conversation between Mizuki Brown and Buzz Anderson when they meet for the first time. They meet in the Festival Theatre before the first film.
5. Roleplaying
You go to Manchester for the festival. You meet another visitor. Act out the conversation, like the one between Mizuki and Buzz, and remember to do the following:

Introduce yourself
Say where you are from
Say what you do (what your job is)
Offer the other person a drink
Offer him/her a cigarette
Ask about his/her interests
Say what your interests are
Suggest that you go into the theatre to get a good seat.

6. Murray Freeman, film director from Focus Films of Manchester, opened the festival with the following speech:

"Good evening, Ladies and Gentlemen. It is my great pleasure, this evening, to open the Fifth International Festival of Documentary Films. Many of you were at the festival last year in Munich. The theme then was 'How People Live'. We had entries from all over the world. We saw some very interesting and professional films and we all learnt a lot about how people live in different countries. This year the theme is 'People at Work' and I am sure that, once again, the festival will be a rewarding experience for all of us.

As one of the film directors at Focus Films, I would like to introduce our own entry for the festival: 'Focus on People at Work'. To make the film, we went to Newcastle, to Coventry, to London and to Bristol. We interviewed a policeman, an engineer, a secretary and a housewife. We went to a police-station, a car factory, a busy London office and an ordinary home. We saw people at work, we saw people in their homes. We saw a lot that was depressing but we did our best to give a balanced picture of the ordinary British worker. We hope that the film will be both interesting and informative. Ladies and gentlemen, may I present the first film, a Focus Film Production: 'Focus on People at Work'."

The date is **November 16th**
The place is **The Palace Theatre Manchester**
The event is **The Fifth International Festival of Documentary Films**

Unit 20

PART 2

1. Put these activities in the right order of time.
go to work
have supper
get up
go home
watch television
have lunch
go to bed
have breakfast
finish work

2. Write the opposite meaning of these words
e.g. single .... return (ticket)
get up ....
start ....
open ....
always ....
beautiful (weather) ....
leave (train) ....
morning ....
black ....

3. Put these words into groups of three
afternoon door   interesting usually
lunch   often   suitcase   bus
sometimes letter   factory   supper
window   morning   envelope   hospital
car   office   breakfast   beautiful
evening   lovely   train   stamp

4. Say these times from a time table
e.g. 16.35 ...Twenty-five to five.
7.45   23.55   14.25
16.40   6.30   7.15
10.20 15.35 12.00
       11.05

5. Fill in the correct prepositions in the gaps. Choose from these:
on at in to by
1. The train arrives .... six o'clock.
2. Are you free .... Saturday evening.
3. His birthday is .... Tuesday.
4. The film starts .... five thirty .... the evening.
5. I go .... work .... car.
6. Can you meet me .... the station?
7. He lives .... Manchester.
8. My birthday is .... December 23rd.
9. The film is .... the Plaza cinema.
10. She has lunch .... home.
11. He goes .... college every day.
12. He has lunch .... the canteen .... work.

6. Fill in the correct form of the verbs in brackets
1. He .... in an office in Manchester. (work)
2. .... he .... in Manchester too? (live)
3. Where .... they .... (live)?
4. He .... work at eight o'clock. (start)
5. We .... work at six o'clock. (finish)
6. When .... you .... lunch? (have)
7. She .... breakfast at seven o'clock. (have)
8. How long .... the journey ....? (take)
9. When .... she ....? (go to bed)
10. It .... about half an hour. (take)
11. He usually .... television after supper. (watch)
12. It .... about 40p. (cost)

7. Fill in the correct personal pronoun in the gaps. Choose between:
me you him her us them
Example: He's busy just now. Can you ring him this evening?
1. I'm busy just now. Can you ring .... tomorrow?
2. I'm afraid she isn't here. Can you ring .... this afternoon?
3. They're at the station. Can you meet ....?
4. We're busy just now. Can you ask .... next week?
5. He isn't at home. Can you ring .... tomorrow?
6. If you're busy now, can I see .... tomorrow?
7. My train arrives at six p.m. Can you meet .... at the station?
8. They're in London today. Ask .... on Monday.

8. Fill in the correct form of the verb in the past tense. Use the verb in brackets
1. I (go) to the theatre on Saturday night.
2. What (you see)?
3. Where (he go) last night?
4. I (see) an old Hitchcock film.
5. What (she have) to eat?
6. She (have) a sandwich and a cup of coffee.
7. What (you do) yesterday?
8. I (do) the washing and the garden.

UNIT 20

9. Fill in the gaps in these dialogues
1. (At the station)
   A: ....
   B: The train to London?
      It leaves at 8.15.
   A: ....
   B: Platform 5.

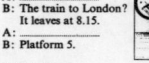

2. (At home)
   A: ....
   B: Yes, of course. What can I get you?
   A: ....
   B: Milk and bread. All right.

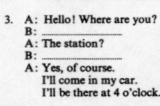

3. A: Hello! Where are you?
   B: ....
   A: The station?
   B: ....
   A: Yes, of course.
      I'll come in my car.
      I'll be there at 4 o'clock.

4. MARIA: 477 9372. Hello?
   JOE: ....
   MARIA: Oh, hello Joe. How are you?
   JOE: ....
   MARIA: Oh, I'm all right.
   JOE: ....
   MARIA: Tonight? Yes, I'd love to. What film is it?
   JOE: ....
   MARIA: Oh yes, I'd like to see 'The Carlton Affair'. What time does it start?
   JOE: ....
   MARIA: Half-past seven! All right but where shall we meet?
   JOE: ....
   MARIA: All right. You know my address, don't you?
   JOE: ....
   MARIA: Yes. Goodbye.

5. A: ....
   B: Oh, usually quite late. About half past seven or eight o'clock.
   A: ....
   B: At nine o'clock. I'm a teacher, you see.
   A: ....
   B: In a school outside Manchester.
   A: ....
   B: At school. In the school canteen. The lunches are quite good.

6. A: ....
   B: By car.
   A: ....
   B: No, never. I don't like buses.
   A: ....
   B: Oh, about five miles.
   A: ....
   B: To get to work? About twenty minutes in the rush-hour.

7. A: What's the matter?
   B: ....
   A: Bored? Well, what do you want to do?
   B: ....
   A: Oh no, not the club. Let's go to the cinema.

8. A: ....
   B: Yes thanks, a very nice evening.
   A: ....
   B: I went to the cinema.
   A: ....
   B: An old Hitchcock film.

Part 2 Exercises

These can be done individually in class or for homework. Oral work could precede written work: some teachers may wish to use this part as a form of end-of-course test.

Key

1 get up/have breakfast/go to work/have lunch/finish work /go home/have supper/watch television/go to bed.

2 go to bed/finish/close/never/awful (terrible) /arrive/ afternoon (evening)/white

3
afternoon	lunch	sometimes	window
evening	breakfast	never	door
morning	supper	usually	suitcase
car	letter	office	lovely
train	envelope	factory	interesting
bus	stamp	hospital	beautiful

4 quarter to eight/twenty past five/twenty past ten/five to twelve/half past six/twenty five to four/five past eleven/ twenty five past two/quarter past seven/twelve o'clock

5
1 at   5 to...by   9 at
2 on   6 at   10 at
3 on   7 in   11 to
4 at...in 8 on   12 in...at

6
1 works   5 finish   9 does...go to bed
2 does...live 6 do...have 10 takes
3 do...live   7 has   11 watches
4 starts   8 does...take 12 costs

7
1 me   5 him
2 her   6 you
3 them 7 me
4 us   8 them

8
1 went   5 did she have
2 did you see 6 had
3 did he go   7 did you do
4 saw   8 did

9 (suggested answers)

(1) What time does the train to London leave?
Which platform does it leave from?

(2) Can you do some shopping for me?
I'd like some milk and some bread.

(3) I'm at the station.
Yes. Can you meet me?

(4) Hallo, Maria. It's Joe here.
Fine thanks. And you?
Would you like to go to the cinema tonight?
The Carlton Affair.
It starts at half past seven.
Let's meet at your house.
Yes I do. See you at
about quarter past seven.

(5) What time do you get up?
What time do you start work?
Where do you work?
Where do you have lunch?

(6) How do you get to work?
Do you ever go by bus?
How far is it to work?
How long does it take you?

Unit 20

(7) I'm bored.
I want to go to the club.
(8) Did you have a nice evening?
What did you do?
What did you see?

Games

The following three games are not part of the test.
Teachers should use them as a form of relaxation after the test has been completed.

1 COFFEE-POTTING

Somebody thinks of an activity e.g. *have lunch*.
The others must guess what activity he is thinking of. They may only ask *yes/no* questions such as:

Do you do this in the morning?   (*No*)
Do you do this every day?   (*Yes*)
Do I do it every day?   (*Yes*) etc.

2 THE SHOPPING LIST

This is a memory game conducted in a chain.
One person starts by saying *When you go shopping can you buy some apples?*
The next person says *When you go shopping can you buy some apples and some oranges?*
Each person has to remember the previous items in order and then add one new item himself.

The words need not be all food and drink, but preferably items preceded by *some* i.e. plurals and uncountables.

3 WHAT DID I DO?

This is an acting/miming game.
The class divides into two teams.
Before the game starts you make a list of different activities (the number of activities should correspond to the number of students in each team) e.g. *I watched television/I went to the cinema/I read the paper* etc. Use familiar vocabulary. Write these activities on separate pieces of paper – one set for each group, though not necessarily in the same order. Both teams start at the same time. They each send one member up to you to get a piece of paper. He/she reads the activity and acts it in front of his/her team. As soon as they guess the activity, they call out e.g. *You watched television!* and the next member of the team goes up to get the next piece of paper and so on.
The team which guesses all the activities first wins.
The aim of the game is that students should call out in the past tense.

ORAL ACTIVITIES

10 Information Sheet

Introduce the timetable showing times and distances of flights from Manchester International Airport. The wall picture/OHP (9) may also be used.
Practise the pronunciation of the names of the cities.
Give an example of the exercise.
Students work in pairs or in a chain round the class.

11 Focus Survey

Students look at the survey silently and note down individually what they believe to be the most popular activity in the evenings for the over-30s in their own country.
They can make a separate list for summer and winter evenings if they wish.
Students then form groups of 4-5 and compare and discuss their notes.

UNIT 20

INFORMATION SHEET

MANCHESTER

is a major centre of commerce and industry. The ease of communication with other commercial and industrial centres abroad is illustrated by the flying times from Manchester International Airport to the following destinations:

Destination	Distance (miles)	Time (hrs/mins)
Amsterdam	312	1.05
Berlin (via Dusseldorf)	712	2.50
Brussels	335	1.05
Copenhagen	624	1.40
Dusseldorf	403	1.15
Geneva	585	1.40
Malta	1459	4.00
Milan	754	3.00
Montreal (via Prestwick)	3199	7.50
Munich	708	1.55
New York	3332	7.30
Paris	366	1.15
Toronto (via Montreal)	3500	8.40
Zurich	627	1.50

FOCUS SURVEY ON LEISURE ACTIVITIES
300 people over the age of 30 were asked what they usually do in the evening after supper. The following figures were obtained:

65% watch TV and read the paper (70% of these watch TV only)

15% do housework

12% go out (to the cinema, to see friends, to the pub etc)

5% listen to the radio, play records or read a book

3% work or study

10. Work with a partner. Ask and answer questions like this:
How long does it take to fly from Manchester to Amsterdam?
It takes one hour five minutes.

How long does it take to fly to Berlin?
It takes two hours fifty minutes.

11. In England it is clear that most people watch television in the evening. What about your country? What do most people do in the evening in your country? Discuss in groups.

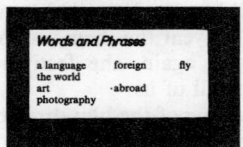

Words and Phrases

a language   foreign   fly
the world
art   abroad
photography

Unit 20

Tapescript

1 LISTENING

Mizuki Brown and Buzz Anderson meet for the first time. They meet in the Festival Theatre before the first film.

BUZZ: Oh, I'm terribly sorry!
MIZUKI: That's all right. It's so crowded in here.
BUZZ: Are you here for the festival?
MIZUKI: Yes, I am.
BUZZ: Oh, well, my name's Buzz. Buzz Anderson.
MIZUKI: Hallo. I'm Mizuki.
BUZZ: Mizuki? Is that your first name?
MIZUKI: Yes, Mizuki Brown. I'm from San Francisco. And you? You aren't American, are you?
BUZZ: No, I'm Australian. I'm from Sydney.
MIZUKI: Oh, what do you do?
BUZZ: I'm a cameraman. And you?
MIZUKI: A journalist.
BUZZ: A journalist, are you? That sounds exciting!
MIZUKI: Oh, I just work for a small newspaper.
BUZZ: Are you interested in the cinema?
MIZUKI: Yes, I'm very interested in the history of the cinema in fact.
BUZZ: Oh are you? Well, my main interest is underwater photography.
MIZUKI: Ah, so you like swimming too, do you?
BUZZ: Oh, I'm interested in all sports really, and stamps actually. I collect rare stamps. Do you have a hobby?
MIZUKI: Not really. I like modern art and, of course, photography in general.
BUZZ: Mmm. Me too. Where are you staying by the way?
MIZUKI: In a hotel very near here.
BUZZ: Oh, I'm just in an ordinary guest house. Bed and breakfast, you know. But that's all right. I like eating out in restaurants and trying different sorts of food.
MIZUKI: Oh, well, I'm vegetarian so it's difficult to find interesting food for me in restaurants.
BUZZ: Yes, I'm sure it is. Well, the first film is starting in a moment. Shall we go in?
MIZUKI: O.K. I'll follow you.

2 LISTENING

Listen to Murray Freeman's speech from the Fifth International Festival of Documentary Films:

Good evening, Ladies and Gentlemen. It is my great pleasure, this evening, to open the Fifth International Festival of Documentary Films. Many of you were at the festival last year in Munich. The theme then was 'How People Live'. We had entries from all over the world. We saw some very interesting and professional films and we all learnt a lot about how people live in different countries. This year the theme is 'People at Work' and I am sure that once again, the festival will be a rewarding experience for all of us.

As one of the film directors at Focus Films, I would like to introduce our own entry for the festival: 'Focus on People at Work'. To make the film, we went to Newcastle, to Coventry, to London and to Bristol. We interviewed a policeman, an engineer, a secretary and a housewife. We went to a police station, a car factory, a busy London office and an ordinary home. We saw people at work, we saw people in their homes. We saw a lot that was depressing but we did our best to give a balanced picture of the ordinary British worker. We hope that the film will be both interesting and informative, Ladies and Gentlemen, may I present the first film, a Focus Film production: 'Focus on People at Work'.

INDEX OF FUNCTIONS: HOW TO SAY IT

	Function	Example Sentence	Unit:Set
Accept	Accept something	Yes please.	10:1
	Accept apologies	That's all right!	11
	Accept invitations to do things	Yes, I'd love to.	17:3
Address	Spell your address		4
Agree	Agree to do something	Yes, of course. / Yes, OK.	14:1
	Agree with suggestions	Yes, that's a good idea!	15:2
Answer	Answer the telephone	872 4679. Hello? / Yes, speaking.	17:1
Apologise	Apologise	Sorry!	11
	Accept apologies	That's all right!	11
Arrange	Arrange to meet somebody	Are you free tomorrow evening? / Yes, I am/No, I'm afraid I'm not.	17:2
Ask for	Ask for things	Can I have a biscuit, please?	10:2
Attention	Attract attention	Excuse me!	1
Can	Say you can't do things	I'm sorry, I can't (just now).	14:1
Conversation	Start a conversation	How are you? / Fine, thanks! And you? / Not too bad.	17:1
Cost	Ask and talk about cost	How much is it? It's £14.	9:3
	Ask and say how much things cost	How much does it cost?	18:5
Count	Count to twenty		9:3
Date	Ask about dates	When's Tessa's birthday?	15:1
	Talk about dates	It's on January 10th. / It's on Monday. / January 10th is a Monday.	15:1
Disagree	Disagree with suggestions	No, not flowers.	15:2
Disappointed	Say you are disappointed	Oh, what a pity!	17:2
Dissatisfaction	Express dissatisfaction	Oh! It isn't very big.	9:2
Do	Ask people to do things	Can you buy some fruit? / Can you open the window? / Can you meet me at the station?	14:1
	Agree to do something	Yes, of course. / Yes, OK.	14:1
	Say you can't do things	I'm sorry, I can't (just now).	14:1
	Ask people what they want to do	What do you want to do?	16:1
	Say what you want to do	I want to go to the cinema.	16:1
	Invite people to do things	Would you like to go to the cinema?	17:3
	Accept invitations to do things	Yes, I'd love to.	17:3
	Refuse invitations to do things	Sorry, I'm afraid I can't.	17:3
Far away	Ask and say how far away places are	How far is it? / It's about seven miles.	18:3
Formal	Thank formally	Thank you.	1
	Greet formally	How do you do!	2:1
	Say goodbye formally	Goodbye!	5
	Accept something	Yes, please.	10:1
From	Ask and say where people are from	Where are you from? / I'm from Melbourne.	7:3
Get	Ask and say how people get to work	How do you get to work? / How does he/she get to work? / He/She goes by car.	18:1
	Say how you get to work	I go by bus.	18:1
Give	Ask for and give things	Can I have a biscuit, please? / Yes, here you are.	10:2
Goodbye	Say goodbye	Goodbye!	3
	Say goodbye formally	Goodbye!	5
	Make parting remarks	Bye! See you later.	17
Greet	Greet formally	How do you do!	2:1
	Greet informally	Hello!	3:1
	Greet somebody in the morning	Good morning!	4

How (see Far away, Get, Long, Much, Often).

Informal	Greet informally	*Hello!*	3:1
	Thank people informally	*Thanks!*	14
Information	Ask for and give specific information	*Which one/ones would you like?*	14:3
		This one./That one over there.	
		These ones./Those ones over there.	
Introduction	Introduce yourself	*My name's Sally Baker.*	2:1
		I'm Sally Baker.	
	Introduce people	*Neville, this is Sally.*	3:1
		Jackie, meet Allan. He's a van driver.	7:1
Invite	Invite people to do things	*Would you like to go to the cinema?*	17:3
	Accept invitations to do things	*Yes, I'd love to.*	17:3
	Refuse invitations to do things	*Sorry, I'm afraid I can't.*	17:3
Job	Ask what somebody's job is	*What do you do?*	2:2
		What does Murray/he do?	
		Is he a film director?	
	Say what your job is	*I'm a journalist.*	2:2
	Say what somebody's job is	*He's a film director.*	2:2
		Sally's a journalist.	3:1
	Ask people about their jobs	*What do you do?/What does she do?*	19:2
Journey	Ask and say how long journeys take	*How long does it take?*	18:4
		It takes about 25 minutes.	
Leave	Say you must leave	*I must go!*	7
Like	Ask what people like	*Do you like tea with lemon?*	11:2
		Does he like tea with lemon?	11:3
	Say what you like	*Yes, I do/No, I don't.*	11:2
		It's all right.	
	Say what other people like	*Yes, he does./No, he doesn't.*	11:3
		He thinks it's all right.	
	Ask what people would like	*What would you like?*	14:2
	Say what you would like	*I'd like some fish/oranges, please.*	14:2
Long	Ask and say how long journeys take	*How long does it take?*	18:4
		It takes about 25 minutes.	
Marital status	Ask and talk about marital status	*Are you married?*	4:1
		Is he/she married?	
		Yes, I am./No, I'm not.	
		Yes, he/she is.	
		No, he/she isn't.	
Meet	Arrange to meet somebody	*Are you free tomorrow evening?*	17:2
		Yes, I am.	
		No, I'm afraid not.	
Much	Ask and say how much things cost	*How much does it cost?*	18:5
		It costs about £1.	
Must	Say you must leave	*I must go!*	7
Name	Ask somebody's name	*What's your name?*	1:1
		What's his/her name?	3:3
	Say your name	*(Sally Baker.)*	1:1
	Say somebody's name	*His/her name's . . . . . .*	3:3
	Spell your name		4:2
	Say your name on the telephone	*It's Allan here.*	17:1
	Introduce yourself	*My name's Sally Baker.*	2:1
Nationality	Ask and talk about nationality	*Are you English?*	7:2
		Yes, I am/No, I'm not. I'm Australian.	
Number	Say your telephone number		4:3
Often	Ask and say how often people do things	*Do you ever go by bus?*	18:2
		Does he ever walk?	
		Yes, always./No, never.	
		She sometimes goes by train.	
	Say how often you do things	*I usually go by train*	18:2
Offer	Offer something	*Would you like a cup of tea?*	10:1
Part	Make parting remarks	*Bye! See you later*	17
Past	Ask about the past	*Where were you yesterday?*	16:2
		What did you do yesterday?	

	Talk about the past	*Where did you go?*	
		What did you see?	
		I was at home.	16:2
		I went to London.	
		I did the washing.	
		I saw 'The Carlton Affair'.	
		I had a cup of coffee.	
		It was quite good.	
People (see Do, Introduce, Invite, Job, Like, Live, Often, Thank, Where, Work)			
Places	Ask where places are	*Where's Kent Road?*	1:2
	Say where places are	*It's over there.*	1:2
		It's next to the station.	5:1
	Show and ask about places	*This is the kitchen.*	9:1
		Is this the kitchen?	
		Yes, it is/No, it isn't.	
	Ask and say how far away places are	*How far is it?*	18:3
		It's about seven miles.	
Pleased	Express pleasure	*What a lovely room!*	15:3
		What beautiful flowers!	
	Say you are pleased	*Oh, good!*	17
Refuse	Refuse invitations to do things	*Sorry, I'm afraid I can't.*	17:3
Satisfaction	Express satisfaction	*Mmm! It's nice and big.*	9:2
Show	Show and ask about places	*This is the kitchen and that's the bathroom.*	9:1
		Is this the kitchen?	
Spell	Spell your address		4
	Spell your name		4:2
Suggestions	Ask for suggestions	*What shall we give her?*	15:2
		What shall we do?	
	Make suggestions	*Let's give her some flowers.*	15:2
		Let's go to the cinema.	
	Agree with suggestions	*Yes, that's a good idea!*	15:2
	Disagree with suggestions	*No, not flowers!*	15:2
Telephone	Say your telephone number	*872 4679. Hello?*	4:3
	Answer the telephone	*Yes, speaking.*	17:1
	Say your name on the telephone	*It's Allan here.*	17:1
Thank	Thank formally	*Thank you.*	1
	Thank somebody	*Thank you very much.*	3
	Thank informally	*Thanks!*	14
	Thank people for things	*Thank you for the beautiful flowers.*	15
Time	Ask the time	*What's the time?*	11:1
	Say the time	*It's two o'clock.*	11:1
		It's half past two.	
		It's quarter past/to two.	
		It's ten past three.	13:1
		It's five to four.	
	Ask what time things happen	*What time does the train leave?*	13:2
	Say what time things happen	*It leaves at five past nine.*	
		It arrives at six o'clock in the morning.	
Want	Ask people what they want to do	*What do you want to do?*	16:1
	Say what you want to do	*I want to go to the cinema.*	16:1
Weather	Make remarks about the weather	*Lovely day, isn't it?*	14:4
		Yes, beautiful.	

What (see Do, Job, Like, Time).
Where (see Places, Live, Work).

Work	Ask and say how people get to work		
	Say how you get to work	*How do you get to work?*	18:1
	Say who people work for and where they work	*How does he/she get to work?*	
		He/she goes by car.	
	Say who you work for and where you work	*I go by bus.*	18:1
		He works for Ford. He works in a car factory in Coventry.	19:2
		I work for Focus Films. I work in a studio in Focus Film Centre.	

GRAMMAR REVIEW

UNIT 1. Set 1

| What's / What is | your name? | (Sally Baker.) |

Set 2

| Where's / Where is | Kent Road? / Mr Freeman? / Mrs Richards? | It's (It is) / He's (He is) / She's (She is) | over there. |

UNIT 2. Set 1

| My name's (name is) / I'm | Sally Baker. / Murray Freeman. |

Set 2

| What | do you / does Murray / Tessa | do? | I'm (I am) / He's (He is) / She's (She is) | a | film director. / journalist. |

UNIT 3. Set 1

| This is | (Sally Baker.) / (Walter Mooney) | Sally's (Sally is) / Walter's (Walter is) | a journalist. / an engineer. |

Set 2

| Is | Neville / he / she | a film director? | Yes, | he / she | is. |
| | | | No, | he / she | isn't (is not). |

| He / She | isn't | a film director. / an engineer. |

| What does | he / she | do? |

| What's (What is) | his / her | name? | His / Her | name's ...... |

UNIT 4. Set 1

| Are | you | married? | Yes, | I am. / he is. / she is. | No, | I'm not. / he isn't. / she isn't. |
| Is | he / she | | | | | |

UNIT 5. Set 1

| Where's the | bank? / post office? / cinema? | It's | next to / behind / in front of / opposite / near | the | station. / park. / hotel. |

UNIT 7. Set 2

| Are | you / they | English? |
| Is | he / she | from | England? / London? |

| Yes, | I am. / we are. / they are. / he is. / she is. | No, | I'm not. / we aren't. / they aren't. / he isn't. / she isn't. | We're / They're / He's / She's | American. / from | America. / New York. |

| Look at | my / your / his / her / our / their | car! |

Set 3

| Where | are you / is he / she | from? | I'm / He's / She's | from | Liverpool / Manchester. / Australia. |

UNIT 8. Set 1 and 2

| Where do | you / they | live? |

I / We / They	live in	London. / England.		
		the	north / south	of England.
		a suburb of		London. / Manchester.
		a suburb	north / south	of	London. / Manchester.

UNIT 9. Set 1

| This is / That's | the | bedroom. / bathroom. / kitchen. |

| Is | this / that | the | bedroom? / bathroom? / kitchen? | Yes, it is. / No, it isn't. |

Set 2

| It's nice and | big. / hot. / cold. |

| It isn't very | big. / hot. / cold. |

Set 3

| How much is it? | It's | £13 / £1 / £20 | a week. |

UNIT 10. Set 1

Would you like a	cup of	tea?
		coffee?
	glass of milk?	
	biscuit?	

Set 2

Can I have a	cup of	tea?
		coffee?
	glass of milk?	
	biscuit?	

one	cup
	glass
	sandwich

two	cups
	glasses
	sandwiches

UNIT 11. Set 2 and 3

Do	you	like	tea with lemon?
Does	he		Frank Sinatra?
	she		Elizabeth Taylor?
			small dogs?

Yes,	I do.	/	No,	I don't.
	he	does.		he	doesn't.
	she			she	

He	thinks	it's	all right.
She		he's	
		she's	
		they're	

UNIT 13. Set 2

What time does	the film	start?
	it	
	the bank	open?
	it	
	the bus	arrive?
	it	

It	starts	at	7.15.
	opens		ten past nine.
	arrives		

It arrives at	4 o'clock	in the	morning.
			afternoon.
	8 o'clock		morning.
			evening.

UNIT 14. Set 1

Can you	buy some	fruit?
		bread?
		stamps?
	meet	me?
		him?
		her?
		us?
		them?
	open	the window?
	close	it?

Set 2

I'd like (I would like) some	fruit.
	bread.
	stamps.

How many	apples	would you like?
	oranges	

Set 3

Which	one	do you mean?	This	one.
			That	
	ones		These	ones.
			Those	

Set 4

Lovely	day, isn't it?
Beautiful	
Awful	
Terrible	

UNIT 15. Set 1

When's (When is)	your	birthday?
	Tessa's	
	your next	English lesson?

It's on	Monday.
	Tuesday (etc.)
	January 10th.
	November 14th.

Set 2

What shall we	give	her?
		him?
		them?
	do?	

Let's (Let us)	give	her	a book.
		him	some chocolates.
		them	
	go to the cinema.		
	have a party.		

What	a	beautiful	film!
		lovely	book!
	an	interesting	

What	beautiful	glasses!
	lovely	people!
	interesting	

UNIT 16. Set 1

What	do	you	want to do?
		they	
	does	he	
		she	

I	want	to	go home.
We			invite some friends to dinner.
They			
He	wants		
She			

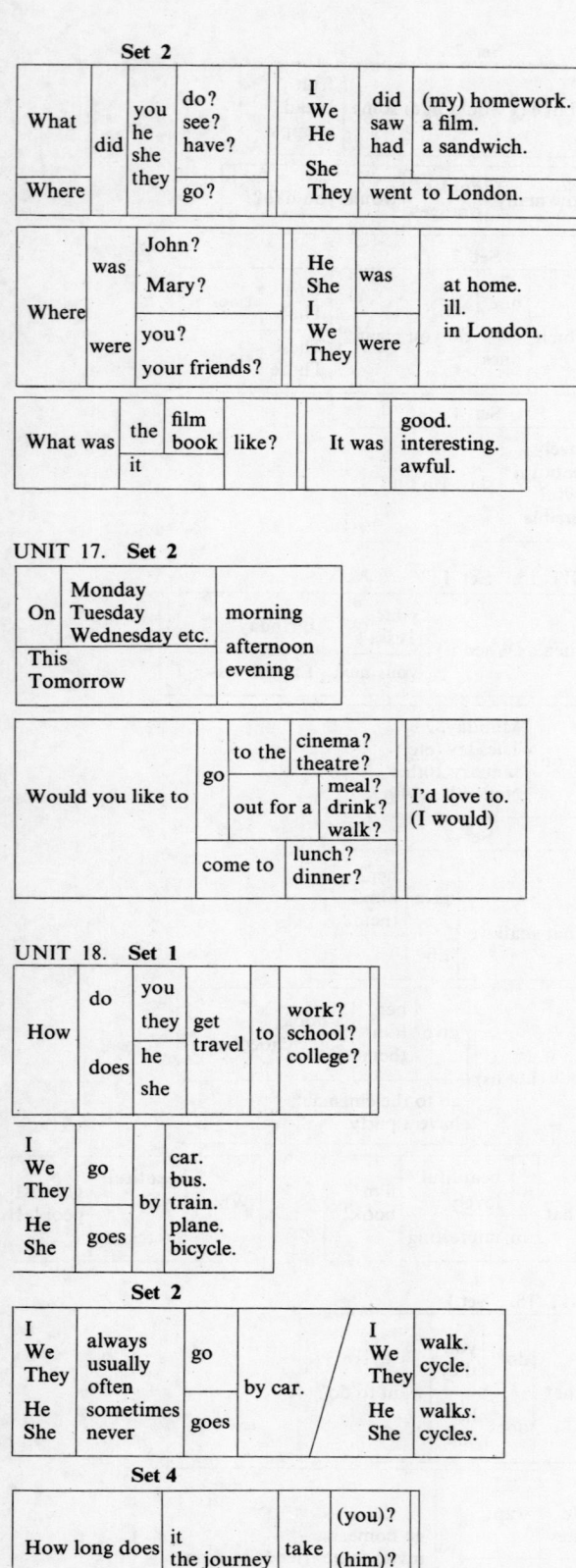

Set 2

What	did	you he she they	do? see? have?		I We He She	did saw had	(my) homework. a film. a sandwich.
Where			go?		They	went to London.	

Where	was	John? Mary?		He She I We They	was	at home. ill. in London.
	were	you? your friends?			were	

What was	the it	film book	like?	It was	good. interesting. awful.

UNIT 17. Set 2

On This Tomorrow	Monday Tuesday Wednesday etc.	morning afternoon evening

Would you like to	go	to the	cinema? theatre?	I'd love to. (I would)
		out for a	meal? drink? walk?	
		come to	lunch? dinner?	

UNIT 18. Set 1

How	do does	you they he she	get travel	to	work? school? college?

I We They	go	by	car. bus. train. plane. bicycle.
He She	goes		

Set 2

I We They	always usually often sometimes never	go	by car.	I We They	walk. cycle.
He She		goes		He She	walks. cycles.

Set 4

How long does	it the journey	take	(you)? (him)? (her)? (them)?

It takes	(me) (us) (him) (her) (them)	about	an hour. 20 minutes.

half	a mile an hour	a mile an hour	and a half

two three (etc.)	and a half	miles. hours.

UNIT 19. Set 1

What time	do does	you he she	get up? start work? finish work? go to bed?

I	get up start work (etc.)	at	7.00. 9.00.
He She	gets up starts work (etc.)		

Where	do does	you he she	have lunch?

I	usually sometimes	have	lunch in the canteen.
He She		has	

What	do does	you he she	do after supper?	I	watch	television.
				He She	watches	

Set 2

Where	do does	you he she	work?	I	work	in an office in Manchester.
				He She	works	

ACTIVE VOCABULARY (IN TOPIC AREAS)

The figure in **bold** beside a word indicates in which Unit the word first occurs as an active vocabulary item.

Occupations
teacher **1**
journalist **2**
film director **2**
cameraman **2**
secretary **2**
technician **2**
van driver **2**
typist **2**
engineer **3**
housewife **3**
student **3**
doctor **3**

Persons
man **5**
woman **5**
girl **7**
boy **7**
child **11**
children **11**
people **15**

Family relatives
sister **7**
brother **7**
mother **7**
father **7**
parents **8**
children **11**
family **15**
husband **19**
wife **19**

Titles
Mr **1**
Mrs **1**
Miss **1**

Countries and Nationalities
England **7**
English **7**
America **7**
American **7**
Canada **7**
Canadian **7**
Ireland **7**
Irish **7**
Australia **7**
Australian **7**
Italian **12**

Places and Buildings
park **1**
road **1**
station **1**
flat **4**
bank **5**
cinema **5**
hotel **5**
school **5**
office **5**

post office **5**
restaurant **5**
police staion **5**
supermarket **5**
cafe **5**
airport **6**
air terminal **6**
centre (city) **6**
shopping centre **6**
car park **6**
bar **6**
hostel **6**
suburb **8**
garden **9**
garage **9**
beach **9**
cafeteria **10**
university **12**
town **12**
club **12**
shop **13**
theatre **16**
church **16**
factory **19**
canteen **19**
hospital **19**
studio **19**
pub **19**
college **19**

Rooms and Furniture
bedroom **4**
room **6**
table **6**
dining room **9**
sitting room **9**
bathroom **9**
kitchen **9**
toilet **9**
hall **9**
garage **9**
classroom **9**
window **14**
door **14**
television **15**

Food, Drink and Meals
food **9**
cup **10**
glass **10**
packet **10**
biscuit **10**
cake **10**
sandwich **10**
coffee **10**
tea **10**
water **10**
milk **10**
wine **10**
beer **10**
orange juice **10**
chocolate **10, 15**

sugar **11**
lemon **11**
whisky **11**
coca-cola **11**
drink **12**
eat *v* **14**
apple **14**
orange **14**
egg **14**
potato **14**
tomato **14**
fruit **14**
bread **14**
meat **14**
fish **14**
cheese **14**
vegetables **14**
menu **14**
lunch **14**
supper **14**
dinner **14**
meal **15**
chips **16**
butter **16**
toast **16**
lunchtime **17**
breakfast **19**
pint **19**

Shops and Shopping
supermarket **5**
shopping centre **6**
price **6**
cheap **6**
expensive **6**
pound **9**
how much? **9**
pence **10**
can I have **10**
here you are **10**
shop **13**
do some shopping **14**

Transport and Traffic
road **1**
station **1**
van driver **2**
car park **6**
taxi **6**
bus **6**
airport **6**
drive **11**
train **13**
plane **13**
flight **13**
platform **13**
ticket **14**
rush-hour **18**
bicycle **18**
petrol **18**
mile **18**
kilometre **18**

traffic 18
accident 18

Travel and Holidays
map 5
tourist 6
airport 6
air terminal 6
taxi 6
hostel 6
river 6
country 6
beach 9
sea 9
sightseeing 11
sunbathing 11
suitcase 14
ticket 14
postcard 16
holiday 16
journey 18
travel 18
foreign 20
language 20
world 20
abroad 20
fly 20

School
teacher 1
student 3
school 11
learn 11
write 11
university 12
lesson 12
class 12
college 19
study 19

Time
week 9
what's the time? 11
o'clock 11
past 11
to 11
quarter 11
half 11
watch 11
a.m. 13
p.m. 13
morning 13
afternoon 13
evening 13
late 13
what time . . . ? 13
date 15
today 15
tomorrow 15
year 15
yesterday 16
last night 16

last week 16
weekend 16
tonight 17
this evening 17
lunchtime 17
minute 18
hour 18

Days of the week
Months of the year
(see Unit 15.)

Numbers
1–10 *(see Unit 4.)*
11–20 *(see Unit 9.)*
20–100 *(see Unit 10.)*
Ordinals: 1st, 2nd etc. *(see Unit 15.)*
double 4
telephone number 4
quarter 11
half 11
single 13
how many? 14
how much? 18

Weather
temperature 9
hot 9
cold 9
warm 9
day 14
beautiful 14
awful 14
terrible 14
lovely 14

Verbs: Daily routine activities
work 6
drink 11
drive 11
smoke 11
cook 11
write 11
sleep 12
dance 12
leave 13
arrive 13
start 13
finish 13
open 13
close 13
buy 14
do some shopping 14
eat 14
pack up 14
drink 14
go to 15
go out for . . . 15
watch (TV) 15
stay at home 15
sit(sat) down 16
go (went) home 16

go (went) to sleep 16
come 17
get to 18
take 18
walk 18
cycle 18
get(got) up 19
go to work 19
go to bed 19
go home 19
have(had) breakfast 19
read(read) the paper 19
do(did) the housework 19
do the ironing 19
do homework 19
mark(marked) homework 19
study(studied) 19
listen(listened) to some music 19
play(played) some records 19
work for 19

Other useful verbs
be(am, is etc.) 1
do 2
send 4
want 5
remember 6
reserve 6
meet 7
guess 7
look at 7
live 8
have 10
like 11
think 11
speak 11
learn 11
give 15
stay 15
see(saw) 16
want(wanted) 5, 16
invite(invited) 16
cost 18
take 18
prefer 19

Useful adjectives
young 5
nice 5
cheap 6
expensive 6
new 7
big 9
hot 9
cold 9
warm 9
clean 9
tasty 9
comfortable 9
red 10
white 10
strong 10

122

black 11
good 12
lonely 12
short 12
little 12
single 13
return 13
late 13
lovely 14
beautiful 14
terrible 14
awful 14
interesting 15
ill 16
bored 16
tired 16
old 16
well 17
free 17
early 19

Adverbs
over there 1
here 3
fairly 6

exactly 8
now 8
very 9
soon 12
quickly 12
quite 16
always 18
usually 18
sometimes 18
often 18
never 18
ever 18

Prepositions
next to 5
behind 5
in front of 5
opposite 5
near 5
from 7
in 8
north 8
south 8
east 8
west 8

with 11
to 11
at 14
on 15
after 17
before 17
by 18

Question words
What 1
Where 1
How much 9
What time 13
How many 14
When 15
Which 14
Who 16
How 18
How far 18
How long 18

Conjunctions
and 3
or 5
but 8
then 14

PASSIVE VOCABULARY (UNIT BY UNIT)
A figure in **bold** beside a word indicates in which Unit the word first occurs as an active vocabulary item.

Unit 1

Dialogue:
doorman
from 7
Manchester 7
news 16
one moment 2
here 3
room 6
one 4

Exercises
surname 4
first 15
signed

Tape:
number 4
two 4
wonder *v*

Unit 2

Extension:
who? 16
meet *v* 7
at 14
Hello! 3
and 3
Hi!
Focus

Tape:
look for
come *v* 17

Unit 3

Dialogue:
call
me 14
all right! 14
mean *v* 14

Extension:
production
produce
by 18
about 18
work
in 8
documentary
sound
lighting
introduce *v*
start *v* 13
well . . .

Tape:
radio 19
twenty 9
question 18
programme 16
host
evening 13

everybody
panel
four 4
guest
left
also 15
last 16
least

Unit 4

Dialogue:
town 12
agency
application form
occupation
size
want *v* 5
offer *v*
man 5
can *v* 10
help *v*
just a minute
that's right 7
code

Exercises:
alphabet
sorry 11
have got
maiden (name)
block
capital

Extension
message
operator
would like 10
spell *v*
read 11
information
day 14
visit *v*
company
people 15
different 15
for example
write *v* 11

Tape:
think *v* 11
once again 12
go 15
see *v* 16
love *v* 9
fine

Unit 5

Dialogue:
I see
let's see 13
exactly 8
look at 7
Oh good! 17

Extension:
mother 7

123

miss *v*
tell *v*
then 14
new 7
with 11
landlady
landlord
give *v* 15
to telephone 17

Tape:
order *v*
cash
traveller's cheques
passport
money 10
pound 9
note

Unit 6
Dialogue:
desk
it doesn't matter
tonight 17
that's all right 11

Activities:
camping
holiday 16
position
single 13
motorway
accommodation
site
stadium
home 16
welcome
manager
at your service
coffee 10
self-service
cafeteria 10
sauna
lounge
boutique
enjoy *v*
stay
leave *v*
key
breakfast 19
lunch 14
dinner 14
here you are 10
firm
hospital 19
place 12
status
(4-star)
reservation

Unit 7
Dialogue:
Morning!

Extension:
birth
date 15
say!
which 14
city
live *v* 8
Britain
British
Jamaican
English-speaking 12
so
non-Europe(an)
Africa(n)
Asia(n)
child(ren) 11

Unit 8
Extension:
quiz
leader
fill in
following
present
actually
really!
big 9
in fact
medium
still
life
very 9
interesting 15
like *v* 11
weekend 16

Tape:
lovely 14
say *v* 16
again 12
down under
to be exact
ready 14
ladies and gentlemen
contestant
pleased to meet you
wonderful
hear *v*
sixty-four 10
dollar

Unit 9
Exercises:
sunshine
tours
Spain
special
reduction
further
details
Dialogue
have *v* 10

cup 10
tea 10
tomorrow 15
Extension:
for sale
family
soon 12
do (= please)
look
floor
usually 18
back
who
alone
sometimes 18
To Let
make

Tape:
beautiful 14
loo (= toilet)
kid
drink 14

Unit 10
Dialogue:
time
Exercises:
list
coca-cola 11
Extension:
listen *v*
late 13
see you later
by the way
ill 16
busy
between
extra
help
while
away
next
before
days of the week 15
months 15
all
other
item
Tape:
quite 16
today 15
hope *v*
cheers 12
good idea 15

Unit 11
Dialogue:
cloth
let's 15

Extension:
assistant
French
German
au-pair
over
years old
yours faithfully
interest
teenager
always 18
same
thing
amusing
worrying
government
typical
watch *v*
television 15
more
than
percent 18
talk to

Tape:
lots of 13
what sort of
best
anything else
apart from
important
sweet (= nice)
sit down 16
class 12
lady
little
cigarette 14
I'm afraid 17
go out 13
at home 15

Unit 12
Dialogue:
member
cloakroom
Extension:
all the time
better
tired 16

Unit 13
Extension:
domestic
passenger
arrival
departure
airline
travel agency
board
practical
pleasant
enjoyable

as soon as possible
department store
hour 18
early closing
night 17
fun
until
performance
take v 18
duty-free
uniform
post
Tape:
attention
request v
proceed to
regret v
owing to
condition
delay
due to
take off
inconvenience
cause v

Unit 14
Dialogue:
I think so
in a hurry
journey 18
afterwards
Extension:
mayonnaise
salad
grilled
roast
fresh
peas
after 17
Tape:
hungry
something
nothing 18
main
course
join v
sound v
pudding
catch v
waiter
eye

Unit 15
Exercises:
everyone
Extension:
concert
tour
outing
come on!

festival
religious
Christmas
Easter
another
bonfire
celebrate
called
try v
blow up
every
adult
light v
burn v
guy
stick
firework
custom
token
gift
spend v
Tape:
old 16
decide v
Good heavens!
boring 16
play 19
anyway
why? 17
somewhere
easily
hard
invite v 16
instead
say v 16

Unit 16
Reading Text:
In the end
a play
exhibition
gallery
back
Dialogue:
What a pity 17
expect v
Extension:
hair
early 19
regards
Tape:
sunny
much
look around
whole
What else?
spaghetti
street
large
see you!

Unit 17
Dialogue:
affair
death
Exercises:
night duty
real
Extension:
What's on
passing
RSVP
informal
event
Tape:
recorded
certificate
announce(ment)
pop
a bit
hush
a break

Unit 18
Reading Text:
problem
increase v
standstill
motorist
turn around
route
one-way
system
improve v
mystery
Dialogue:
pollution
I suppose
Exercises:
method
transport
distance
Extension:
graph
way
protest
placard
build
enough
primary
complain v
on time
dark
homework 19
support v
campaign
Tape:
survey
go ahead
the rest

in all
high
though
reckon v
include v
keep v
pleasure
look out for
fast
had better

Unit 19
Exercises:
institution
company
authority
council
National Health
Extension:
actor
leading
role
reporter
rehearse
Tape:
details
daily
routine
first of all

Unit 20
Letter:
USSR
People's Republic of China
Cuba
Hungary
theme
film-maker
hold v
fill in
attached
best wishes
Chart:
domicile
professional
personal
history
full-board
underwater
ordinary
Speech:
speech
great
entry
sure
rewarding
experience
depressing
balanced
picture
worker

125

informative
present *v*
Extension:
major
commerce/ial
industry/ial/

ease
communication
illustrate
destination
leisure
activity

obtain
Tape:
terribly
crowded
exciting

interested
rare
hobby
in general
difficult
follow *v*

ALPHABETICAL LIST OF BOTH ACTIVE AND PASSIVE VOCABULARY

A figure in *italic* beside a word indicates in which Unit the word first appears as a passive vocabulary item.
A figure in **bold** beside a word indicates in which Unit the word first occurs as an active vocabulary item. The letter *v* beside a word indicates the *verbal* form of the word.

A
about *3*, **18**
abroad *19*
accident **18**
accommodation *6*
activity *20*
actor *19*
actually *8*
address **4**
adult **15**
affair *17*
Africa(n) *7*
after *14*, *17*
afternoon **13**
aftershave **15**
afterwards *14*
again **8**, **12**
agency *4*
airline *13*
airport **6**
airterminal **6**
alphabet **4**
all *10*
all right! *3*, **14**
all the time **12**
all right (he's . . .) *11*
alone *9*
also *3*, **15**
always *11*, **18**
America **7**
American **7**
amusing *11*
and *2*, **3**
angry *18*
announce(ment) *17*
another **15**
answer *v* **11**
anything else *11*
anyway **15**
apart from *11*
apple **14**
application form *4*
April **15**
arrival *13*
arrive *v* **13**
art *20*
article *18*
Asia(n) *7*
ask *v* *11*
assistant *11*

as soon as possible *13*
at *2*, **14**
at home *11*, **15**
attached *20*
attention *13*
at your service *6*
August **15**
au pair *11*
Australia **7**
Australian **7**
authority *19*
away *10*
awful **14**

B
back *9*, *16*
balanced *20*
bank **5**
bar **6**
bathroom **9**
beach **9**
beautiful *9*, **14**
bed *19*
bedroom **4**
beer **10**
before *10*, *17*
behind **5**
best *11*
best wishes *20*
better **12**
between *10*
bicycle **18**
big *8*, **9**
birth *7*
birthday *15*
biscuit **10**
bit *17*
black (black coffee) **11**
blow up *15*
board *13*
bonfire *15*
book **15**
bored *16*
boring *15*, *16*
bottle **14**
boutique *6*
boy *7*
bread **14**
break *17*

breakfast *6*, *19*
Brighton **8**
bring (brought) *v* *17*
Bristol **8**
Britain **7**
British **7**
brother **7**
build *18*
burn *v* *15*
bus **6**
busy *10*
but **8**
butter **16**
buy *v* **14**
by (by bus) **18**
by *3*, **18**
by the way *10*
Bye *10*

C
cafe **5**
cafeteria *6*, **10**
cake **10**
call **3**
called *15*
Cambridge **8**
cameraman **2**
campaign *18*
camping *6*
Canada **7**
Canadian **7**
Can I have . . . **10**
can *v* **4**, **10**
canteen *19*
capital *4*
car **7**
car park **6**
cash *5*
catch *v* **14**
cause *v* *13*
celebrate *15*
centre **6**
certificate *17*
cheap **6**
cheers! *10*, **12**
cheese **14**
child **11**
children *7*, **11**
chips *16*
chocolate *10*, **15**

Christmas *15*
church *16*
cigarette *11*, **14**
cinema **5**
city *7*
class *11*, *12*
classical music **11**
classroom **9**
clean *v* **9**
cloakroom *12*
close *v* *13*
closed *14*
cloth *11*
clothes **11**
club *12*
coca-cola *10*, **11**
code *4*
coffee *6*, **10**
cold **9**
college *19*
come *v* **2**, *17*
come on! *15*
comfortable **9**
commerce/ial *20*
communication *20*
company *4*
complain *v* *18*
concert *15*
condition *15*
congratulations *4*
contestant **8**
cook *v* **11**
cooking *11*
cost *18*
council *19*
country **6**
course *14*
Cuba *20*
cup *9*, **10**
custom *15*
crowded *20*
cycle *18*

D
daily *19*
dance *v* **12**
dark *18*
date *7*, **15**
day *4*, *14*
days of the week *10*, *15*

126

Dear 9
death 17
December 15
decide v 15
delay 13
department store 13
departure 13
depressing 20
desk 6
destination 20
details 9
detective story 11
diary 17
different 4, 15
difficult 20
dining room 9
dinner 6, 14
distance 18
do 2
do (=please) 9
doctor 3
documentary 3, 16
dog 11
dollar 8
domestic 13
domicile 20
don't laugh! 16
don't worry 10
door 14
doorman 1
do some shopping 14
do the ironing 19
double 4
downstairs 9
down under 8
drink 12
drink v 9, 14
drive v 11
due to 13
duty free 13

E
each 10
early 16, 19
early closing 13
ease 20
easily 15
east 8
Easter 15
easy 7
eat v 14
Edinburgh 8
egg 14
eight 4
eighteen 9
eighth 15
eighty 10
eleven 9
engineer 3
England 7
English 7
English-speaking 7, 12

enjoy v 6
enjoyable 13
enough 18
entry 20
envelope 14
Europe(an) 7
evening 3, 13
event 17
every 15
everybody 3
everyone 15
exactly 5, 8
exciting 20
excuse me! 1
exhibition 16
expect v 16
experience 20
expensive 6
extra 10
eye 14

F
factory
fairly
family 9, 15
fast 18
father 7
February 15
festival 15
fifteen 7
fifth 15
fifty 10
fill in 8
film 13
film director 2
find v 16
fine 4
fine thanks! 17
finish v 13
firework 15
firm 6
first 1, 15
first of all 19
fish v 14
five 4
flat 4
flight 13
floor 9
flower 15
fly 19
Focus 2
follow v 20
following 8
food 9
football 17
for example 4
foreign 19
for sale 9
forth 15
forty 10
four 3, 4
four-star 6

fourteen 9
free 17
French 11
fresh 14
Friday 15
friend 3
from 1, 7
fruit 14
full board 20
fun 13
further 9

G
gallery 16
garage 9
garden 9
German 11
get v 11
get to 18
get up 19
gift 15
girl 7
give v 5, 15
glass 10
go 4, 15
go ahead 18
go home 16
good 12
good bye 3
Good heavens! 15
good idea 10, 15
good morning 4
go out 11, 13
go out for... 15
go to 15
go to bed 19
go to sleep 16
go to work 19
government 11
graph 18
great 20
grilled 14
guess v 7
guest 3
guy 15

H
had better 18
hair 16
half 11
hall 9
Happy Birthday 15
hard 15
have v 9, 10
have got 4
have breakfast 19
Health 19
hear v 8
Hello! 2, 3
help v 4
help 10
her 3

here 1, 3
here you are 6, 10
Hi! 2
his 3
history 20
hobby 20
holiday 6, 16
home 6, 15
hope v 10
hospital 6, 19
host 3
hostel 6
hot 9
hotel 5
hour 13, 18
house 9
housewife 3
housework 19
how? 18
how are you? 17
How do you do! 12
however 18
how far? 18
how long? 18
how many? 14
how much? 9
hundred 10
Hungary 20
hungry 14
hush 17
hurry up 13
husband 19

I
I'd love to 17
I don't know 5
ill 10, 16
illustrate 20
I'm afraid 11, 17
important 11
improve v 18
I must go! 7
in 3, 8
include 18
inconvenience 13
increase v 18
industry/ial/ 20
in fact 8
informal 17
information 4
informative 20
in a hurry 14
in all 18
in front of 5
in general 20
I see 5
instead 15
I suppose 18
institution 19
insurance 18
interest 11
interested 20

127

interesting 8, **15**
in the end 16
I think so 14
introduce v 3
invitation 17
invite v 15, **16**
Ireland 7
Irish 7
ironing 19
it doesn't matter 6
item 10

J
Jamaican 7
January 15
jazz 11
job 3
join v 14
journalist 2
journey 14, 18
July 15
June 15
just 10
just a minute 4

K
keep v 18
key 6
kid 9
kilometre 18
kitchen 9

L
ladies and gentlemen 8
lady 11
landlady 5
landlord 5
language 19
large 16
last 3, **16**
last night 16
last week 16
late 10, **13**
leader 8
leading 19
learn v 11
least 3
leisure 20
leave v 13
Leeds 8
left 3
lemon 11
lesson 12
letter 11
let's 10, **15**
let's see 5, **13**
life 8
light v 15
lighting 3
like v 8, **11**
list 10
listen v 10
listen to the radio 19

little 11, **12**
live v 7, **8**
Liverpool 7
London 7
lonely 12
loo (=toilet) 9
look 9
look around 16
look at 5, **7**
look for 2
look out for 18
lot(s) of 11, **13**
lounge 6
love v 4, **9**
lovely 8, **14**
lunch 6, **14**
lunchtime 17

M
maiden (name) 4
main 14
major 20
make 9
man 4, **5**
manager 6
Manchester 1, **7**
many 7
map 5
March 15
mark homework 19
married 4
match 13
May 15
mayonnaise 14
me 3, **14**
meal 15
mean v 3, **14**
meat 14
medium 8
meet v 2, **7**
Melbourne 7
member 12
menu 14
message 4
method 18
mile 18
milk 10
minute 18
Miss 1
miss v 5
modern 10
Monday 15
money 5, **10**
months 10, **15**
more 11
morning 13
Morning! 7
mother 5, **7**
motorist 18
motorway 6
Mr 1
Mrs 1

much 16
musical 16
my 2
mystery 18

N
name 1
National 19
near 5
never 18
new 5, **7**
news 1, **16**
newspaper 19
Newcastle 8
New York City 7
next 10, **5**
next to 5
nice 5
night 13, **17**
night duty! 17
nine 4
nineteen 9
ninety 10
ninth 15
no 3
no, thanks 10
non- 7
north 8
not 7
note 5
nothing 14, **18**
November 15
now 8
number 1, **4**

O
obtain 20
occupation 4
o'clock (one o'clock) 11
October 15
of course 7
offer v 4
office 5
often 18
Oh good! 5, **17**
old 15, **16**
once again 4, **12**
on time 18
one 1, **4**
one moment 1, **2**
one way 18
only 4
open v 13
operator 4
opposite 5
or 5
orange 14
orange juice 10
order v 5
ordinary 20
other 10
over 11
over there 1

our 7
outing 15
outside 6
owing to 13

P
packet 10
pack up 14
panel 3
passenger 13
passing 17
passport 5
past (quarter past) 11
parents 8
park 1
party 15
pay v 10
peas 14
pen 14
pence 10
people 4, **15**
People's Republic of China 20
per cent 11, **18**
performance 13
perfume 15
personal 20
petrol 18
photography 19
picture 20
pint 19
placard 18
place 6, **12**
plane 13
plate 15
platform 13
play 15, **19**
pleasant 13
please 1
pleased to meet you 8
pleasure 18
p.m. 13
pop 17
police station 5
pollution 18
position 6
post 13
post-card 16
poster 15
post office 5
potato 14
pound 5, **9**
prefer v 19
practical 13
present 8
present v 20
primary 18
problem 18
proceed to 13
produce 3
production 3
professional 20

programme *3*, **16**
protest *18*
pudding *14*

Q
quarter **11**
question *3*, **18**
quickly **12**
quite *10*, **16**
quiz **8**

R
radio *3*, **19**
rare *20*
read *v 4*, **11**
reading **11**
ready *8*, **14**
real *17*
really! *8*
reckon *v 18*
record **11**
recorded *17*
reduction *9*
rehearse *19*
regards *16*
regret *v 13*
religious *15*
remember *v 6*
reporter *19*
request *v 13*
reserve *v 6*
reservation *6*
restaurant **5**
return *v 13*
rewarding *20*
right **10**
ring *v 17*
river *6*
road *1*
roast *14*
role *19*
room *1*, **6**
route *18*
routine *19*
R.S.V.P. *17*
rush-hour *18*

S
salad *14*
same *11*
sandwich **10**
sat *16*
Saturday *15*
sauna *6*
say *v 15*, *16*
say! *7*
school **5**
sea *9*
second *15*
secretary **2**
see *v 4*, *16*
see you (on Friday) *16*, *17*

see you later *10*
self service *6*
send *4*
September *19*
seven *4*
seventeen *9*
seventh *15*
seventy **10**
shampoo *14*
shop **13**
shopping *14*
shopping centre *6*
short **12**
show *9*
sightseeing **11**
signed *1*
single *6*, **13**
sister *7*
site *6*
sit down *11*, **16**
sitting room *9*
six *4*
sixteen *9*
sixth *15*
sixty **10**
size *4*
sleep *v 12*
small *4*
smoke *v 11*
so *7*
soap *14*
something *14*
sometimes *9*, *18*
somewhere *15*
soon *9*, **12**
sorry *4*, **11**
sound *3*
sound *v 14*
south *8*
Southampton *8*
spaghetti *16*
Spain *9*
speak *v 11*
speaking! *17*
special *9*
speech *20*
spell *v 4*
spend *v 15*
spider **11**
sports *6*
stadium *6*
stamp *14*
standstill *18*
start *v 3*, **13**
station *1*
status *6*
stay *6*
stay at home *15*
stick *15*
still *8*
stop *v 16*
street *16*

strong **10**
student *3*
study *v 19*
studio *19*
suburb *8*
sugar **11**
suitcase *14*
sunbathing **11**
Sunday *15*
sunny *16*
sunshine *9*
supermarket **5**
supper *14*
support *v 18*
sure *20*
surname *1*, *4*
survey *18*
sweet (= nice) *11*
Sydney *7*
system *18*

T
table *6*
take *v 13*, *18*
take off *13*
talk to *11*
tasty *9*
tax *18*
taxi *6*
tea *9*, **10**
teacher *1*
technician **2**
teenager *11*
telegram *4*
telephone number *4*
television *11*, *15*
tell *v 5*
temperature *9*
ten *9*
tenth *15*
terrace *9*
terrible *14*
terribly *20*
than *11*
thanks *14*
thank you *1*
thank you very much **5**
that *14*
That's a good idea *15*
that's all right! *6*, **11**
that's right *4*, *7*
theatre *16*
their *7*
theme *20*
then *5*, *14*
the rest *18*
these *14*
thing *11*
think *v 4*, **11**
third *15*
thirteen *9*
thirty **10**

this *3*
this evening *17*
those *14*
though *18*
three *4*
Thursday *15*
ticket *14*
time *10*
tired *12*, *16*
toast *16*
toilet *9*
token *15*
to (quarter to) **11**
to be exact *8*
today *10*, *15*
To Let *9*
tomato *14*
tomorrow *9*, *15*
tonight *6*, *17*
too **2**
toothpaste *14*
tourist *6*
tour *9*
town *4*, **12**
traffic *18*
train *13*
transport *18*
travel *v 18*
travel agency *13*
traveller's cheques **5**
try *v 15*
T-shirt *15*
Tuesday *15*
turn around *18*
twelve *9*
twenty *3*, *9*
twenty-one **10**
two *1*, *4*
typical *11*
typist **2**

U
underwater *20*
uniform *13*
university **12**
until *13*
upstairs *9*
usually *9*, *18*
U.S.S.R. *20*

V
van driver **2**
variety programme *16*
vegetables *14*
vegetarian *20*
very *8*, *9*
visit *v 4*

W
wait a moment *17*
waiter *14*
walk *15*

want *v* 4, 5
warm 9
washing 16
watch *v* 11
watch T.V. 15
water 10
way 18
weather 13
Wednesday 15
week 9
weekend 8, 16
welcome 6
well . . . 3
well 17
west 8

what? 1
what about? 8
what a pity! 16, 17
what else? 16
what's on? 17
what sort of? 11
what's the matter? 16
what's the time? 11
what time . . ? 13
where? 1
whereas 18
which? 7, 14
while 10
whisky 11
who? 2, 16

who 9
whole 16
why? 15, 17
wife 19
window 14
wine 10
with 5, 11
woman 5
wonder *v* 1
wonderful 8
work *v* 6
work 3, 19
worker 20
work for 19
world 19

worrying 11
would like 4, 10
write *v* 4, 11
writing 11
wrong 11

Y
yawn *v* 16
year 15
years old 11
yes 1
yesterday 16
young 5
your 1
yours faithfully 11